Music Theory Workbook
for Guitar

Volume One
Chord and Interval
Construction

by
Bruce Arnold

Muse Eek Publishing Company
New York, New York

ISBN 1890944-52-1

Printed in the United States

This publication can be purchased from your local bookstore or by contacting:
Muse Eek Publishing Company
P.O. Box 509
New York, NY 10276, USA
Phone: 212-473-7030
Fax: 212-473-4601
http://www.muse-eek.com
sales@muse-eek.com

Table Of Contents

Acknowledgments

The author would like to thank Michal Shapiro for her patience and help in proof reading and helpful suggestions. A very special thank you to Tina Sobin for her editing and proof reading which saved the author many many hours of work.

About the Author

Bruce Arnold is from Sioux Falls, South Dakota. His educational background started with 3 years of music study at the University of South Dakota; he then attended the Berklee College of Music where he received a Bachelor of Music degree in composition. During that time he also studied privately with Jerry Bergonzi and Charlie Banacos.

Mr. Arnold has taught at some of the most prestigious music schools in America, including the New England Conservatory of Music, Dartmouth College, Berklee College of Music, Princeton University and New York University. He is a performer, composer, jazz clinician and has an extensive private instruction practice.

Currently Mr. Arnold is performing with his own "The Bruce Arnold Trio," and "Eye Contact" with Harvie Swartz, as well as with two experimental bands, "Release the Hounds" a free improv group, and "Spooky Actions" which re-interprets the work of 20th Century classical masters.

His debut CD "Blue Eleven" (MMC 2036J) received great critical acclaim, and his most recent CD "A Few Dozen" was released in January 2000. The Los Angeles Times said of this release "Mr. Arnold deserves credit for his effort to expand the jazz palette."

For more information about Mr. Arnold check his website at http://www.arnoldjazz.com This website contains audio examples of Mr. Arnold's compositions and a workshop section with free downloadable music exercises.

Foreword

Many of my students have asked me how they can improve their music theory and fretboard knowledge. This book is an attempt to fill those needs.

Learning the language of music is imperative to becoming a professional musician who can communicate intelligently with other musicians. More importantly, applying this knowledge to your instrument will give you the ability to create music with greater flexibility, coherence, and confidence. In order to help you apply the information presented in this book I've created a small booklet that can be downloaded for free at the muse-eek.com website. This booklet gives you exercises specifically designed to help you apply the theory information to your instrument. The booklet can be found in the "member's area" at www.muse-eek.com. The "member's area" also contains other educational files which can help you in your musical studies.

Future volumes of this Music Theory Workbook series will cover scales and diatonic chords of a key both of which are very important to playing and understanding music. See the final pages of this book for a complete listing and description of current music related publications.

Muse Eek Publishing has created a website with a FAQ forum for all my books. If you have any questions about anything contained in this book feel free to contact me at FAQ@muse-eek.com and I will happy to post an answer to your question. My goal is to educate and help you reach a higher degree of musical ability.

A very special thank you goes to Tina Sobin for her patient and meticulous work in editing this book.

Bruce Arnold
New York, New York

Theory Workbook for Guitar Volume One

This theory workbook is designed to teach you the basic building blocks of music theory and how to apply them to the guitar fretboard. Each exercise presents a group of intervals or chords which must be written using staff notation and guitar chord diagrams. This method will instill the information in your head and your hands. Direct physical application of music theory makes it more relevant and greatly helps in learning the guitar fretboard.

Background theory information needed to complete each exercise is presented in easy to understand language. This is followed by exercises for learning intervals and triads, 7th chords (4 note chords) and chords with tensions. The answers are in the back of the book.

The notes contained in each chord will fit into the chord diagram supplied with each exercise. Make sure to fit your answer into this diagram. You can place more than one note on each string. The answers are not meant to be played as a chord but as an arpeggio (one note after another).

For each exercise in this book you will need to find the intervals or chord tones/tensions. Each example will require you to figure out where the notes would be on a staff and where these notes would be located on a guitar. Remember that memorizing the notes contained in each chord presented combined with knowing where these notes are on the guitar will open up a whole new understanding of music. Example One shows how the music staff and chord diagram will appear for each exercise:

Example 1

A full explanation of the chord diagrams can be found on page 14.

A total beginner should keep in mind that there is a lot of information presented here and it can get overwhelming after a while. It is important for you to pace yourself. If you take on to much information in "one gulp" you will end up with learning fatigue, so divide your work into sensible amounts. For example, once you have read up to page 6, do the "Basic Intervals" exercise on page 16 while this information is fresh in your mind. Refer back to pages 1-6 as you do the "Basic Intervals" exercise on page 16 if you need help in remembering the chromatic scale or how many half steps are in a particular interval. As you work further through this book you will find that over time you will start to remember many of the concepts presented in the theory section just from using them so many times. I've also included a blank sheet in the back of the book if you feel you want to redo certain pages.

Whether you are a beginner, or an advanced student seeking to improve your music theory knowledge, the only way you will make music theory a coherent natural process is by working with it repeatedly until it becomes as automatic as speaking in your own language. Music schools raise students to this ability by giving them the same information presented in the music theory section, and then spending 1 to 2 years giving them theory assignments in order to ingrain the information. This book does the same thing by giving you 100 pages of exercises. It's not enough to understand how each chord and interval is built; you need to do all the exercises. That is how you will gain a command over the information and will be able to instantaneously say what the notes in a chord are in any key. At that point, your proficiency with music theory becomes a reflex and is very much like speaking. You don't think of every word when you say a sentence, yet you could easily stop and explain any word that you are using. This is the same process that happens when you master the music theory information presented in this book.

With all this in mind, let's get started.

Music theory and chord construction

The first thing a student must tackle is learning how to read music. A detailed description of the development of music notation is beyond the scope of this book and some inconsistencies (which will appear in italics) have stayed in musical notation, in the course of that development. For the beginner these inconsistencies can be confusing but inconsistent as it may be, music notation does have a standard for expressing itself visually and by understanding this system the world of western music is open to you.

Example 2 shows a series of lines and spaces which are employed to create a visual representation of sound. Each line and space corresponds to a pitch. Each pitch is given a name A, B, C, D, E, F, or G. A clef sign is also used to designate what names each line and space will receive. The reason for the many types of clefs will be explained momentarily. First let us look at the treble clef. The treble clef places the note sequence in the order listed below. This complete system of lines and spaces with a clef sign is called a staff.

Example 2

As can be seen in Example 2, each line and space corresponds to a different tone. If you want to have pitches higher or lower than the 5 lines and four spaces you can extend the staff by using ledger lines. Ledger lines give you the ability to represent higher and lower pitches by extending the staff; these extended pitches are called ledger line notes. (See Example 3)

Example 3

If we extend this idea we run into trouble as can be seen in Example 4. When excessive ledger lines are used, reading music becomes very difficult. To alleviate this problem other clefs are employed to make reading these notes that are out of the treble clef's range easier. The note in Example 4 would be found in the bass or F clef on the 2nd space. (See Example 5)

Example 4   C note

Example 5   The same C in bass clef

Example 6 shows where the notes fall in the bass clef. We will only use the treble clef in this book but a basic understanding of the bass clef is important.

Example 6

If we look at our treble clef again (Example 2) we notice that there is an "e" on the first line and a "e" on the 4th space. Our ear recognizes these pitches as being the same pitch but the "e" on the 4th space sounds like a higher version of the low "e". In musical terminology the higher "e" is said to sound an octave higher than the lower "e". If we play these two "e's" on the guitar it would be the 2nd fret on the D string and fifth fret on the B string. (See Example 7)

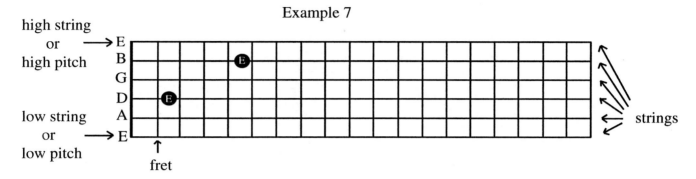

Example 7

high string
or → E
high pitch   B
              G
              D
low string   A
or → E
low pitch

fret

strings

To summarize what we have learned so far: there are 7 pitches which are represented on a staff with the letter names A,B,C,D,E,F,G. These 7 pitches keep repeating themselves in different octaves. To represent these notes in other octaves we need to use ledger lines or other clefs.

One of the inconsistencies of the notation system we have learned so far is that it doesn't show all the available notes in western music. There are a total of 12 pitches used in western music which of course as we have learned can be found in many different octaves. To show all 12 notes in the system, "sharp"(#) and "flat" (b) symbols are used to represent the tones that occur between the letter names of the notes. For example between the note C and D there exists a pitch which can be called either C sharp or D flat. These notes are represented as follows: C# or Db. The (#) and (b) symbols work in the following way, the flat (b) lowers a pitch and a sharp (#) which raises the pitch. If a note is sharped it is said to have been raised a half step; if it is flatted it is said to have been lowered a half step. **A half step is the smallest distance possible in western music.** If we show all 12 notes on the staff within one octave we get what is called the chromatic scale. (See example 8) This scale contains all possible notes in the western system of music. Notice that there is no sharp or flat between E and F and B and C which is just one of those inconsistencies you have to accept with this notational system. Both chromatic scales shown below sound the same on the guitar; the decision to use sharps or flats depends on the musical situation. You will notice that the D in the chromatic scale with flats has a symbol in front of it. This symbol is called a natural sign. It is used to cancel the flat that appears before the previous D. **In written music, measures are used to delineate time, and sharps and flats carry through the whole measure until a new measure starts, unless a natural symbol is used to cancel it.**

Example 8

Chromatic Scale

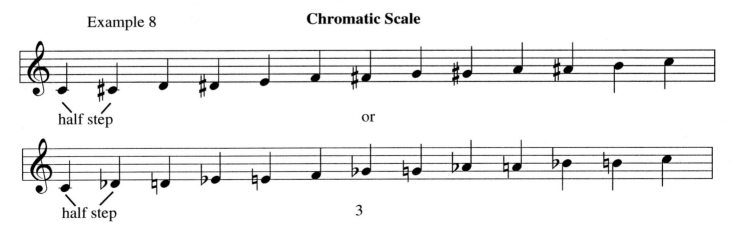

half step

or

half step

3

The 12 note chromatic scale can be represented using either method found in Example 8. Remember a C# is the same note as a Db on the guitar. If you play on only one string of the guitar and move consecutively up each fret you will be playing a chromatic scale (See Example 9). If you were to play the chromatic scale found in example 8 on the guitar you would start on the A string 3rd fret and move up each fret until you reach the 15th fret to complete the chromatic scale.

Example 9

Guitar Fretboard

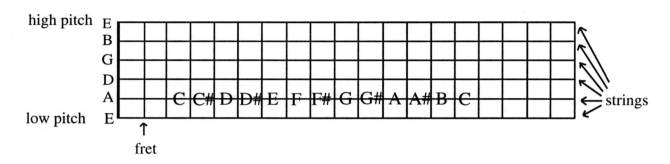

Though the chromatic scale represents all 12 notes, much of western music of the last few centuries has been based around only 7 tones. If we extract these 7 notes as shown in example 10 we end up with a major scale.

Example 10

Major scale derived from Chromatic scale

Chromatic Scale

Major Scale

If we look at the distance in half steps between the notes of a major scale we see a pattern; whole, whole, half, whole, whole, whole, half. **All major scales are based on these intervals** (See Example 11).

Example 11   **C Major Scale**

whole step   whole step   half step   whole step   whole step   whole step   half step

4

If we apply the major scale to the guitar fretboard the system works out as follows: start on any note on the guitar and move up on one string starting with a whole step (2 frets), whole step, half step (1 fret), whole step, whole step, whole step, half step. This is one way to play a major scale on the guitar. Example 12 shows this system starting on C, which creates a C major scale.

Example 12   **Guitar Fretboard**

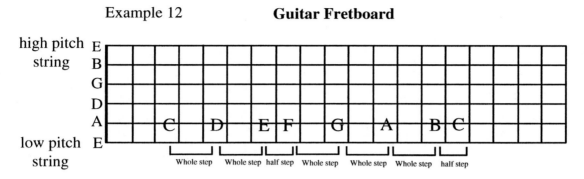

With this information you could play any major scale by following the pattern of whole step, whole step, half step, whole step, whole step, whole step, half step. Example 13 shows a D major scale.

Example 13   **Guitar Fretboard**

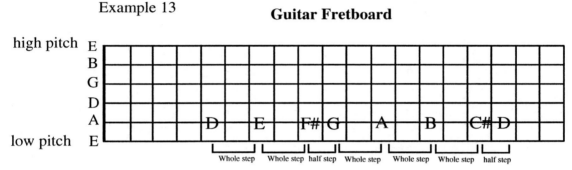

The notes of a C major scale C, D, E, F, G, A, B are commonly referred to as the diatonic notes of the key of C major. If we had the key of D major the diatonic notes would be D, E, F#, G, A, B, C#.

If we use the major scale formula (1,1,1/2,1,1,1,1/2) we can figure out every major scale. We will find that each key has a different number of sharps or flats. If a piece of music uses a particular key, its key signature is placed at the beginning of the piece of music. Example 14 shows a list of all the sharps and flats found in various keys. These are commonly referred to as the key signatures, and they occur after the clef sign and at the beginning of each line of music. "Music Theory Workbook for Guitar Volume Two" covers learning all scales and their associated keys.

Example 14

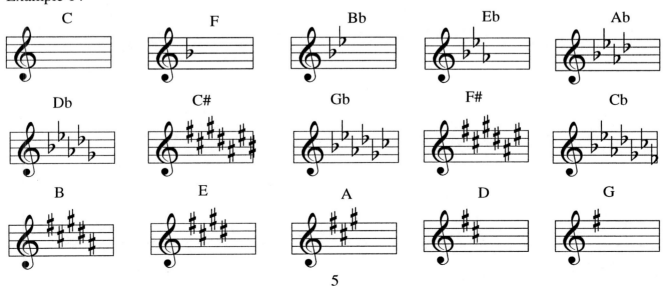

5

Whole steps and half steps are the basic building blocks for the major scale. The whole step equals two half steps. The distance between two notes is called an interval. For example the distance between C and D is a whole step. This is also called a major second interval. It is important to know intervals because chords are frequently named for the intervals in their internal structure. All two note interval combinations from the root of the major scale are listed below in example 15.

Example 15

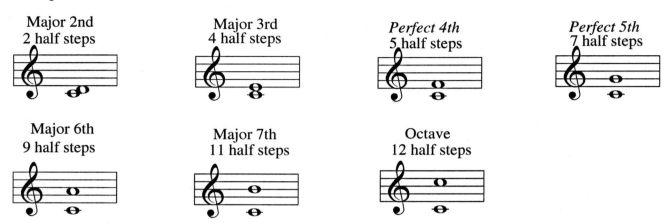

If we sharp any of these intervals we create an augmented interval. If we flat a major second, third, sixth, or seventh, we create a minor interval. If we flat a perfect fourth, a fifth, or an octave, we get a diminished interval, and *if we double flat the major 7th we have a diminished 7th.* * Example 16 shows a list of some of the more common augmented, minor and diminished intervals. These are explored in all keys with the "Basic Intervals" exercise on page 16.

Example 16

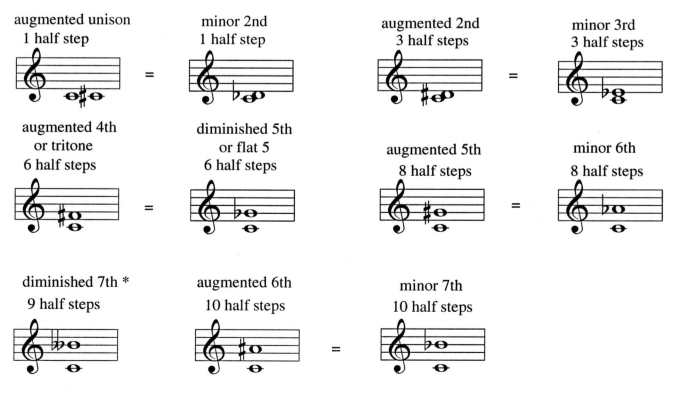

* A double flat (bb) lowers a note two half steps. A double sharp (X) raises a pitch two half steps.

6

If we continue past the octave, intervals are given new names to show that they are more than an octave apart (See example 17). The larger intervals exercise on page 17 covers these intervals.

Example 17

| 9th | 10th | 11th | 12th | 13th |
| 14 half steps | 16 half steps | 17 half steps | 19 half steps | 21 half steps |

An augmented interval may be written in different ways. A (+) may appear before the number, or a (#) or (aug). If the interval is flatted it is usually indicated with a flat. Example 18 shows some of the common interval names you will need to know.

Example 18

| b9 | #9th | #11th | b13th | b15th |
| 13 half steps | 15 half steps | 18 half steps | 20 half steps | 23 half steps |

This knowledge of the chromatic scale, major scale and the construction of intervals is a crucial tool to understanding the internal structure of chords. The process of learning all this information will take some time to memorize. Be patient with yourself. Through a combination of rereading these theory pages and working on the exercises you will find your theoretical knowledge will improve.

So far we have discussed 2 note intervals, sometimes called diads. When we add one more note to our 2 note interval we create a chord. A chord can be a combination of any 3 or more notes played at the same time. Western music can build chords using a wide variety of intervals. One of the most common ways to build chords is to stack up diatonic 3rd intervals. For example if we took C in the key of C and stacked up 3rds we would get C, E, and G because all of those notes are in the key of C and are a 3rd apart (See Example 18). **These structures built in thirds are commonly referred to as triads and the C note is said to be the root of the chord.**

Example 18   **C Major Triad**

If we continue this process and build up diatonic triads above all the notes of C major we get the following 3 note structures (See Example 19)

Example 19

Triads derived from stacking 3rds above a C major scale

These seven chords structures have a certain internal structure. The first structure C, E, and G form what is called a major chord, if we measure the distance or interval between each note using our chromatic scale we can find the formula for building major chords. Between C and E is 4 half steps or a major third. Between E and G is 3 half steps or a minor third (See example 20). Therefore to create a major chord we need to combine a major third on the bottom and a minor third on the top. You will notice that the chord starting on F and on G are also major chords. The exercise on page 18 covers major triads.

C major chord

minor 3rd
3 half steps

Example 20

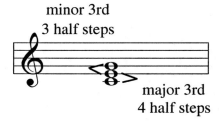

major 3rd
4 half steps

The second structure D, F, and A form what is called a minor chord. Using the chromatic scale once again we can find the formula for building minor chords. Between D and F is 3 half steps or a minor third. Between F and A is 4 half steps or a major third (See example 21). Therefore to create a minor chord we need to combine a minor third on the bottom and a major third on the top. You will notice that the chord starting on E and on A are also minor chords. The exercise on page 19 covers minor triads.

D minor chord

major 3rd
4 half steps

Example 21

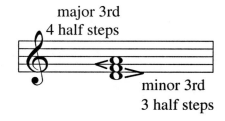

minor 3rd
3 half steps

This leaves us with one last structure, B, D, F which forms what is called a diminished chord. Using the same method we find that the distance between B and D is 3 half steps or a minor third. Between D and F is 3 half steps or a minor third (See example 22). Therefore to create a diminished chord we need to combine a minor third on the bottom and a minor third on the top. The exercise on page 20 will cover diminished triads.

B diminished chord

Example 22

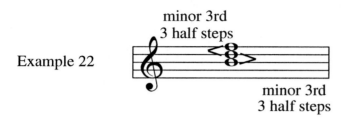

Example 23 shows a list of all the triads and their chord names. These chords are referred to as the diatonic triad or chords of a major key. You will see each of these chords labeled in many ways. C major could be shown as: C major, CMaj, C, CM, D minor could be shown as: D minor, Dmin, D-, Dm, B diminished could be shown as: B diminished, B dim, or B°.

They are also numbered sequentially which allows someone to refer to the D minor chord in the key of C, as a "II chord". Because many contemporary tunes are written using only the diatonic chords of a key it is a very common practice among musicians to learn the diatonic chords of every key using numbers and letters to aid in the memorization and quick learning of new songs. "Music Theory Workbook for Guitar Volume Three" will cover learning these Diatonic Chords in all keys.

Example 23

Diatonic chords of C Major

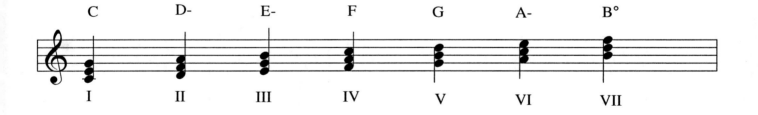

The practice of numbering each of the diatonic chords is very commonly used by musicians to communicate with each other. For example, you might go into a jam session and the piano player might say. "Let's play this new song I've written. It goes 1, 6, 2, 5 in C major." If you know the diatonic chords of the key of C major, you will know that the chords will be C major to A minor to D minor to G Major. So you can see why it would be extremely useful to memorize the diatonic chords of all keys.

If we take the three types of chords learned so far and write them out with C as the root we come up with (Example 24) C, E, G for a C major chord which is a major third stacked below a minor third, (Example 25) C, Eb, G for a C minor chord which has just the opposite interval combination; a minor third stacked below a major third, and (Example 26) C, Eb, Gb for a diminished chord which is two minor third intervals. You may notice that we have not yet discussed the combination of a major third and major third which is shown in (Example 27) C, E, G#. This combination is called an augmented chord and is written as follows: C augmented, C aug, C+. The augmented chord can be found as a diatonic chord in other scales which are discussed in the "Music Theory Workbook for Guitar Volume Two." The exercise on page 21 covers augmented chords.

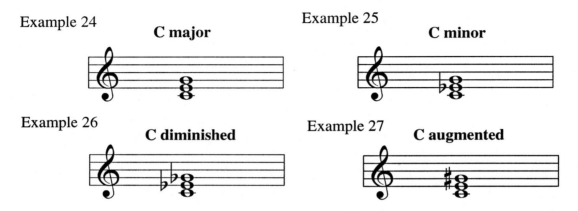

Example 24
C major

Example 25
C minor

Example 26
C diminished

Example 27
C augmented

There are two more triad chord structures that are commonly found in contemporary music; the suspended 4th chord (sus 4, Example 28) and the add 9th (add 9, Example 29). The sus 4 is a triad in which the 4th has replaced the 3rd. This creates an unusual structure of 5 half steps or a 4th and 2 half steps or a major 2nd. The suspended chord can be a diatonic chord built on the 1st, 2nd, 3rd, 5th, or 6th degrees. It is common to see the suspended chord written as C4, C sus or C sus4. The add 9 replaces the 3rd with the second. The interval structure of this chord would be 2 half steps or a major 2nd and 5 half steps or a perfect 4th. The add 9 chord can be a diatonic chord built on the 1st, 2nd, 4th 5th or 6th degrees of the scale. The exercise on page 22 covers sus 4, and the exercises on page 23 covers the add 9 triads.

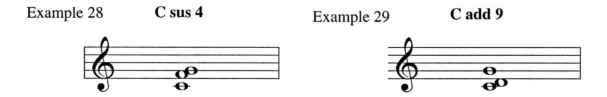

Example 28   **C sus 4**

Example 29   **C add 9**

The notes of each chord are called the chord tones. For example, the chord tones of a C major chord are C, E, and G. It is also possible to build chords that contain more notes. The next most common chord type is a four note structure which is commonly referred to as a 7th chord (Example 30). To build a 7th chord you add a note a third above the triads we have just discussed. If we add a major third above our C major triad we get C, E, G B

Example 30

If we go back to our diatonic triads of C major and add a diatonic third above each chord we now have the diatonic 7th chords of the key of C major (See Example 31).

Example 31

7th Chords derived from C major scale

These seven 7th chords structures have a certain internal structure just as our triads did. The first structure (C, E, G and B) contains the triad C, E and G plus another major third up to B. This structure is called a major 7th chord. If we again measure the distance or interval between each note using our chromatic scale we can find the formula for building major 7th chords. Between C and E is 4 half steps or a major third, between E and G is 3 half steps or a minor third, G to B is 4 half steps or a major third (See example 32). **Therefore to create a major 7th chord we need to combine a major third on the bottom and a minor third in the middle and a major third on the top.** You will notice that the chord starting on F is also a major 7th chord. The exercise on page 25 covers major 7th chords.

C major 7th chord

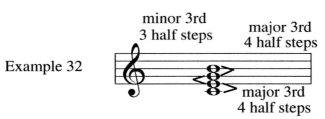

The second structure (D, F, A and C), forms what is called a minor 7th chord. Using the chromatic scale once again, we can find the formula for building minor 7th chords. Between D and F is 3 half steps or a minor third. Between F and A is 4 half steps or a major third; between A and C is 3 half steps or a minor third (See Example 33). **Therefore to create a minor 7th chord we need to combine a minor third on the bottom and a major third in the middle and a minor third on the top.** You will notice that the chord starting on E and on A are also minor 7th chords. The exercise on page 26 covers minor 7th chords.

D minor 7th chord

11

The third new structure (G, B, D and F), forms a dominant 7th chord. Using the chromatic scale we can find the formula for building dominant 7th chords. Between G and B is 4 half steps or a major third, between B and D is 3 half steps or a minor third, between D and F is 3 half steps or a minor third (See Example 34). **Therefore to create a dominant 7th chord we need to combine a major third on the bottom and a minor third in the middle and a minor third on the top.** Only one dominant seventh chord can appear naturally within any major key. The exercise on page 27 covers dominant 7th chords.

G dominant 7th chord

Example 34

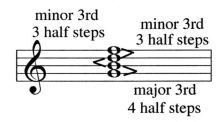

The last structure (B, D, F and A) forms what is called a minor 7 flat 5, also referred to as the "half diminished" chord. Using the chromatic scale we can find the formula for building minor 7 flat 5 chords. Between B and D is 3 half steps or a minor third, between D and F is 3 half steps or a minor third and between F and A is 4 half steps or a major third (See example 35). **Therefore to create a minor 7b5 chord we need to combine a minor third on the bottom and a minor third in the middle and a major third on the top.** The minor 7b5, like the dominant 7th, happens only once in diatonic 7th chords of a major key. The exercise on page 29 covers minor 7b5 chords.

B minor 7 flat 5 chord

Example 35

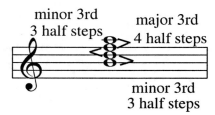

The 7th chords can be organized in the same manner as our triads were. Below is a list of the diatonic 7th chords of a major key. Again these chords can be labeled in many ways: C major 7 could be shown as C major 7, CMaj7, CΔ7, CM7. D minor 7 could be shown as D minor 7, Dmin 7, D-7, Dm7. G dominant 7th could be shown as G dominant, G dom7, or G7. B minor 7th flat 5 can be shown as B minor 7b5, Bmin7b5, and B-7b5.

The same numbering system applies for the 7th chords as for the triads.

Example 36 show the chords listed sequentially with their chord names and degrees.

Example 36   **Diatonic 7th chords of C Major**

Most styles of music generally use triads or 7th chords with or without tensions. For instance, folk music gravitates toward triads while jazz tends to use more 7th chords and even more complicated structures.

If we extend the idea of adding more notes to chords by extending up another 3rd above our 7th tone we create 9th chords. Therefore CΔ7 (C, E, G, B) becomes CΔ79 (C, E, G, B, D), the interval formula would be maj3, min3, maj3, min3 (See Example 37). The 9th is a tension, not a chord tone. A tension in contemporary music is a non chord tone which adds color to our basic triads and 7th chords.

The method of using intervals by calculating half steps gets very time consuming as the chord structures get larger and larger. **There is a faster way to calculate which notes are contained in any chord but this requires that you first memorize the major scale.** If we go back and look at our C major scale we can see that to find for example, a major 7 chord which is C, E, G, and B we need only to think the 1, 3, 5, 7 degrees of the C major scale. To add on a tension like the 9th we simply add the 2nd degree of the C major scale which is a D. When the 2nd is placed above the 7th it is called the 9th. We need only to add the 2nd degree of C (which we have learned is the same note as the 9th). The exercises starting on page 39 cover chords with tensions.

Δ9th chord

Example 37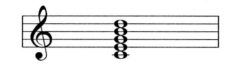

If we use the major scale as our reference point in figuring out chord tones we only need to know the formula for each chord type. For example: a C-7 chord would be C, Eb, G, Bb which would be 1, b3, 5 and b7 in the key of C. Therefore by memorizing the structure of each chord and altering the notes from the major scale we can quickly find the correct notes for any chord. Example 38 shows a list of the triads and seventh chords found in this book and their relationship to a C major scale.

Example 38

triad chords (exercises found on page 18 to 23)

major	(1 3 5)
minor	(1 b3 5)
diminished	(1 b3 b5)
augmented	(1 3 #5)
sus4	(1,4,5)

7th chords (exercises found on page 25 to 37)

Δ7	(1 3 5 7)
-7	(1 b3 5 b7)
7	(1 3 5 b7)
-7b5	(1 b3 b5 b7)
°7	(1 b3 b5 bb7)
-Δ7	(1 b3 5 7)
7sus4	(1 4 5 b7)
Δ7#5	(1 3 #5 7)
7#5	(1 3 #5 b7)
Δ7#11	(1 3 #4 7)
7#11	(1 3 #4 b7)
6	(1 3 5 6)
-6	(1 b3 5 6)

When we add even more tensions to our triads or seventh chords we simply have to add the appropriate note from our reference major scale. For example: Cdom9 would be C, E, G, Bb, D or 1, 3, 5, b7, and 9th degrees of a C major scale (See Example 39). Tensions are applied in the exercises starting on page 39.

Example 39

C reference scale

flat the (B) for b7

*   *   *   *   *

1   2   3   4   5   6   7   1

or   or   or

9   11   13

As each chord type is presented in this book a review is made of the available tensions for each chord type. A brief overview of how each chord type is used is also included.

The chord diagrams used in this book are explained in Example 40. When completing the exercises you do not have to put the name of the notes within each black circle.

Example 40

chord diagrams

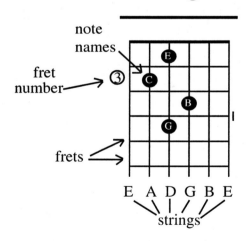

Many students become confused once they start the exercises on page 16. Keep in mind that there are many places to play the same note on the guitar. To help you understand all these possibilites you can download alternate answers for each exercise from the "member's section" of the muse-eek.com website. As an owner of this book you have free access to this resource and it is recommended you take advantage of it. To further help you see all the possible places each note can be played you can also check the 6 pages of fretboard charts in the back of this book. These charts will give you all the different places each pitch can be found on the guitar and its corresponding placement on the music staff. Don't be discouraged, eventually all these different locations of notes on the fretboard will become second nature.

It must be mentioned that the guitar is a transposing instrument sounding an octave (12 half steps) lower than written. Therefore middle C on a piano appears as the C one ledger line below the staff (Example 41) while the actual sound of middle C on the guitar is 1st fret on the B string (See Example 42). So if you see a middle C written for guitar (See Example 43) you will play it on the 3rd fret of the A string (See Example 44). All staff notation in this book is transposed.

Example 41

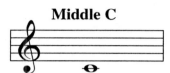

Example 43

Middle C in guitar notation

Example 42

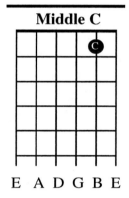

Example 44

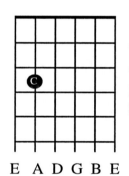

When you see middle C on the staff you play this note on the guitar.

Example 45 shows how the open strings on the guitar would be written.

Example 45

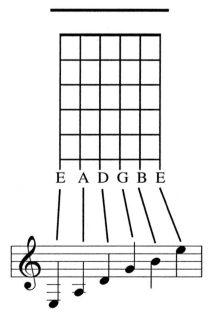

15

Basic Intervals

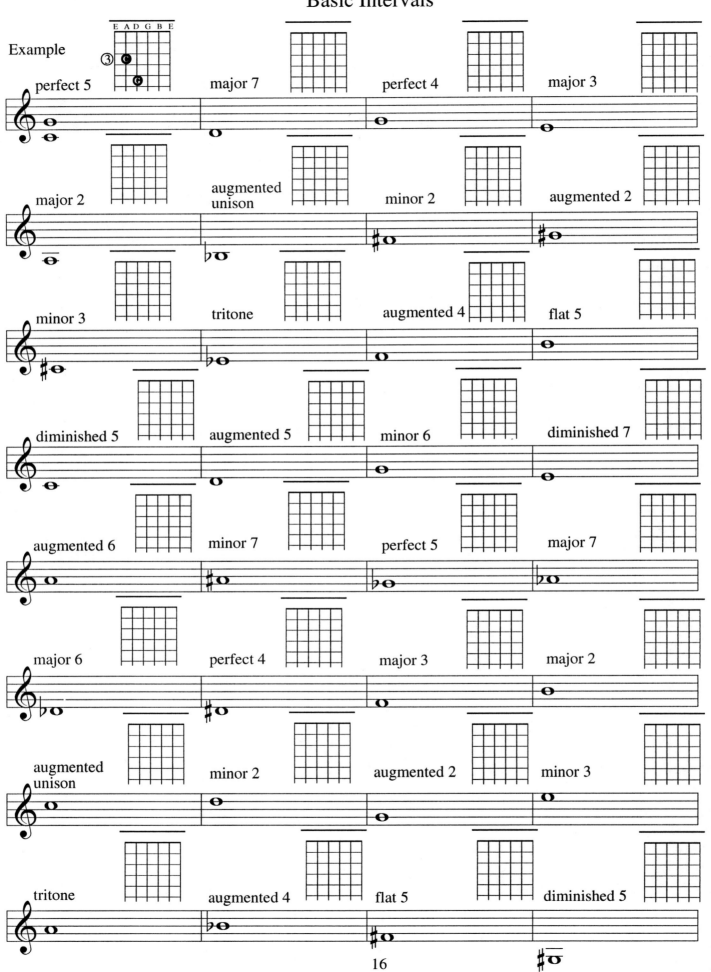

Larger Intervals

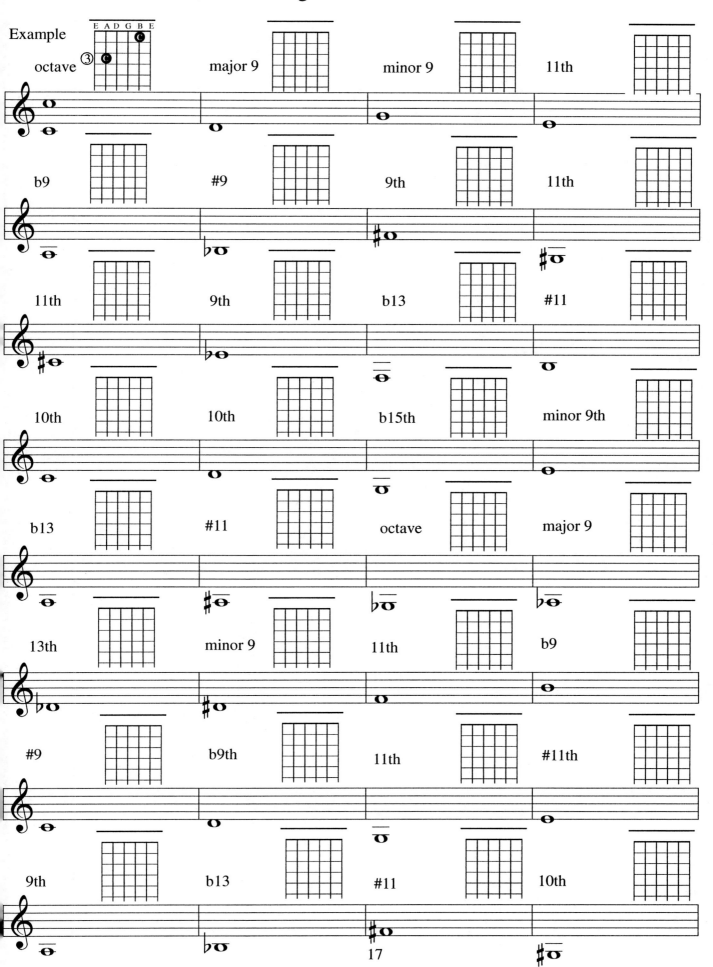

Major Triads

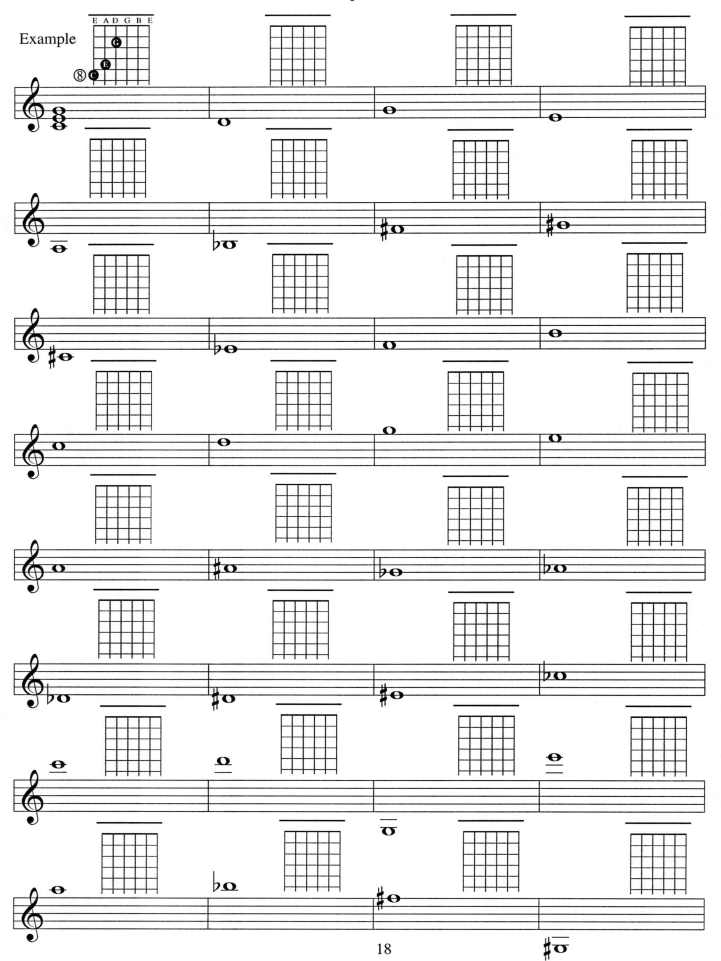

Minor Triads

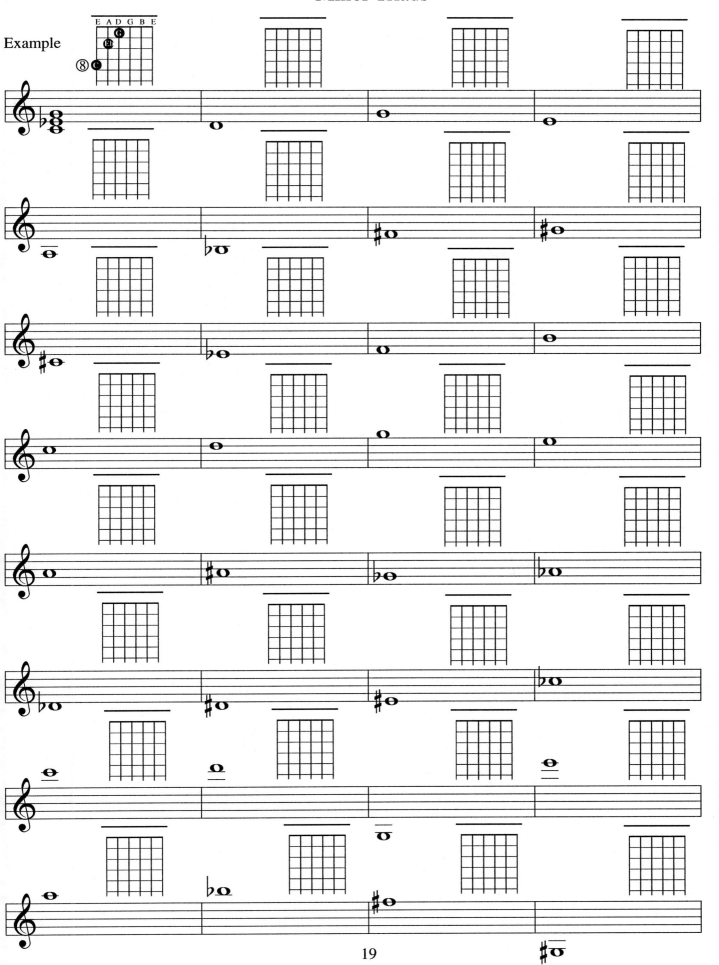

Diminished Triads

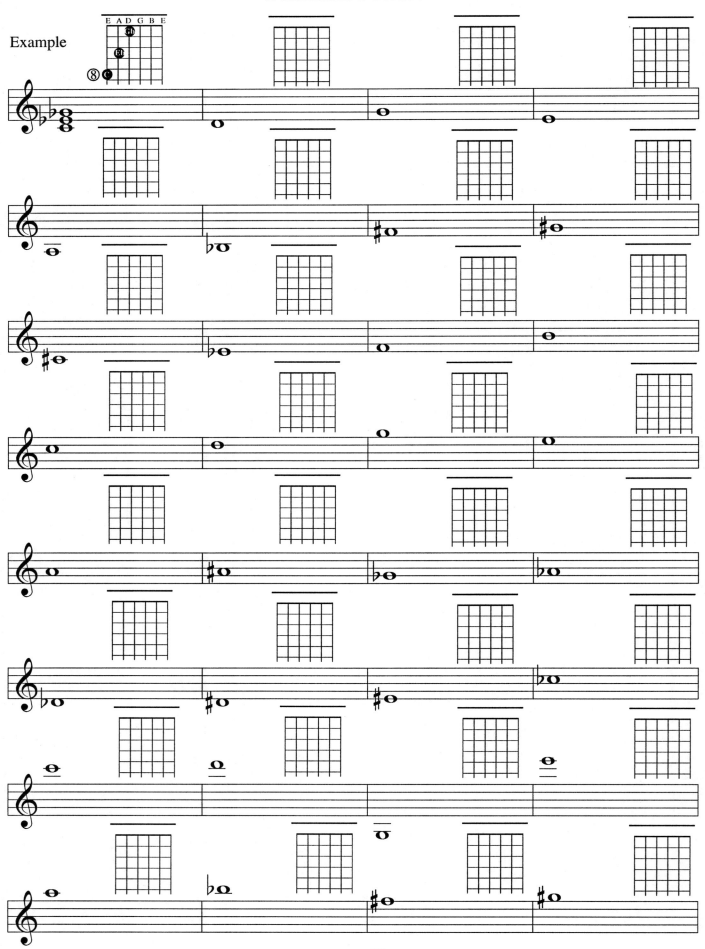

Augmented Triads

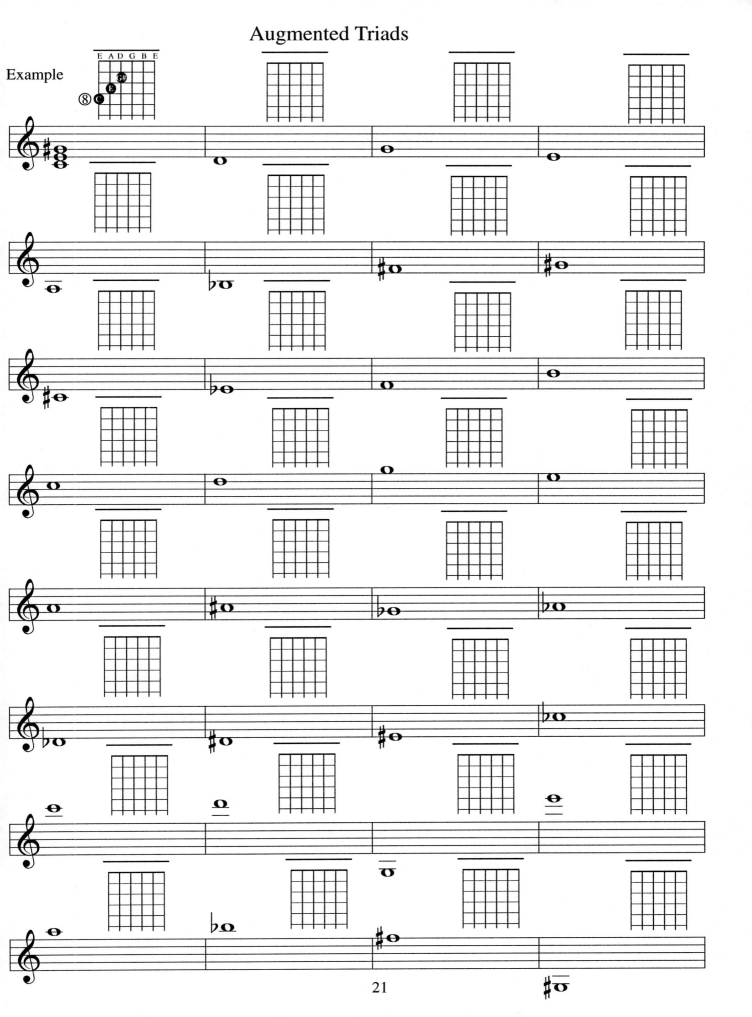

Suspended 4th Triads

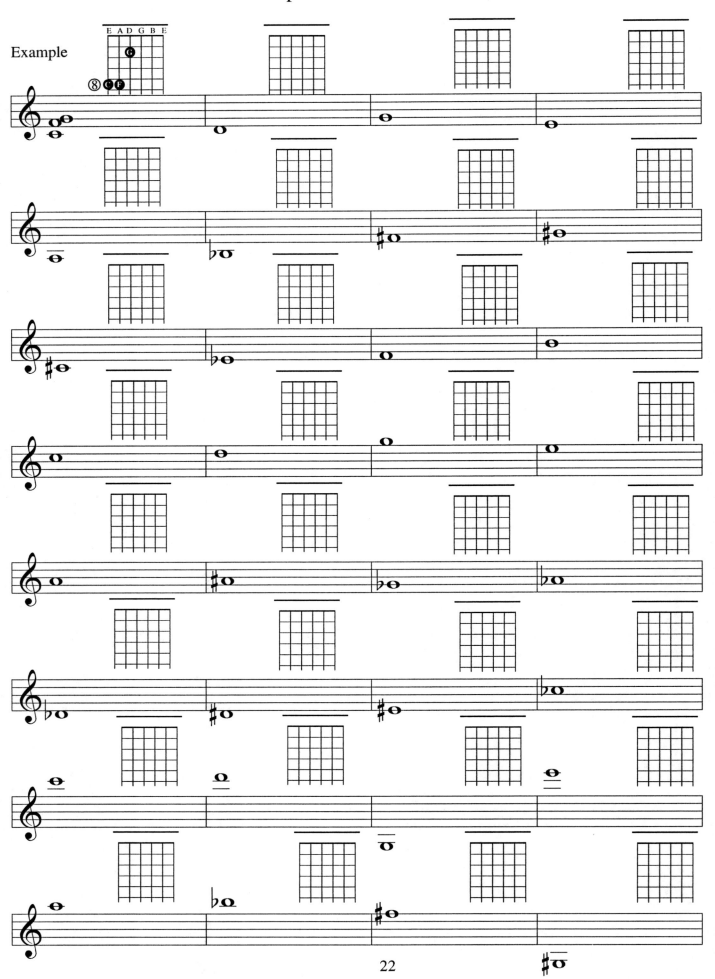

Add 9 Chords

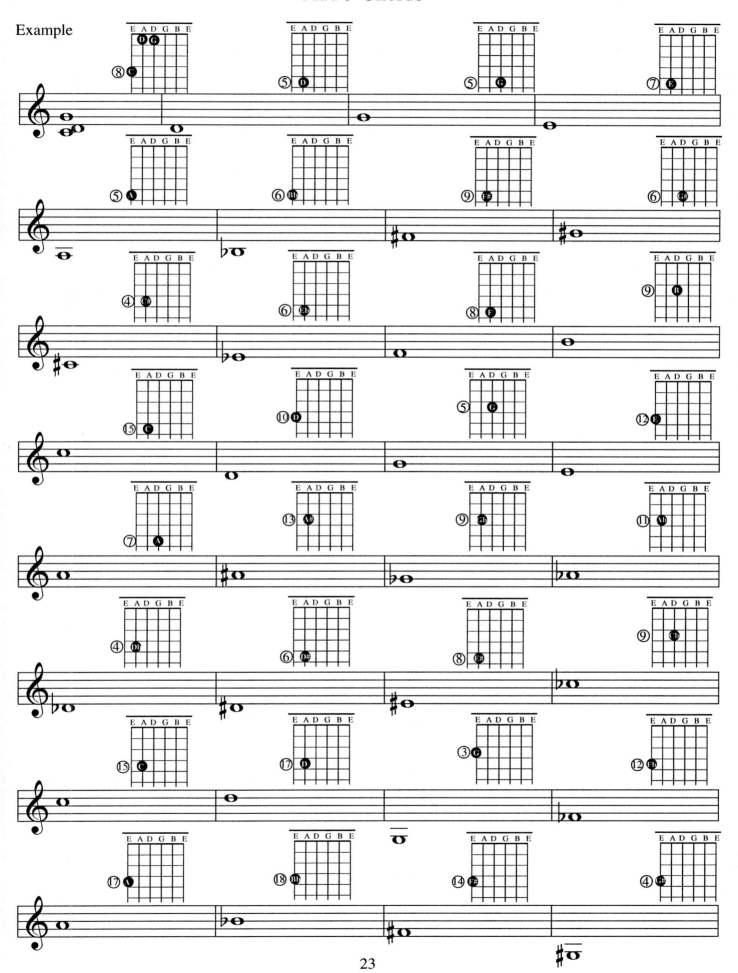

Seventh Chords

Pages 25 to 37 will present exercises covering seventh chords. A complete list of the 7th chords is found below. Make sure you understand each chord type before proceeding to the exercises. If you need to review 7th chords and their construction they can be found on page 11 and 12.

There are 13 basic Seventh chord types:

Δ7	1,3,5,7
-7	1,b3,5,b7
7	1,3,5,b7
7sus4	1,4,5,b7
-7b5	1,b3,b5,b7
°7	1,b3,b5,bb7
-Δ7	1,b3,5,7
Δ7#11	1,3,#4,7
Δ7#5	1,3,#5,7
7b5	1,3,b5,b7
7#5	1,3,#5,b7
6th	1,3,5,6
-6	1,b3,5,6

It is a very good idea to memorize the structures of these chords. I find that relating them all back to the major seventh is a good idea. Therefore a -7 is a major seventh with a flatted 3 and flatted 5th.

Major Seventh Chords

Example

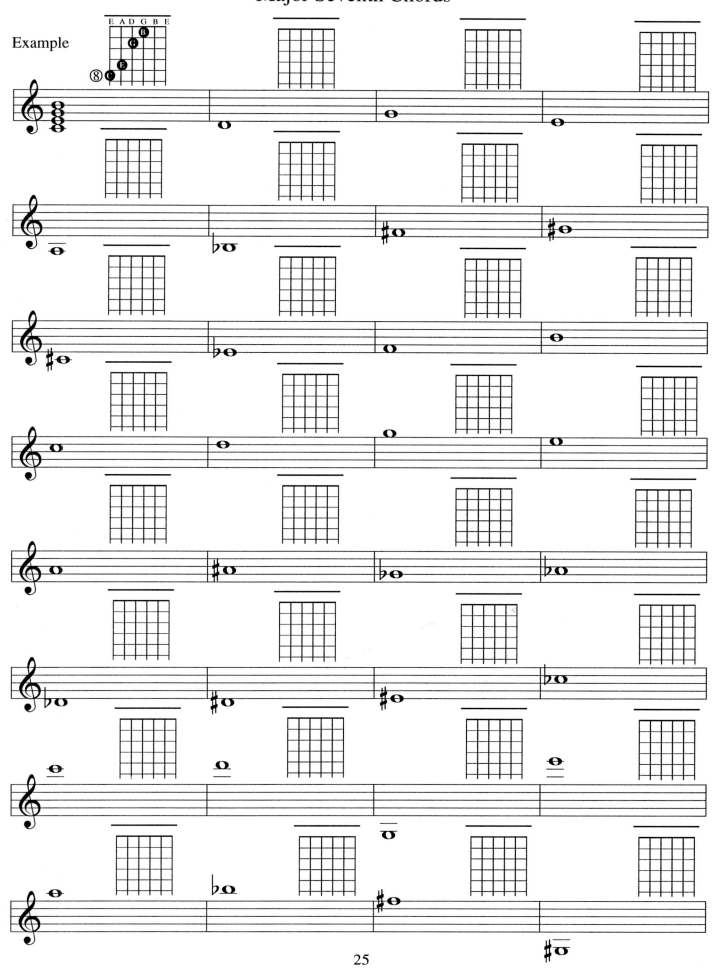

25

Minor Seventh Chords

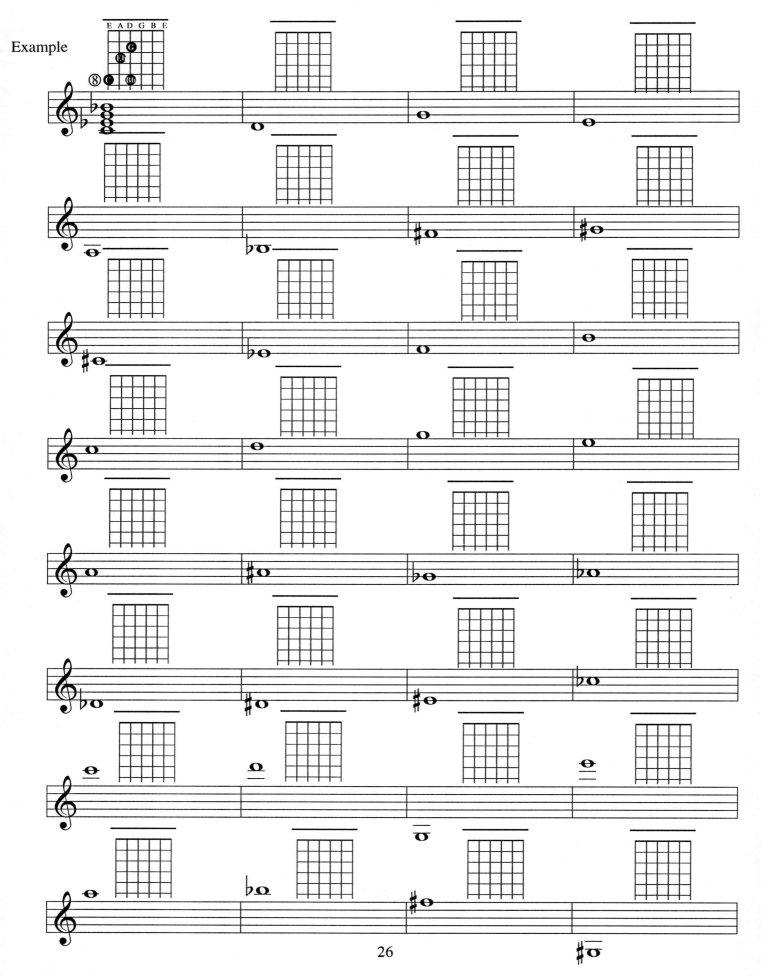

Dominant Seventh Chords

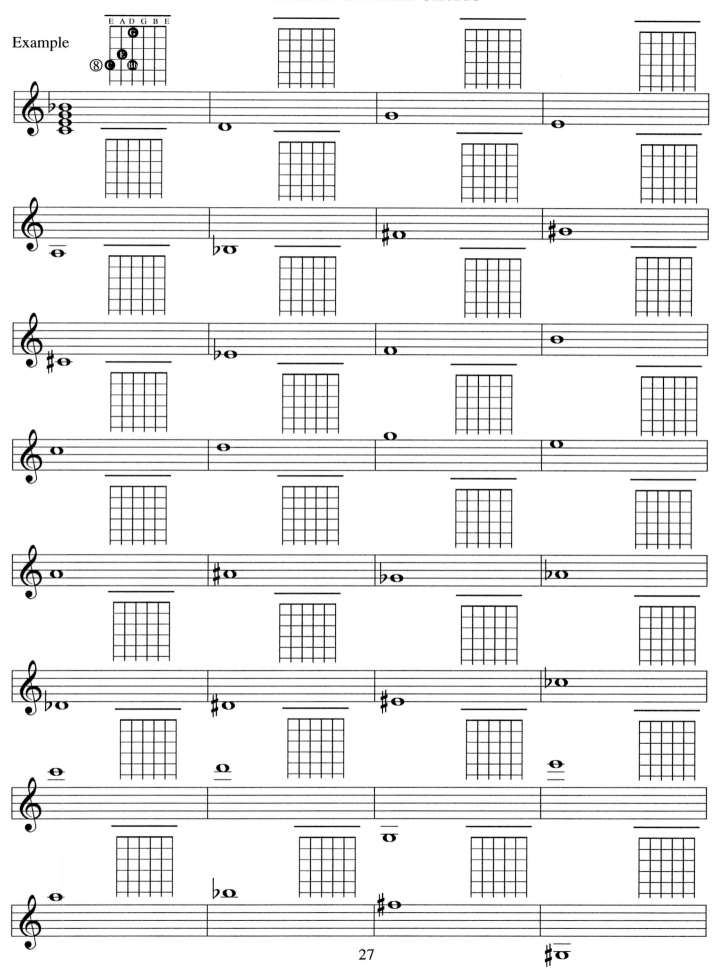

Dominant Seventh Sus4 Chords

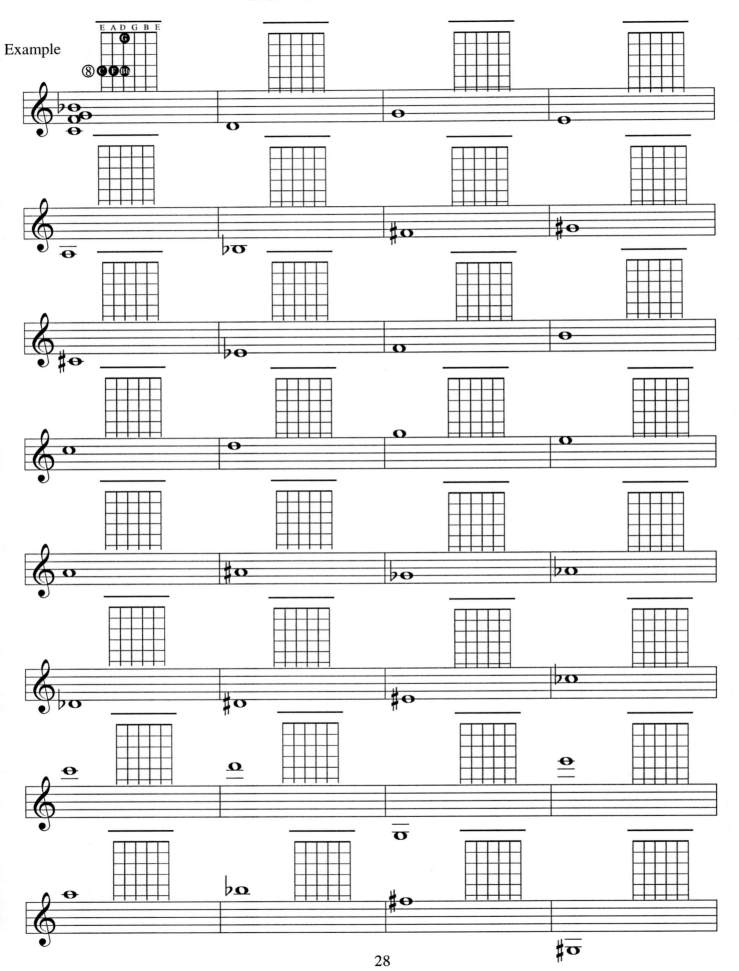

Minor 7b5 Chords

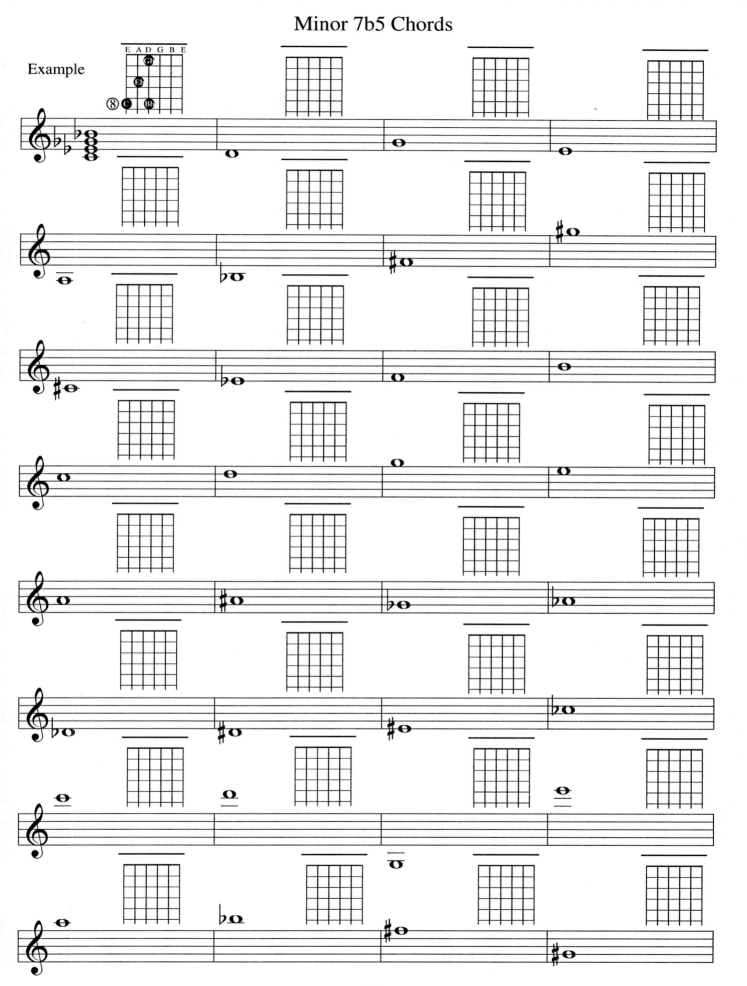

29

Diminished 7th Chords

Example

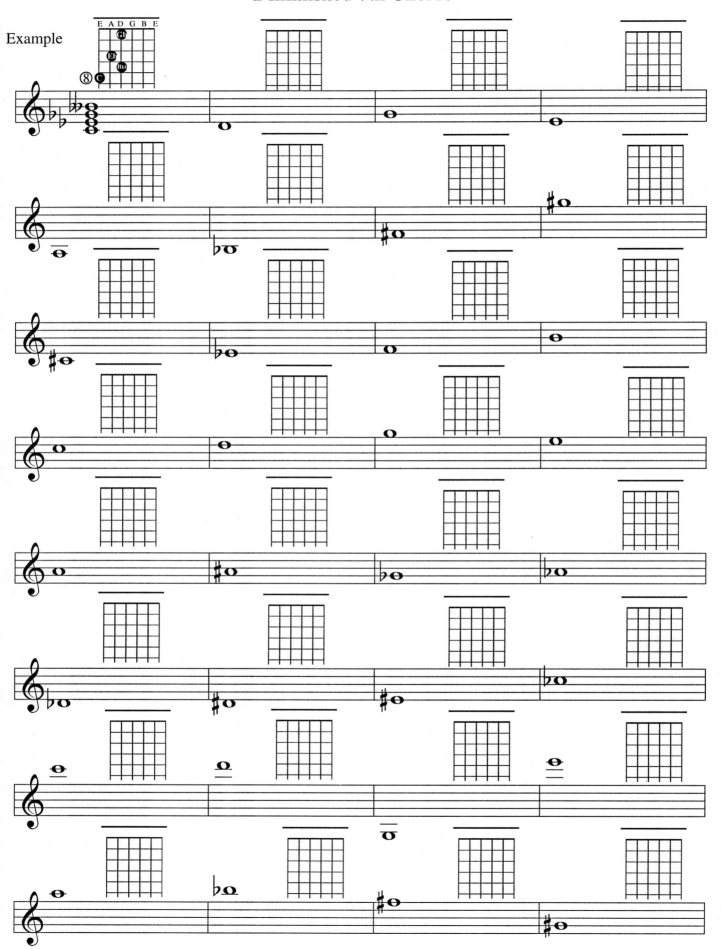

Minor Major Seventh Chords

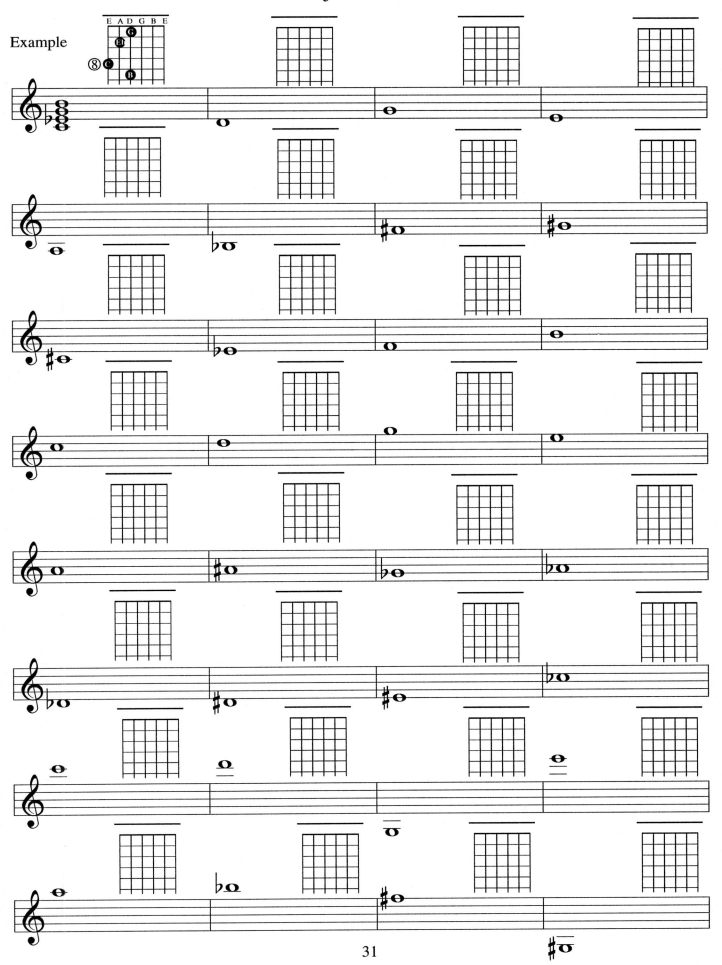

Major 7#11 Chords

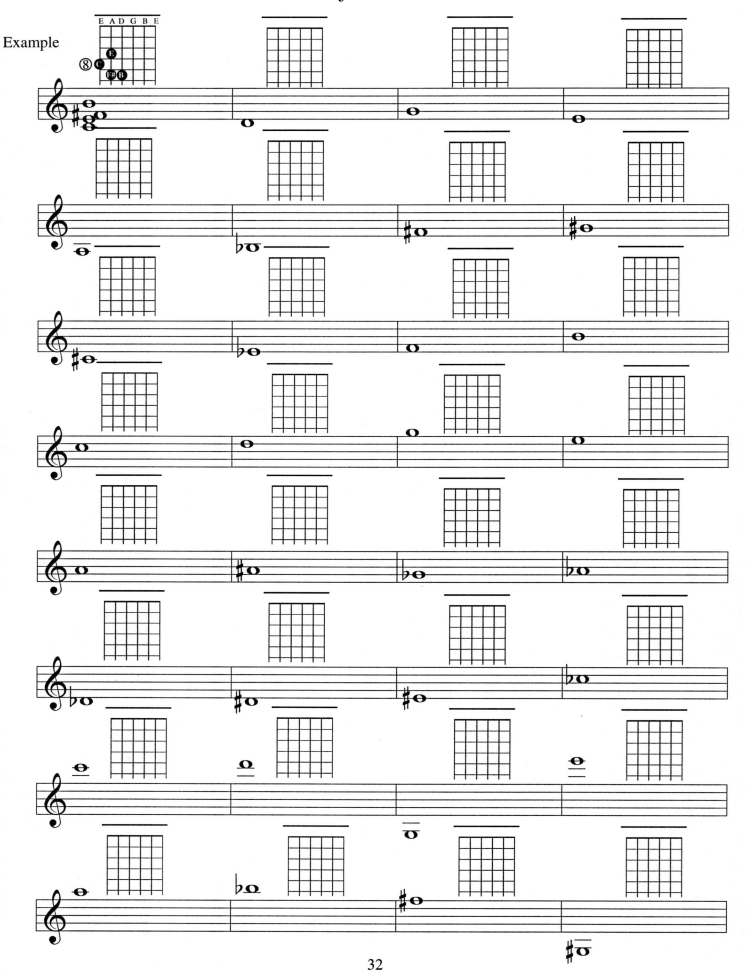

Major 7#5 Chords

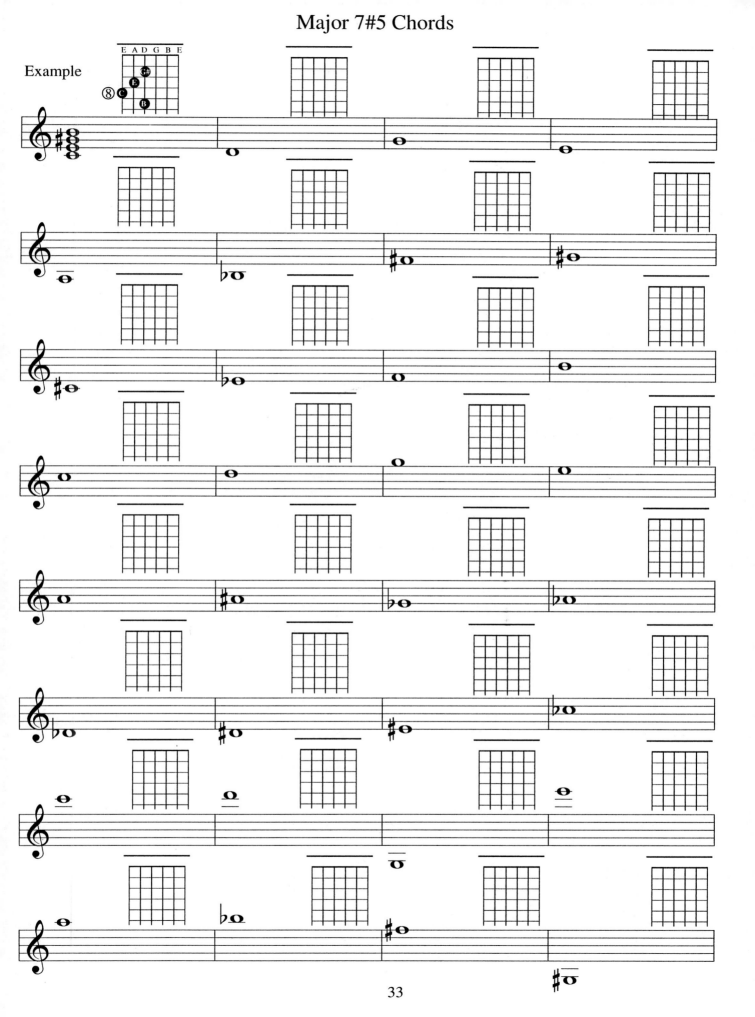

Dominant Seventh b5 Chords

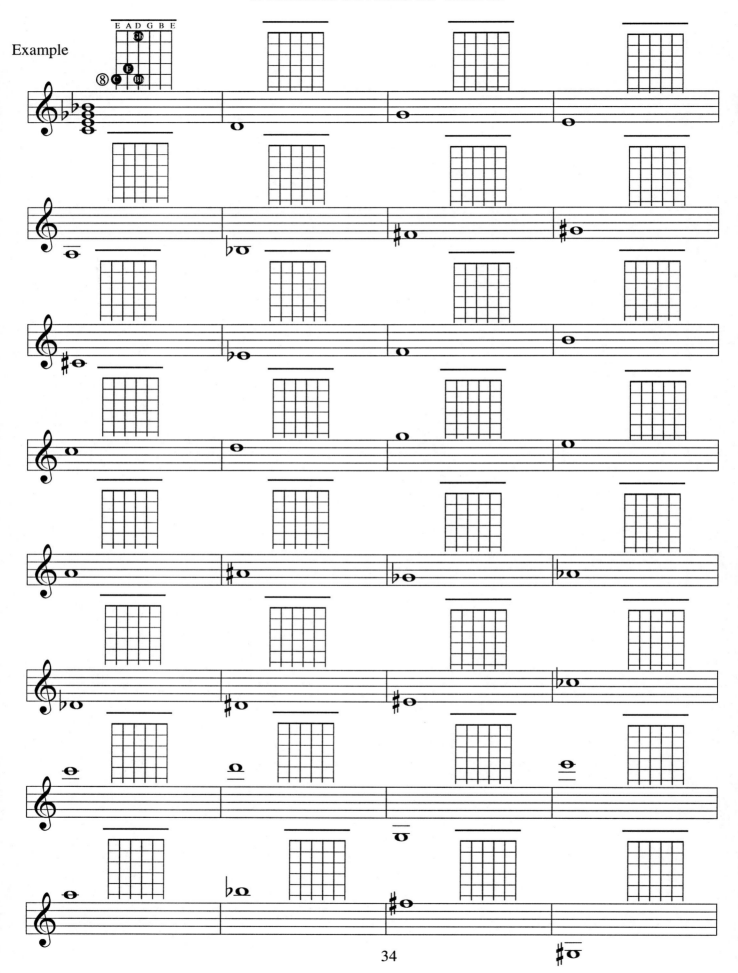

Dominant Seventh #5 Chords

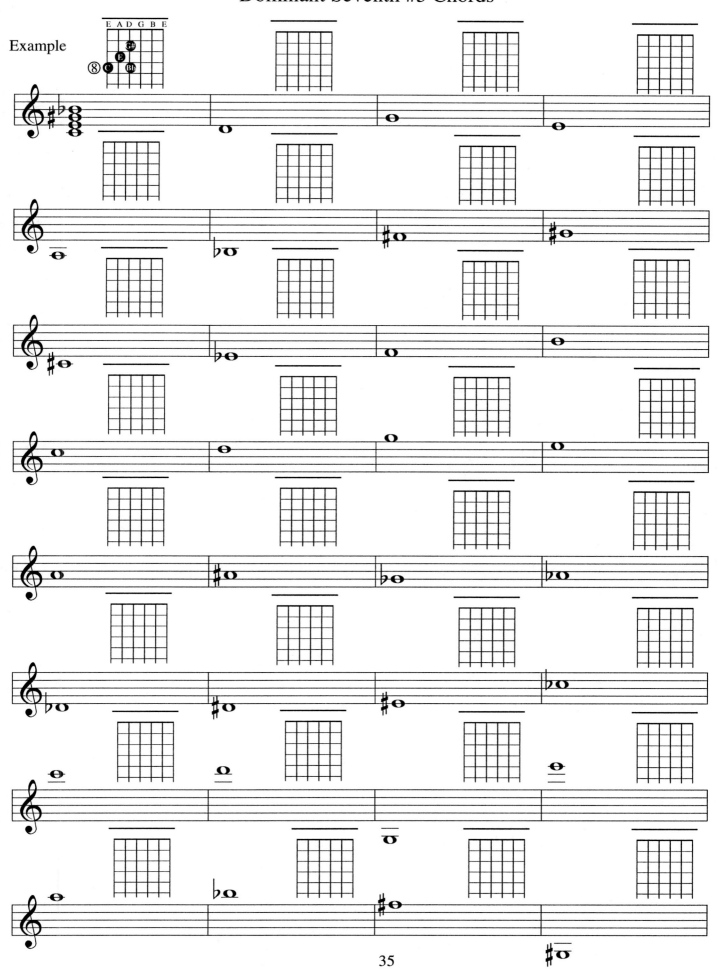

Major 6th Chords

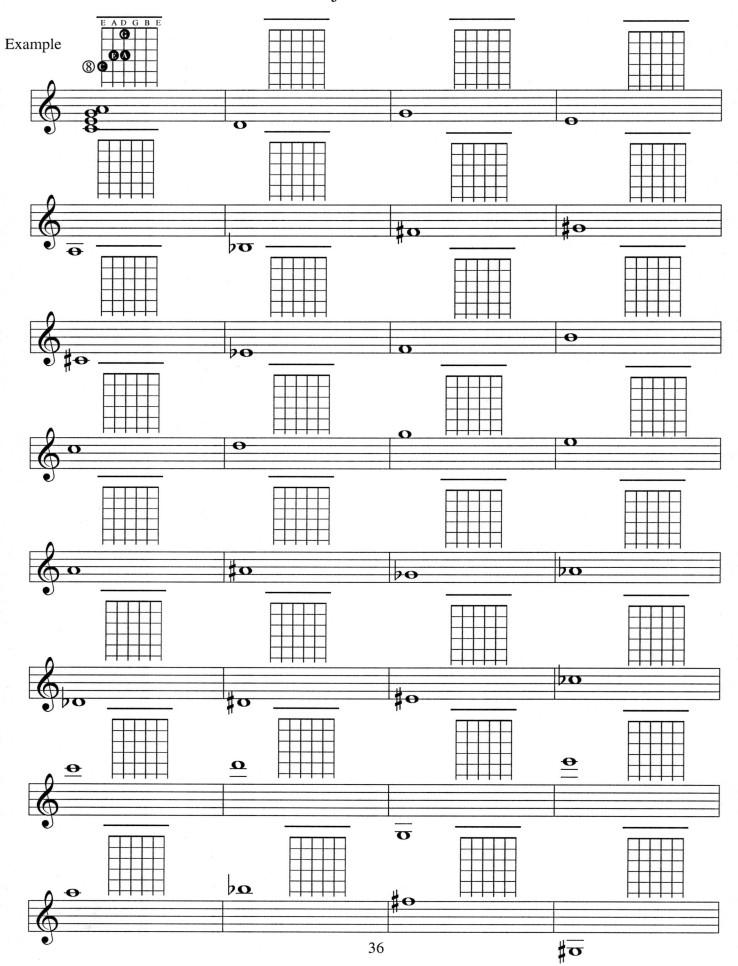

Minor 6th Chords

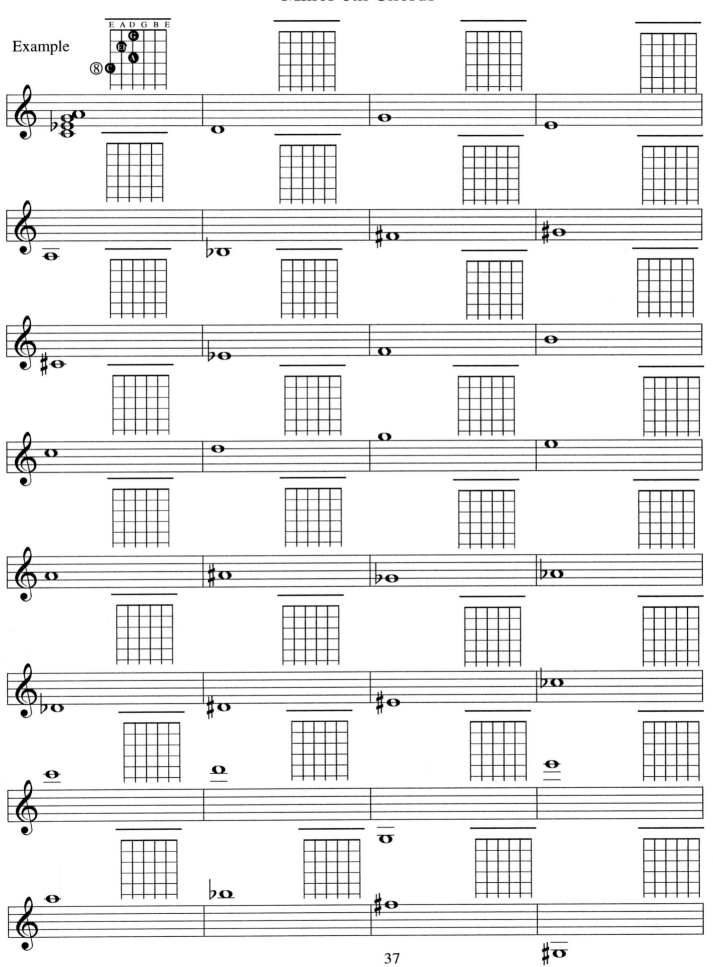

Chord Tones and Tensions
Major 7th
Δ7
Chord Tones 1 3 5 7
Tensions 9 #11 13

Chords with Tensions

As has been previously discussed "tensions" can be added to chords to give them more "color". Before each chord type is shown, the possible tensions for that chord will be given. The chord tones and tensions for CΔ7 are as follows:

All the tensions that we learn for each chord can be used as a substitute for the basic chord type. For instance if we have a C chord we could substitute CΔ7 or CΔ79, etc. Theoretically this will work, but you must use your ear to decide whether the sound is appropriate for the chords before and after it, and for the style of music you are playing.

Major 7 9 Chords

Example

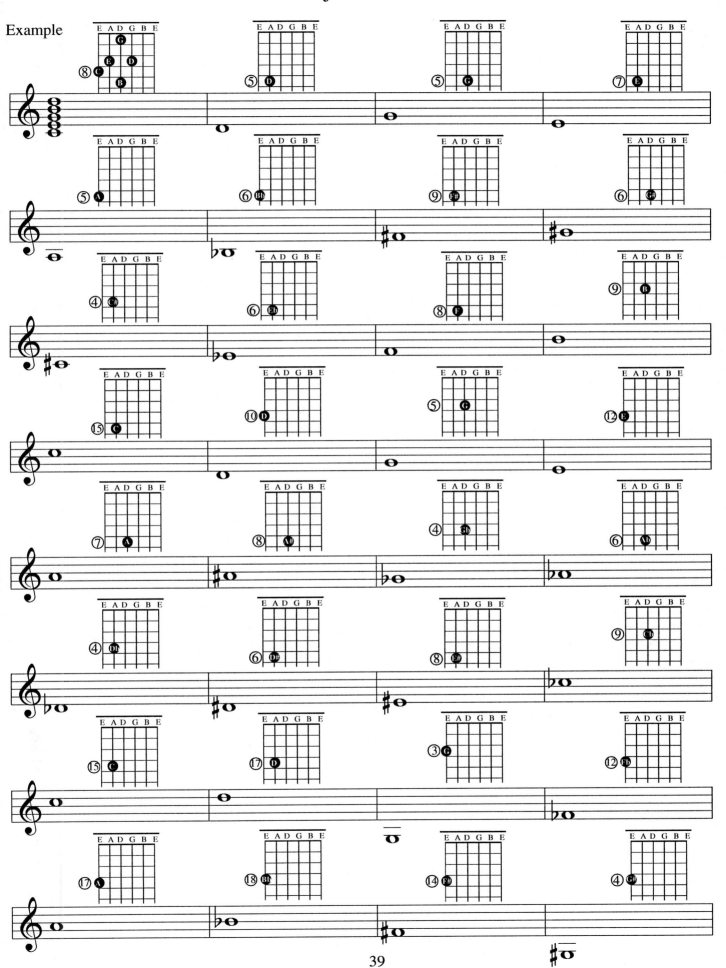

Major 7 6 Chords

Example

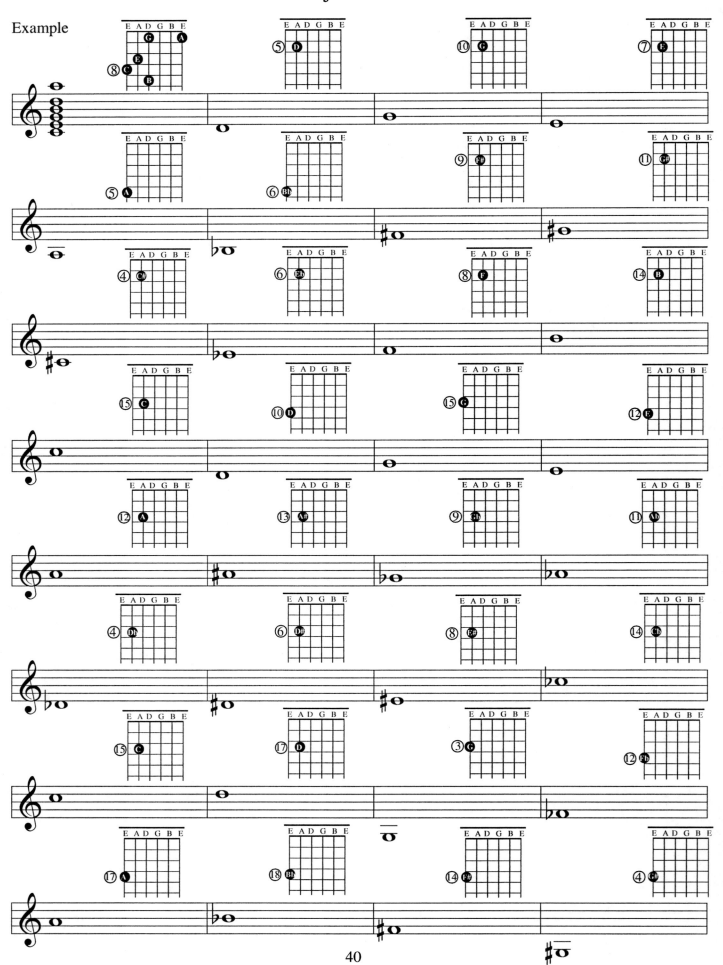

Major 7 6 #11 Chords

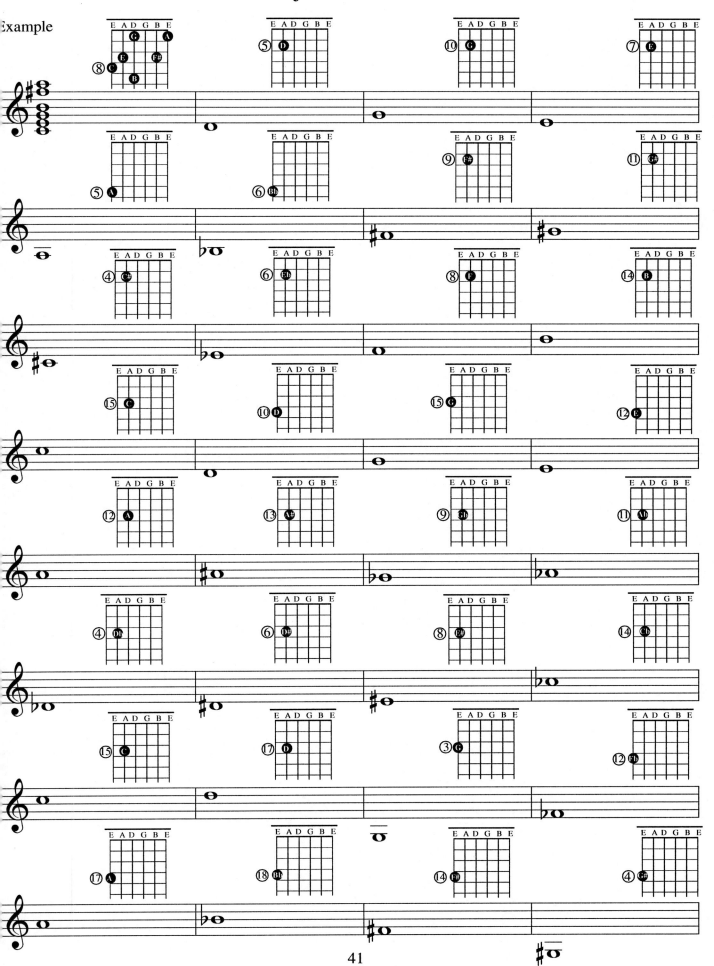

41

Major 7 9 #11 Chords

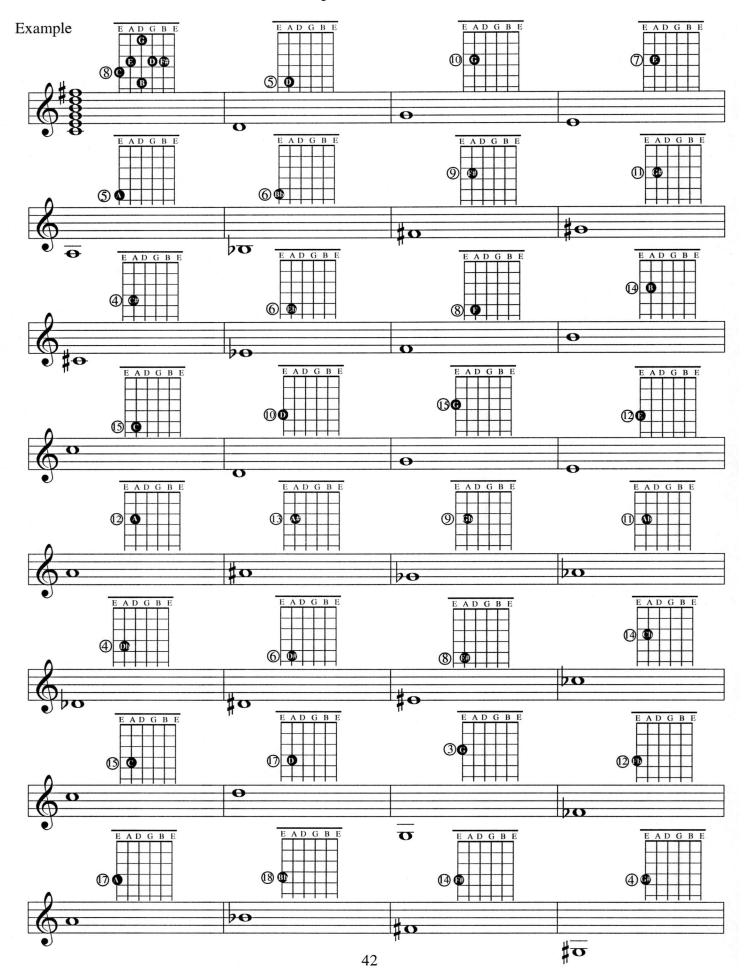

Major 7 6 9 Chords

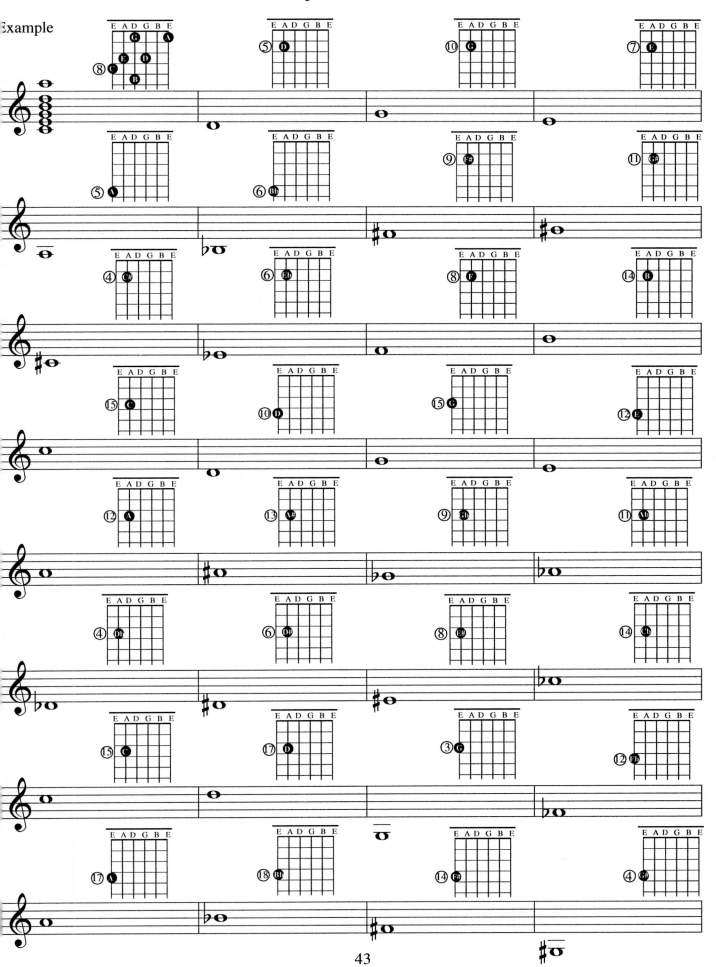

Major 6 9 Chords

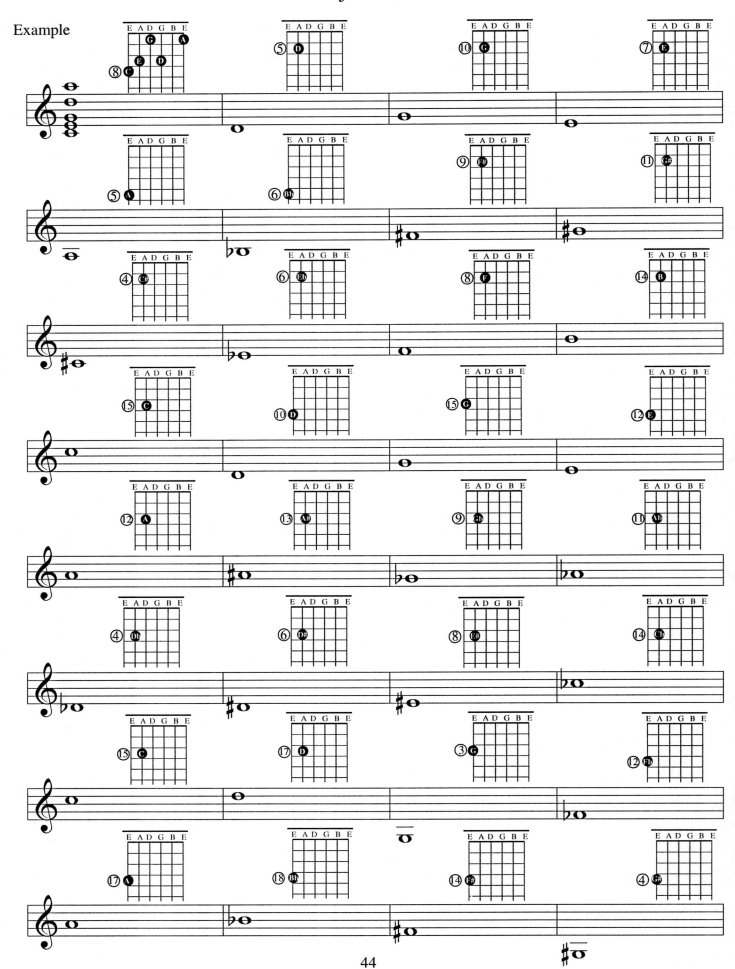

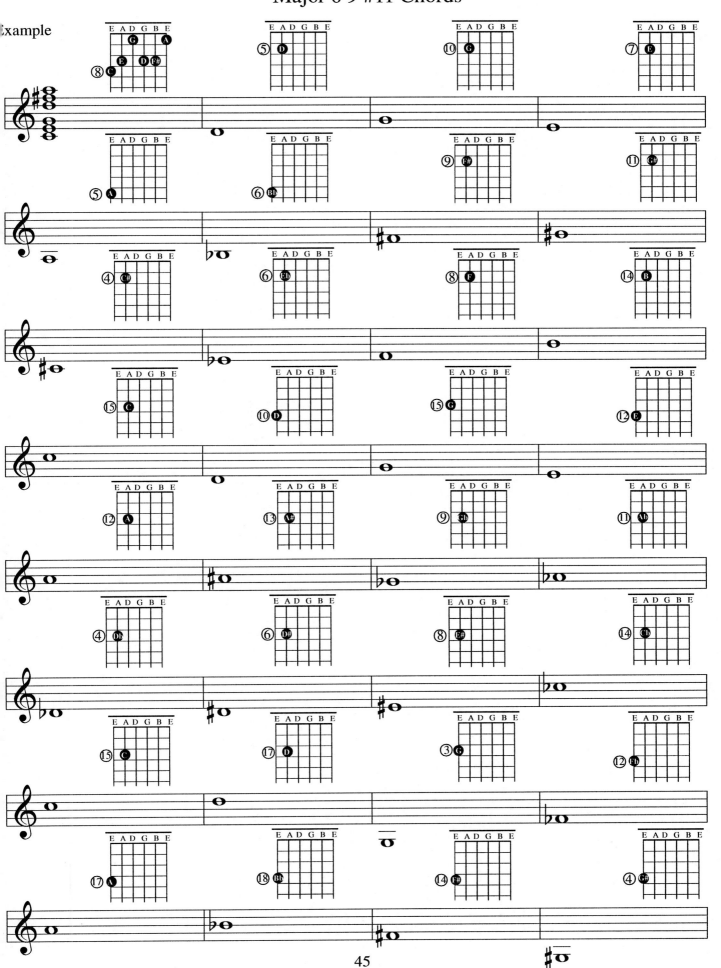

Major add 9 Chords

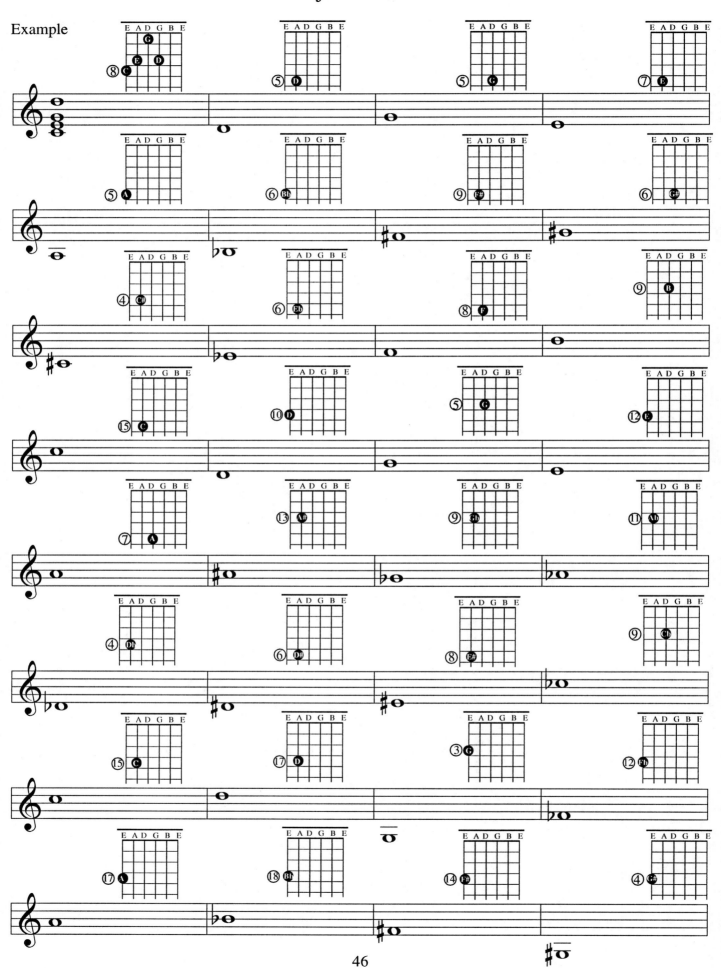

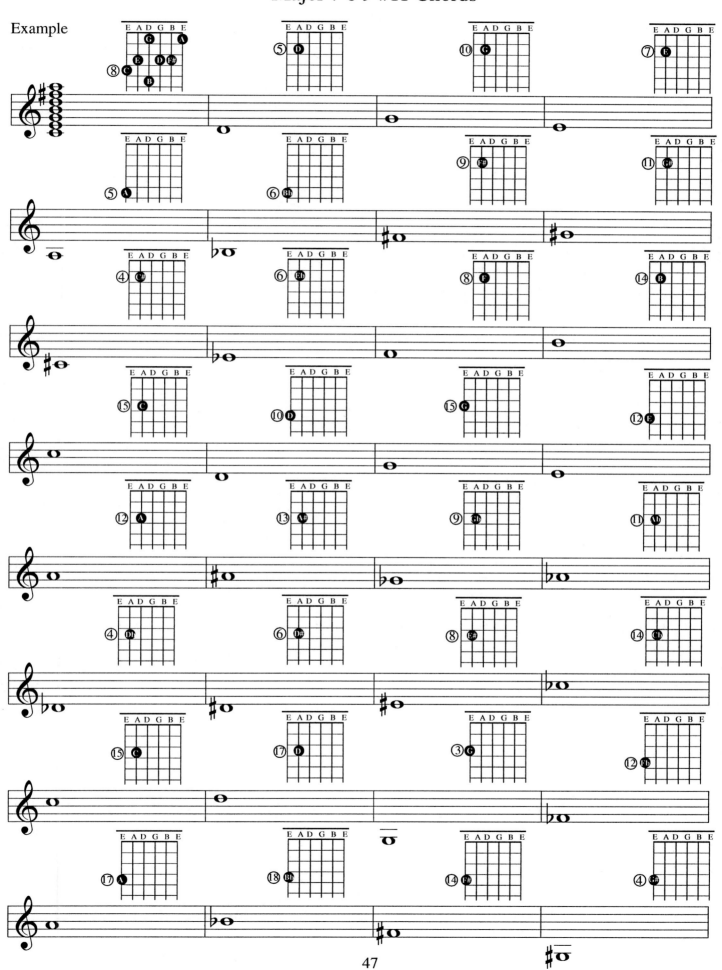

Chord Tones and Tensions
Minor 7th
-7
Chord Tones 1 b3 5 b7
Tensions 9 11 13

Chords with Tensions

Below is a list of the chord tones and tensions for a minor 7th chord. When used in a jazz context it is common to add tensions to the -7 to give it more "color". When used in a jazz tune the minor 7th chord can sound fine if it is used without tensions. This is especially true when it is the II chord of a II V I progression; however if a minor 7th is the I minor, a minor chord that is part of a vamp, or is in a ballad it is more common to add tensions.

The chord tones and tensions for C-7 are as follows:

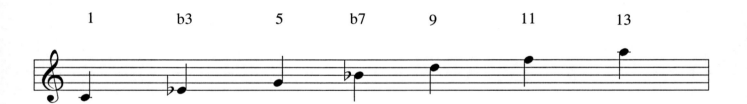

Be careful when adding tensions to a minor chord especially when adding the 9th. Sometimes the 9th can conflict, especially when the minor chord is build on the 3rd degree of a key. As always you must use your ear to decide whether the added tension is appropriate and if it sounds good with the chords before and after it. Again, different styles will affect which tensions sound the best.

Minor 9th Chords

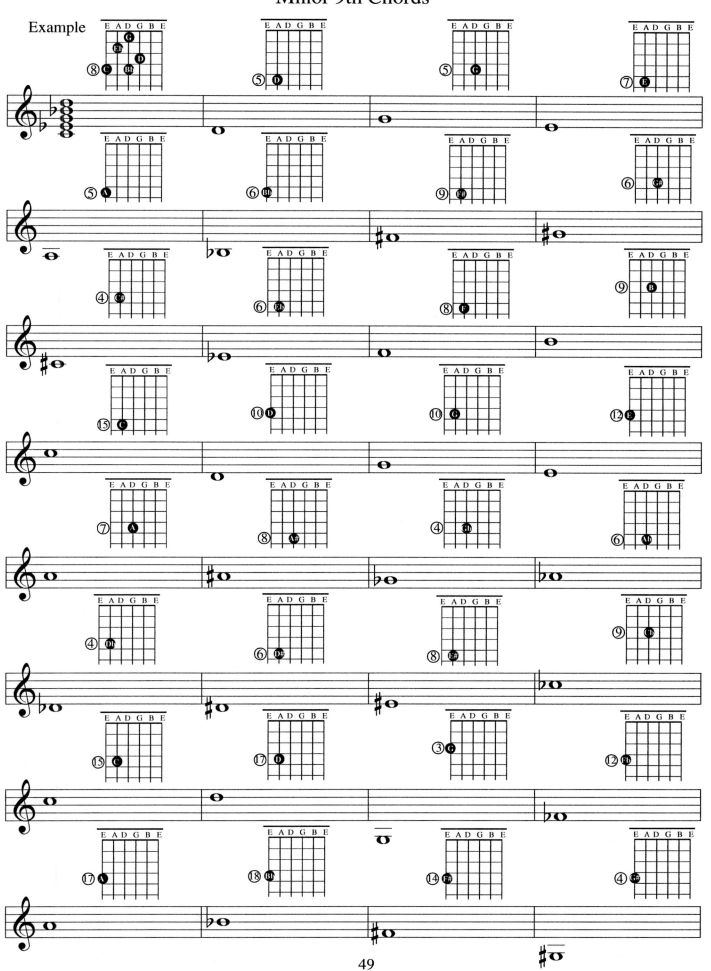

Minor 9 11 Chords

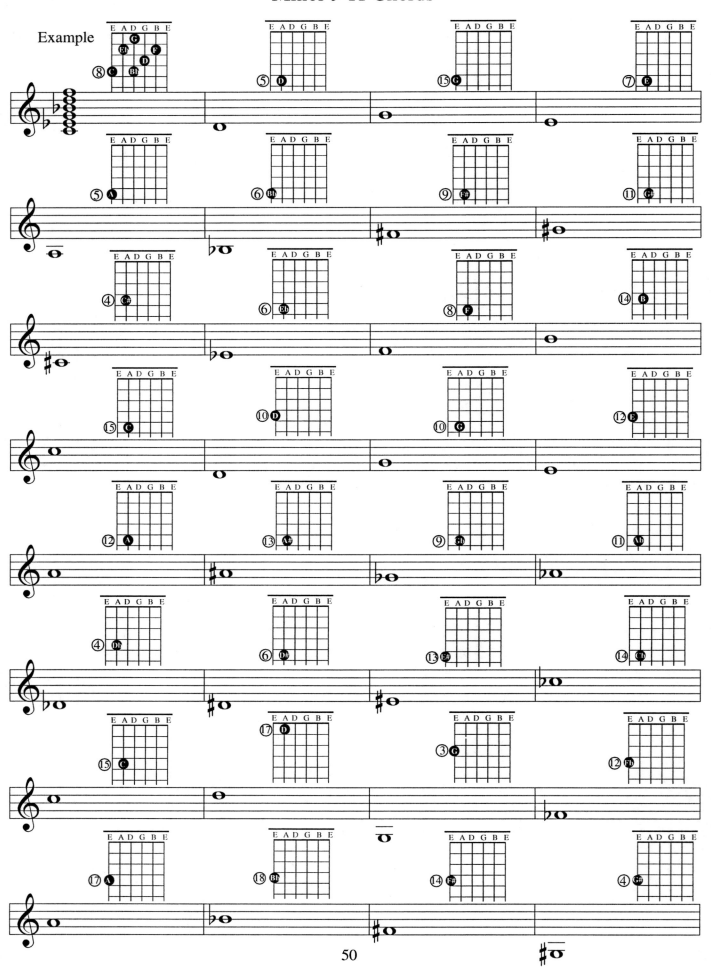

Minor 6 9 Chords

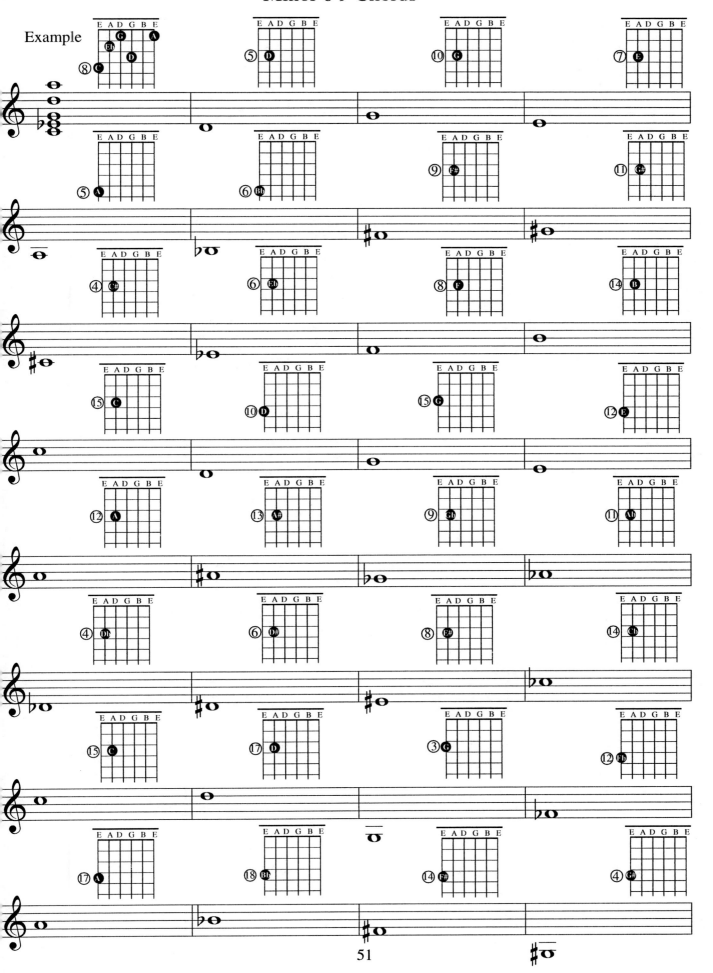

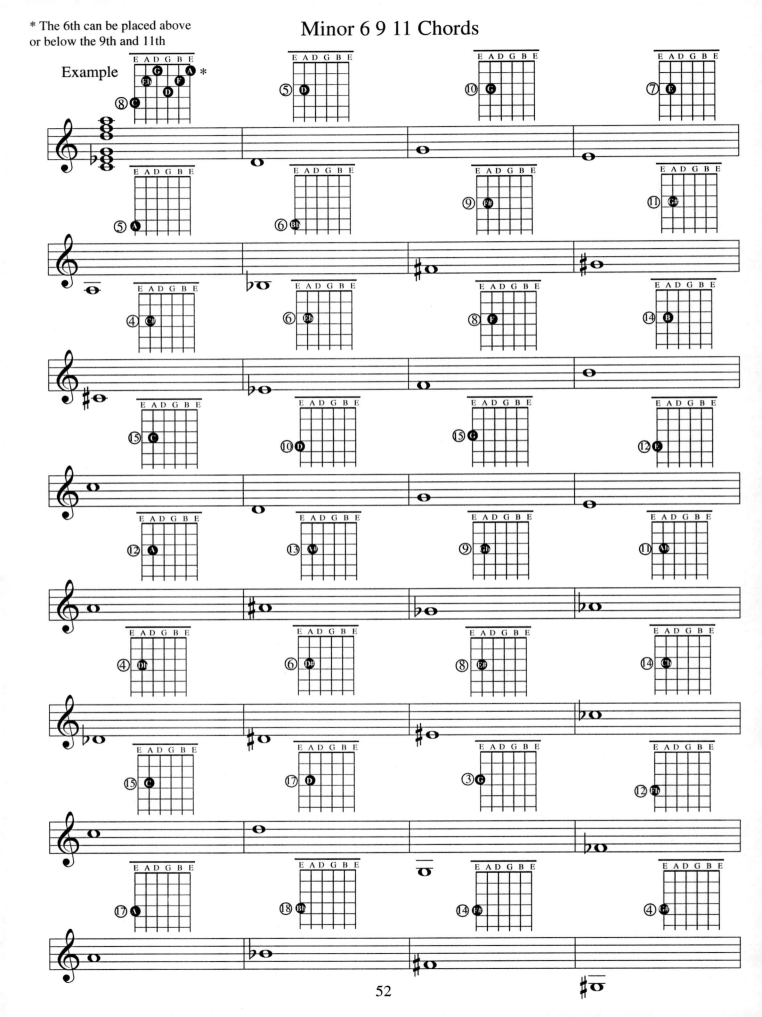

Minor 11 Chords

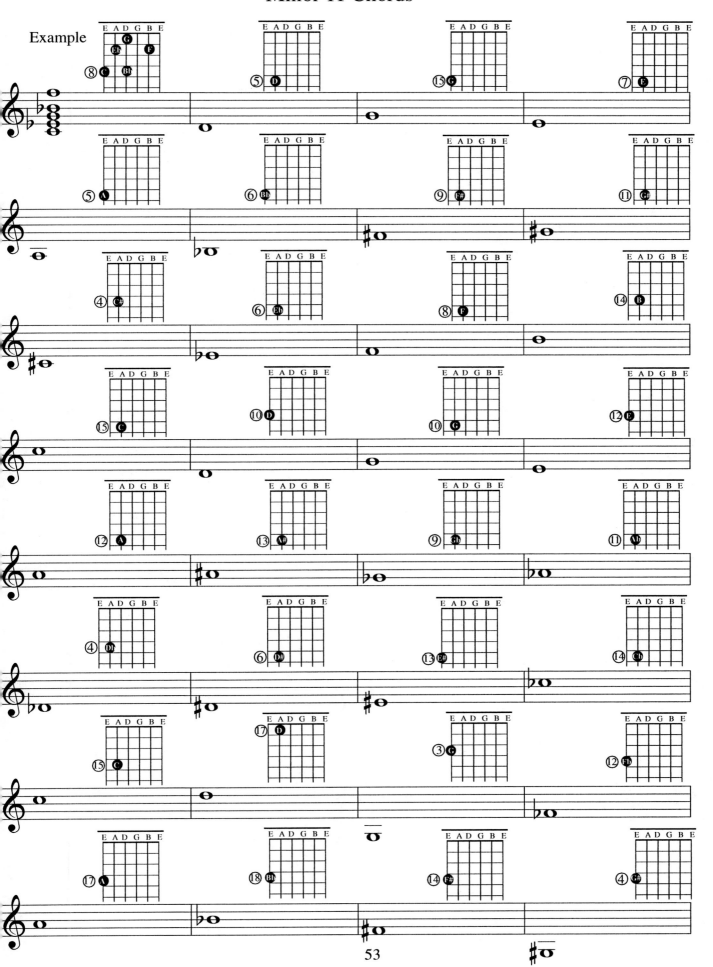

Minor 6 11 Chords

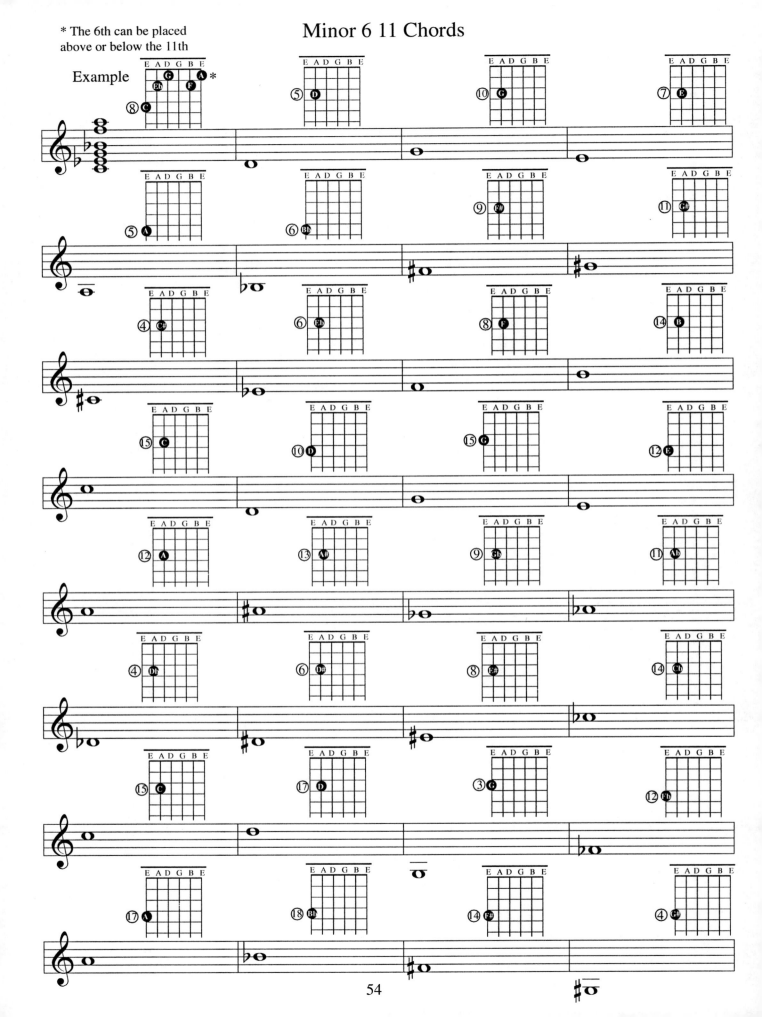

* The 6th can be placed above or below the 11th

54

Minor 6 7 Chords

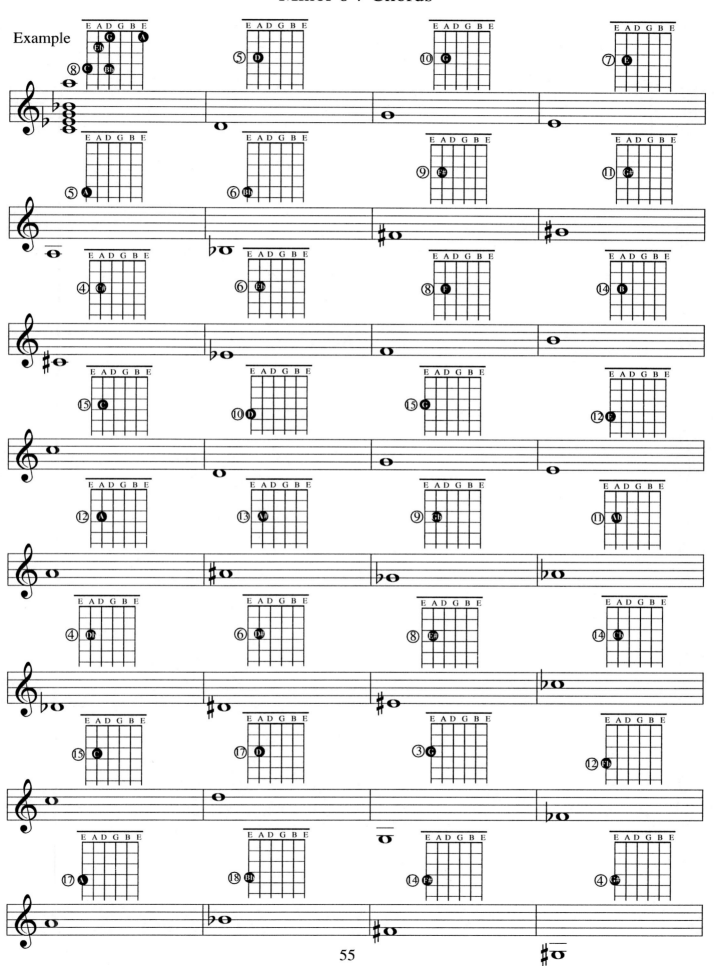

Minor 7 6 9 Chords

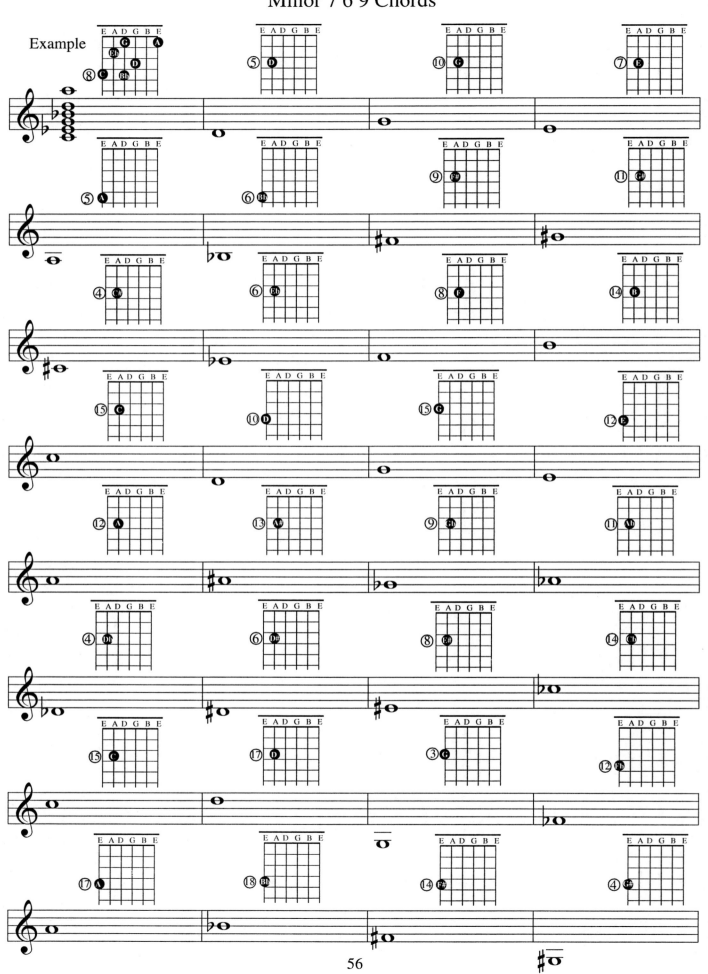

Chord Tones and Tensions
Dominant 7th
7
Chord Tones 1 3 5 b7
Tensions b9 9 #9 #11 #5 13

Chords with Tensions

Below is a list of the chord tones and tensions for a dominant chord. There is no limit to how many tensions can be in a chord, but because the guitar has only 6 strings we are limited to 6 notes.

The chord tones and tensions for C7 are as follows:

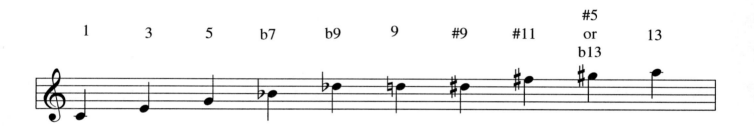

All the tensions that we learn for each chord can be used as a substitute for the basic chord type. Dominant chords have many possibilities for adding and combining tensions. For instance if we have a C7 chord we could substitute C7#11 or C7#9b13 etc. Theoretically any combination is possible. Usually tensions are not combined that are a half step apart. For example, you usually don't have a dominant chord which contains "b9" and natural 9. Also most of these half step possibilities make for difficult and awkward playing on the guitar.

Although any tension combination is possible, there are common situations where certain tensions are preferred over others. When a dominant chord resolves up a fourth to a major chord i.e. C7 to FΔ7 it is common to use natural tensions 9 or 13. When a dominant chord resolves up a fourth to a minor chord i.e. C7 to F-7 it is common to use the altered tensions b9, #9, #11, b13. The reason C7 to FΔ7 uses natural tension is that the 9 and 13 (in this case, on C7 that would be D and A), are diatonic to the F major scale therefore creating an expectation of an impending major resolution. On the other hand if C7 resolves to an F minor chord, the altered tensions (in this case, on C7 they would be Db, Eb, Ab) are commonly used because they are found in various F minor scales. Db and Ab could be from the F harmonic minor scale and Eb from the natural minor scale. There are of course many other F minor scales that these three notes are found in. You can find many examples of these different tension combinations in the progression section found at the end of "Chord Workbook for Guitar Volume One."

Dominant 9th Chords

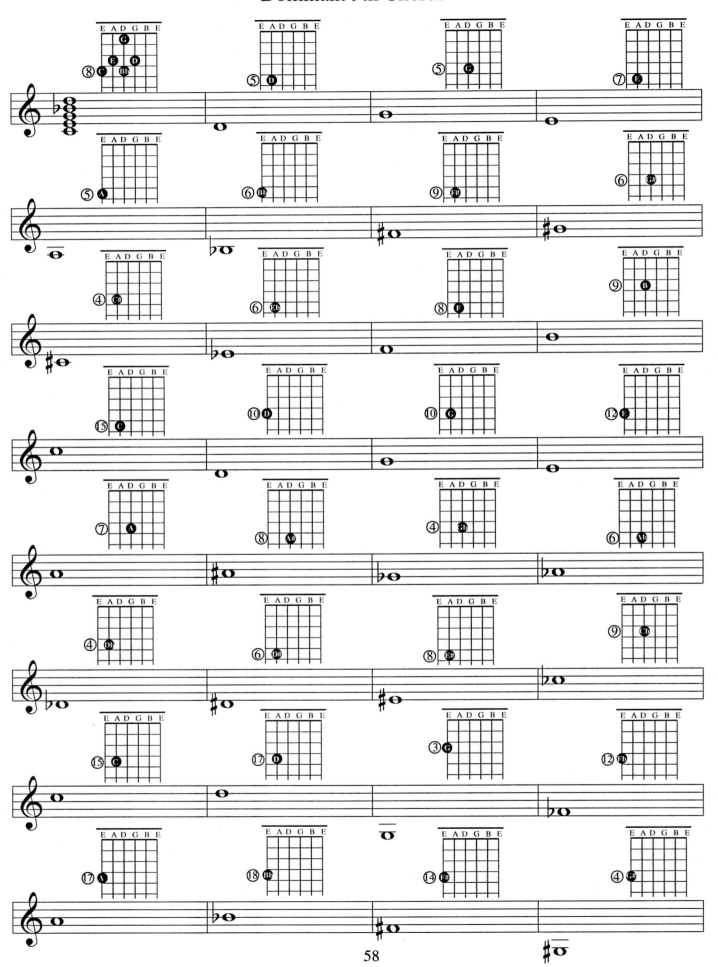

Dominant 7b9 Chords

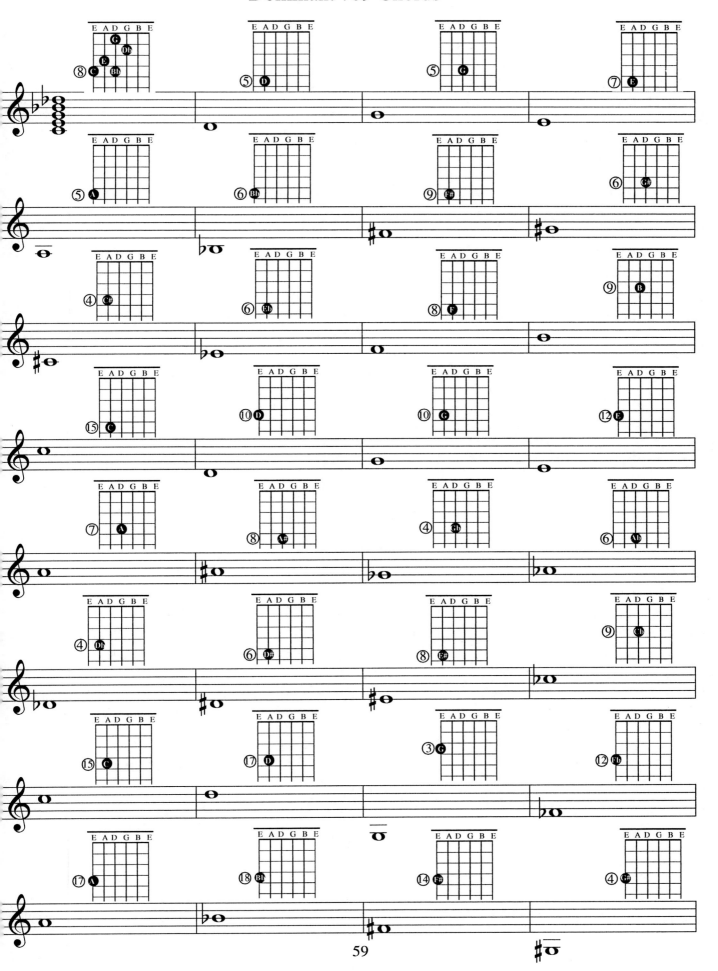

Dominant 7#9 Chords

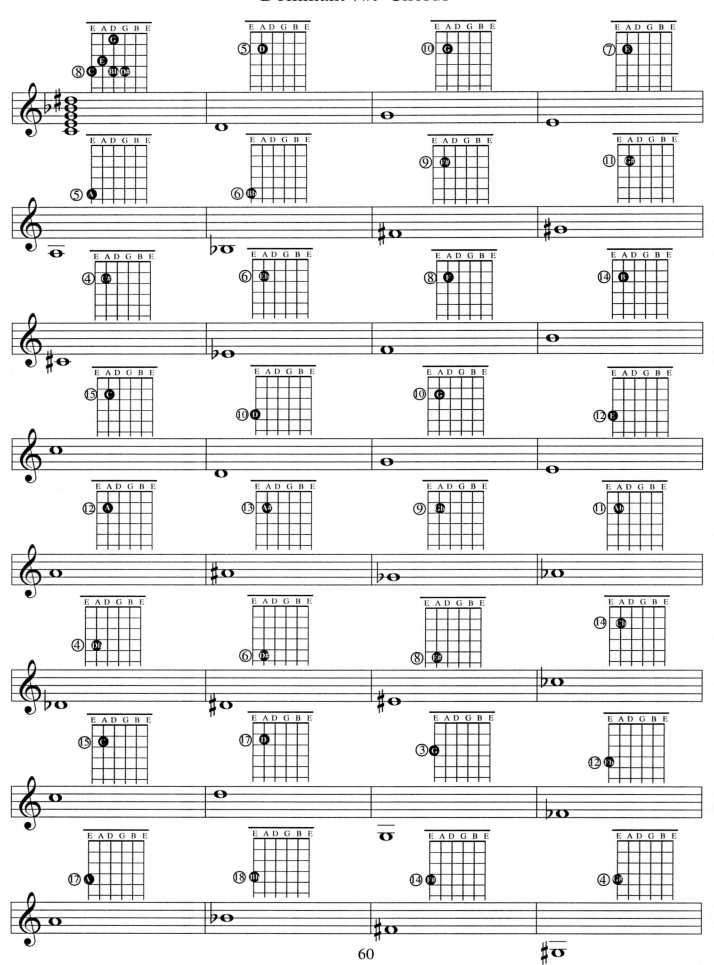

Dominant 13 Chords

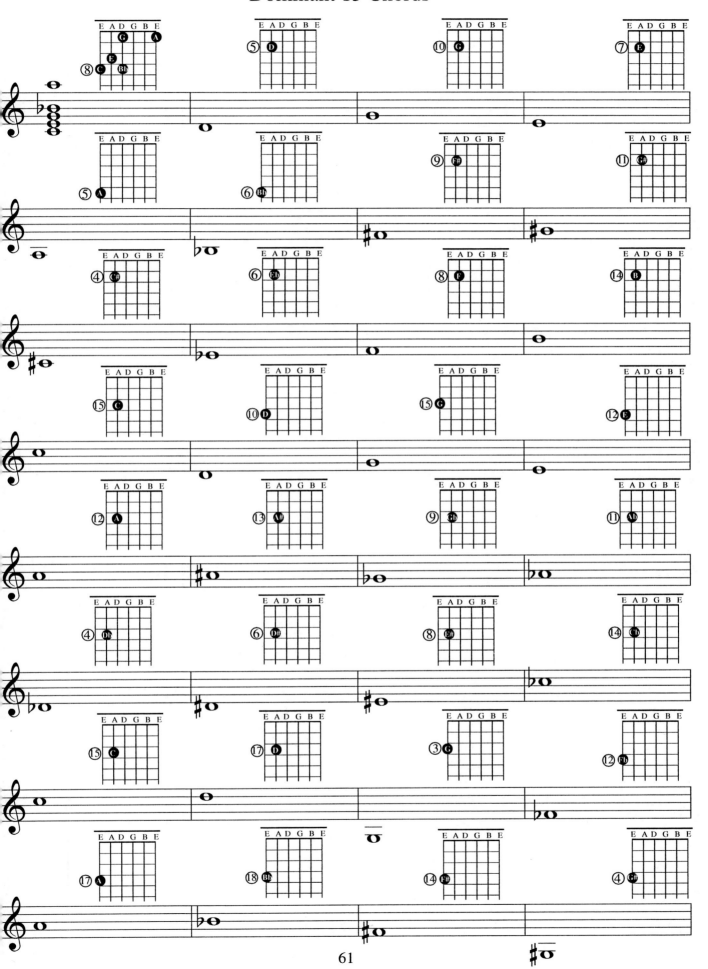

Dominant 7b13 Chords

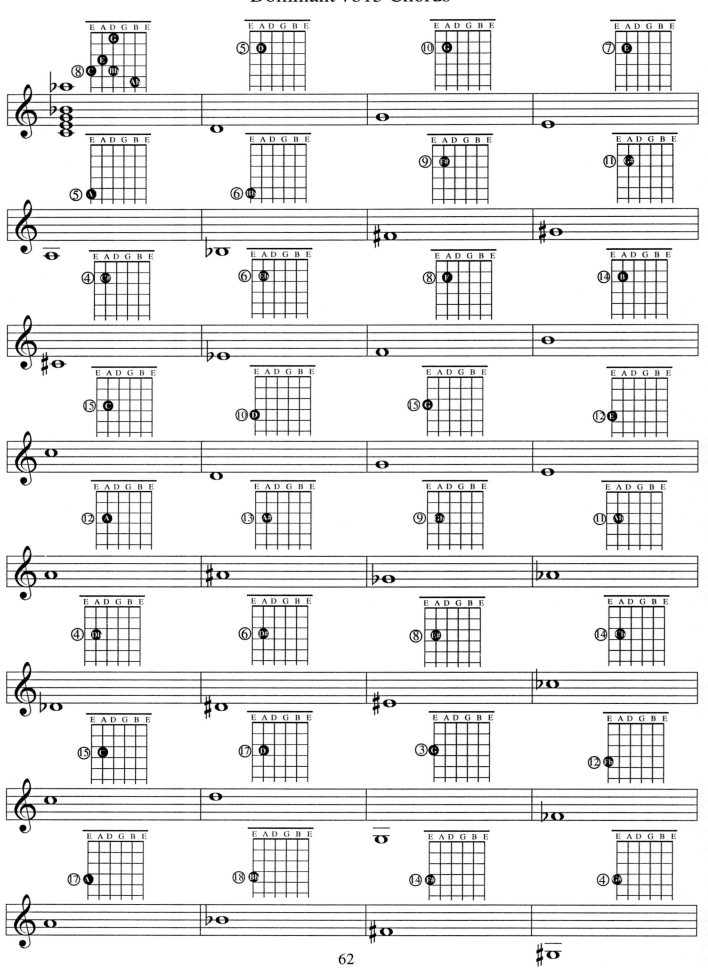

Dominant 9 13 Chords

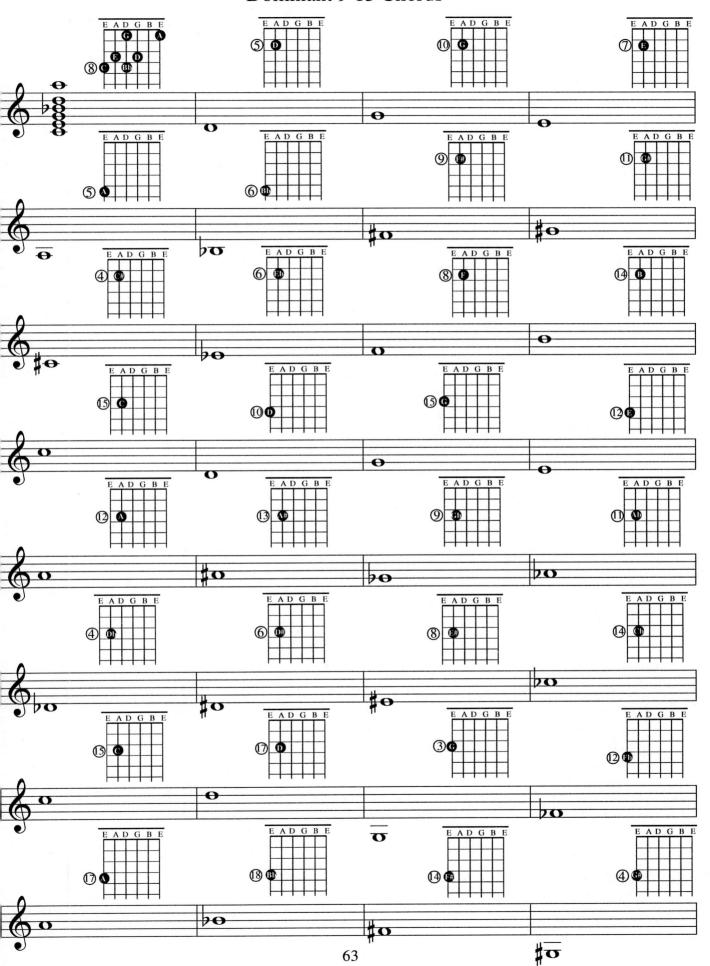

Dominant 9 b13 Chords

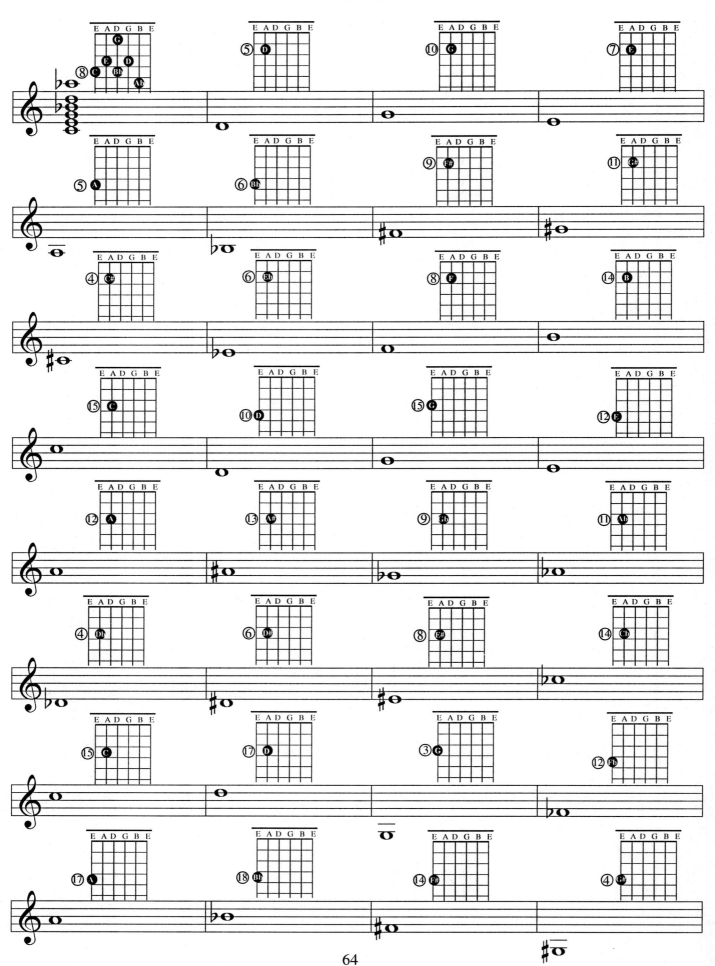

Dominant 7 b9 13 Chords

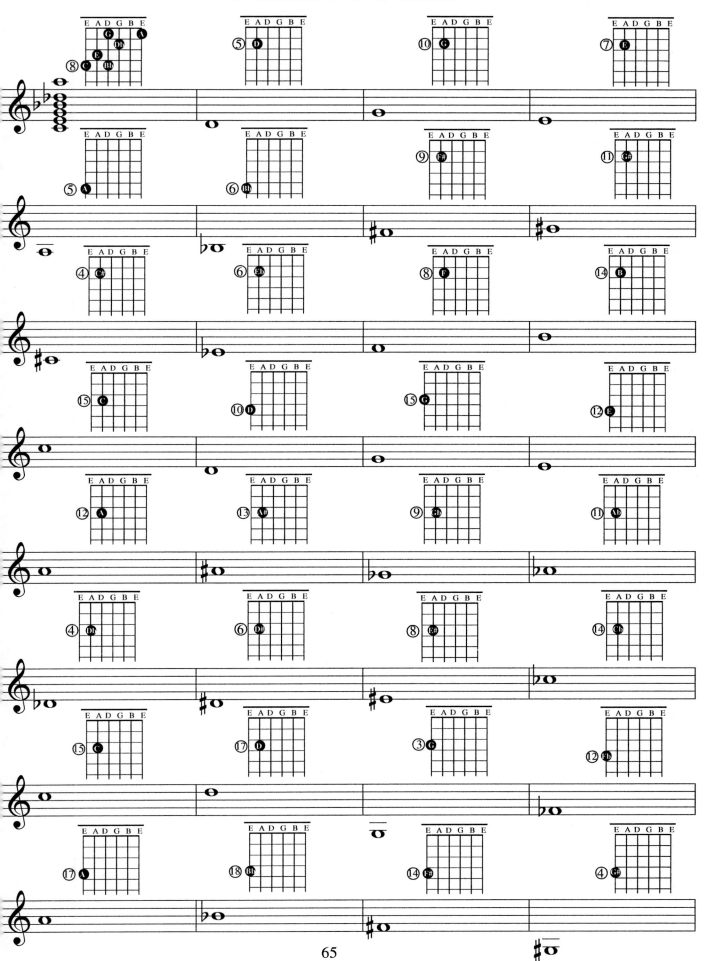

Dominant 7 #9 13 Chords

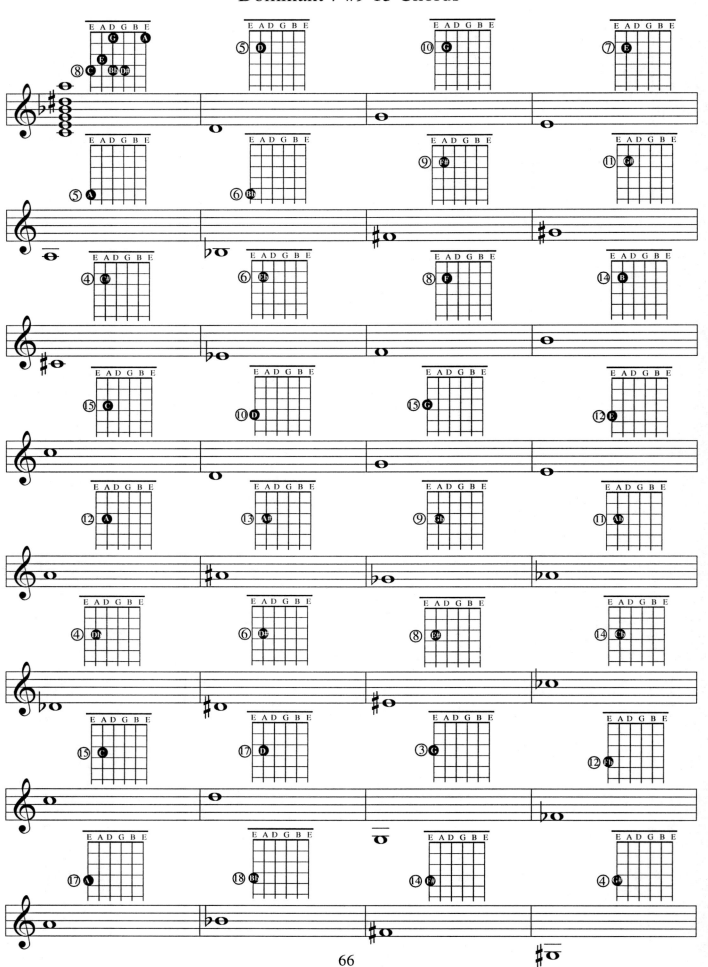

Dominant 7 b9 b13 Chords

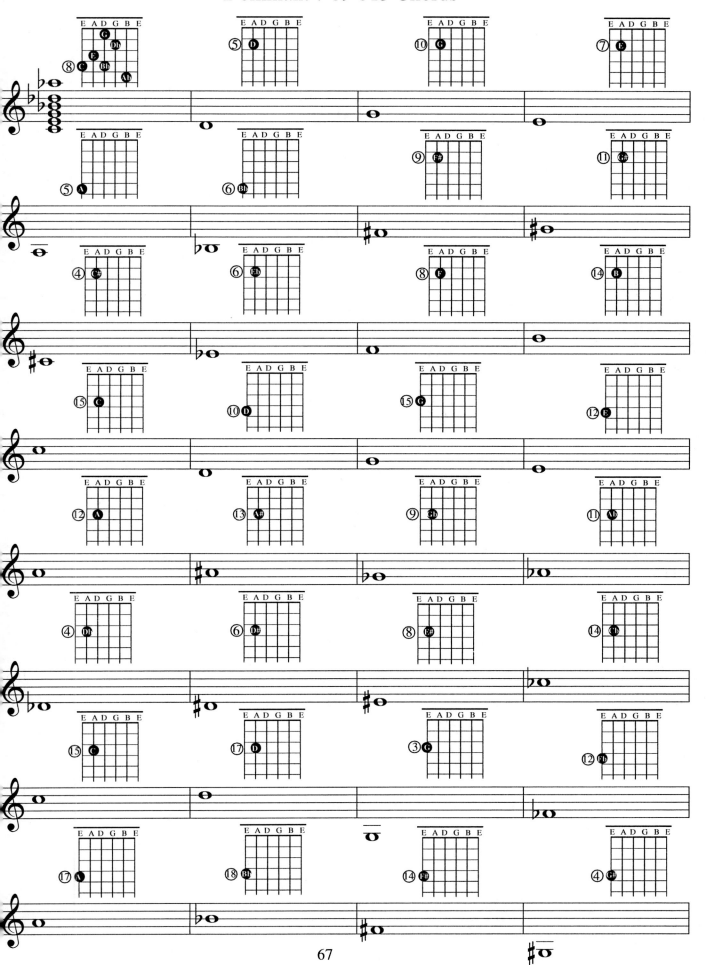

Dominant 7 #9 b13 Chords

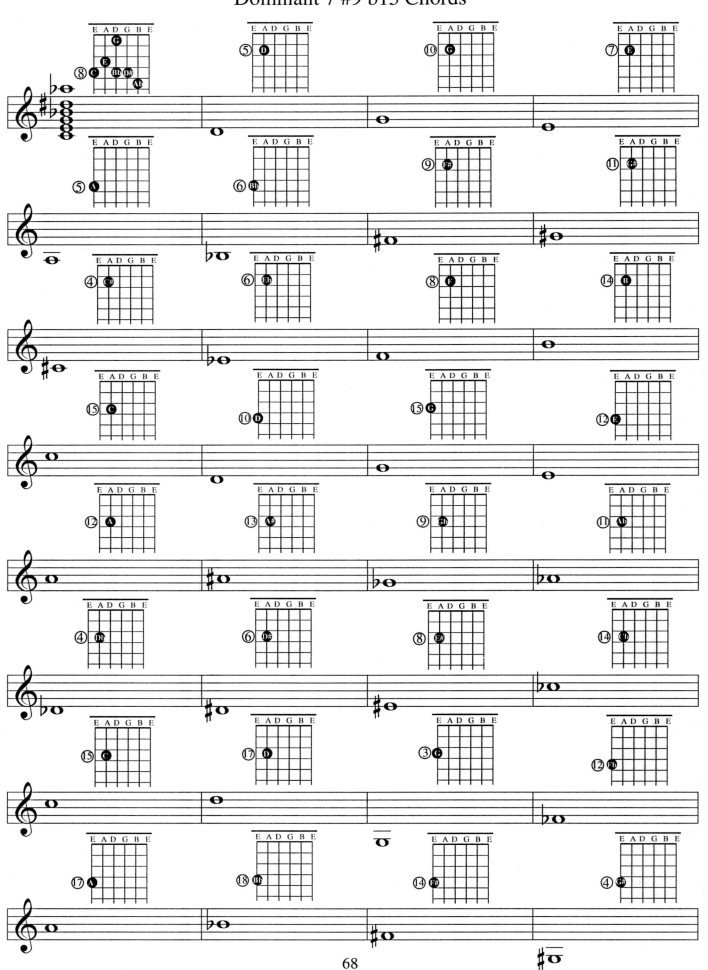

Dominant 9 #11 Chords

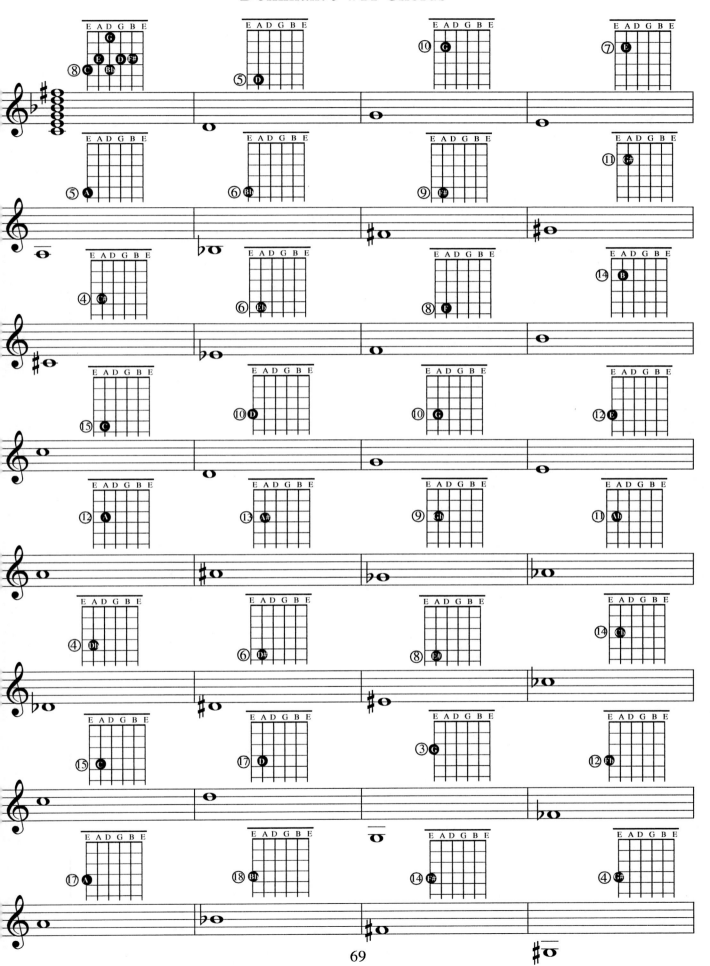

Dominant 7 b9 #11 Chords

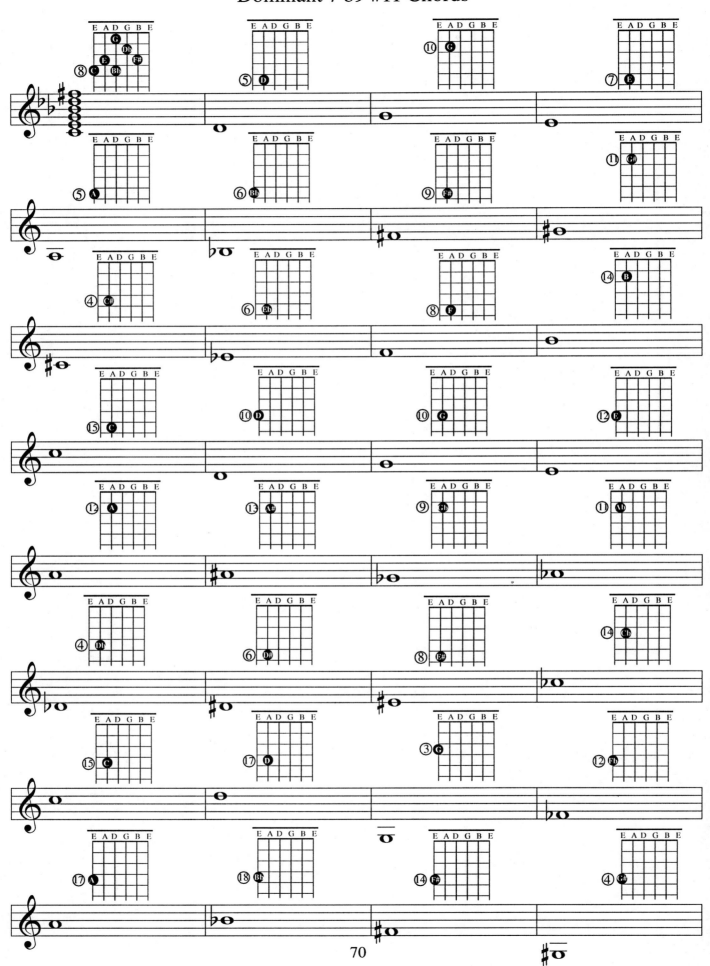

Dominant 7 #9 #11 Chords

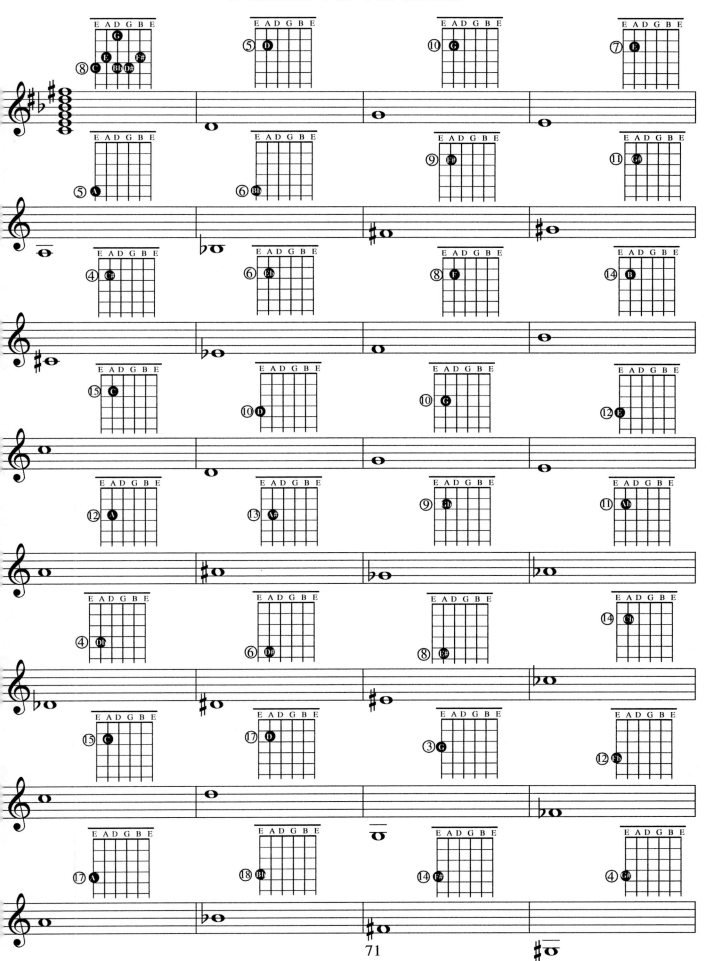

71

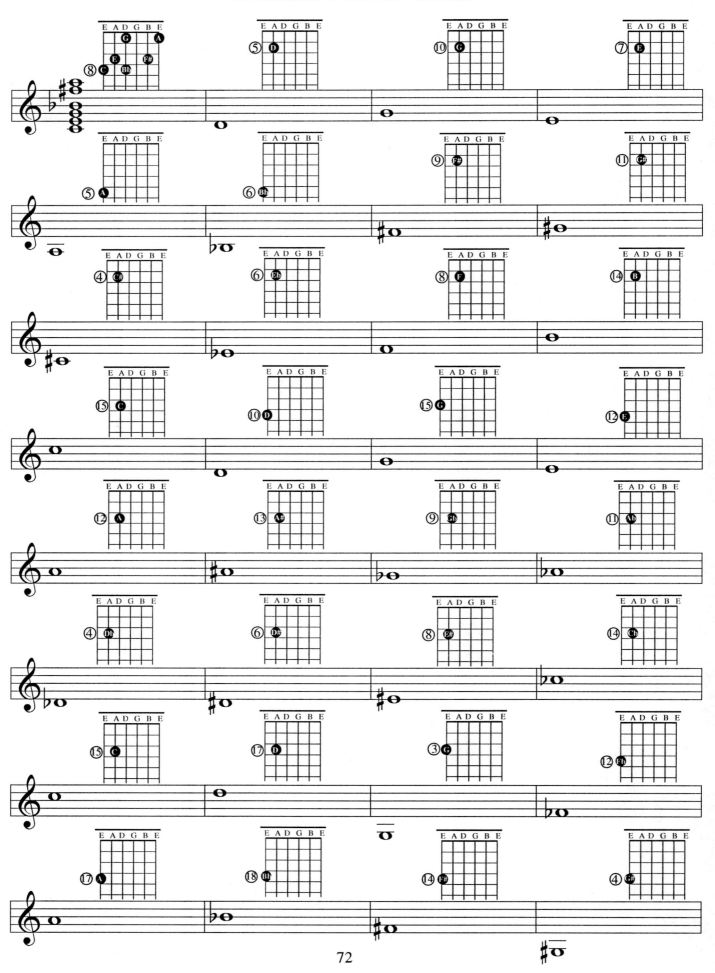

Dominant 7 #11 b13 Chords

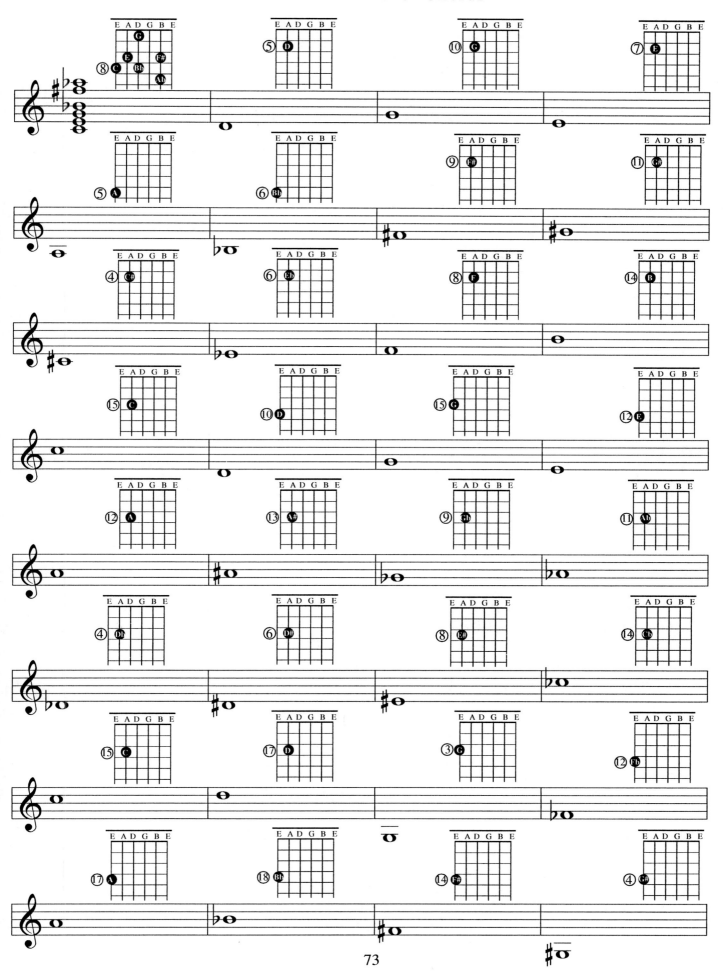

Chord Tones and Tensions
Dominant 7th sus4
7sus4
Chord Tones 1 4 5 b7
Tensions b9 9 #9 10 b13 13

Chords with Tensions

Below is a list of the chord tones and tensions for a dominant 7th sus4 chord. Dominant 7th sus4 is commonly found in jazz where there is a vamp or when it is placed before a dominant 7th. For example, C7sus4 to C7. Like the minor 7th chord the 7sus4 chord can sound fine if it is used without tensions.

The chord tones and tensions for C7sus4 are as follows:

Many of the voicings of the dominant 7sus4 chords on guitar contain a lot of 4th intervals. This creates a very "open" sound and is commonly used for vamps. It is also common to use the 7sus4 voicing as a vehicle to slide in and out of a key center by moving the chord up and down a half step or to other intervals. An example of this application can be found in the E minor blues progression on page 117 of the Chord Workbook for Guitar Volume 1.

Dominant 9sus4 Chords

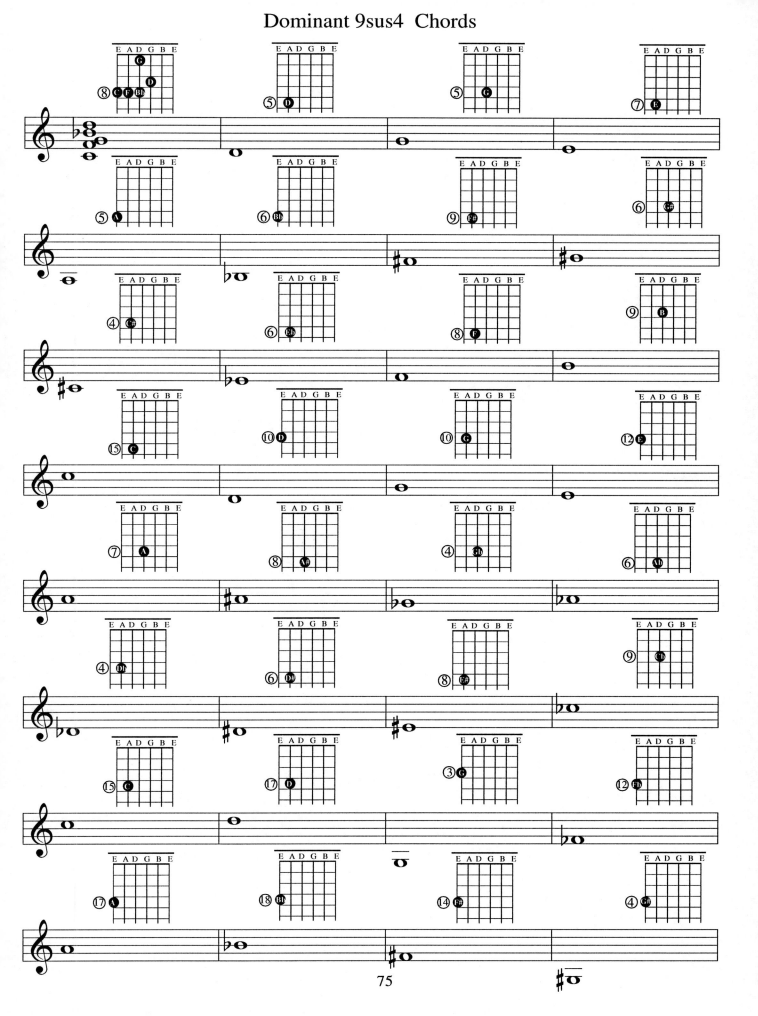

Dominant 7sus4b9 Chords

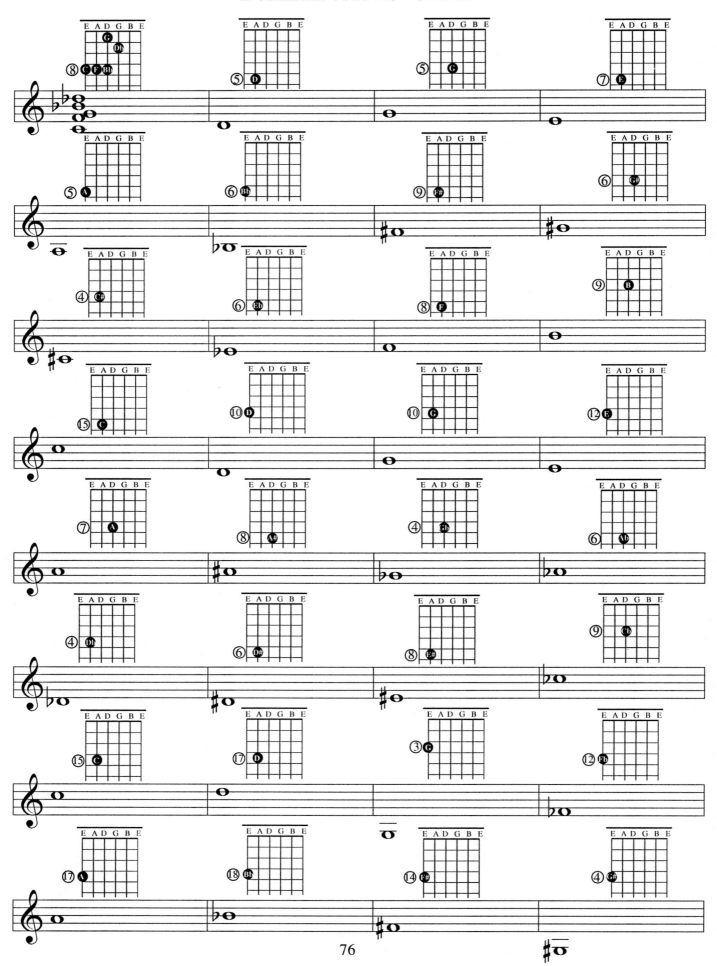

Dominant 7sus4#9 Chords

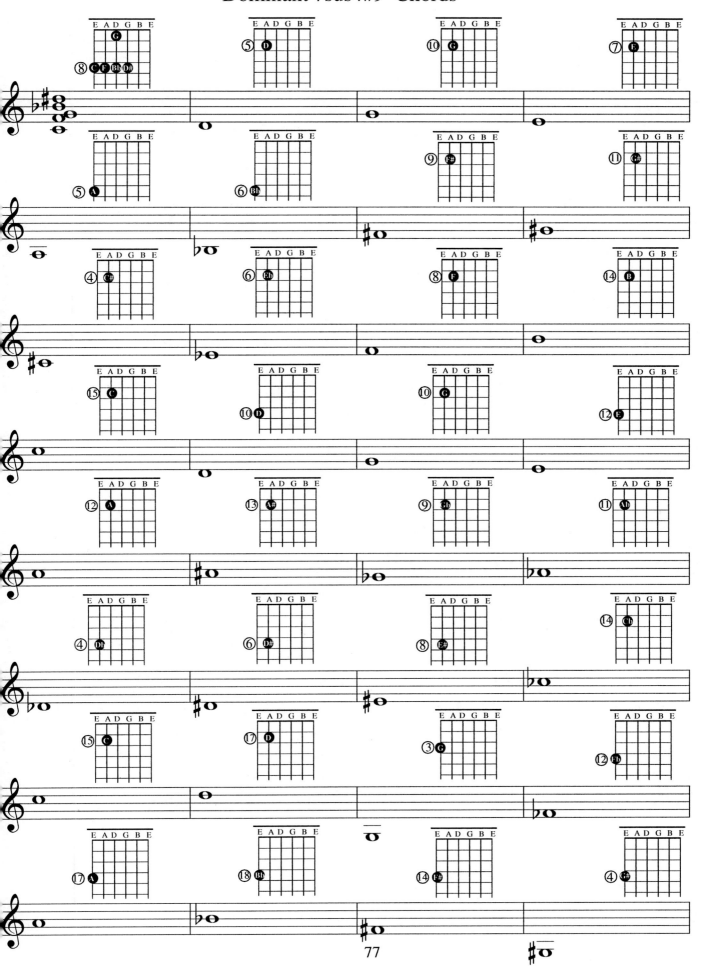

Dominant 13sus4 Chords

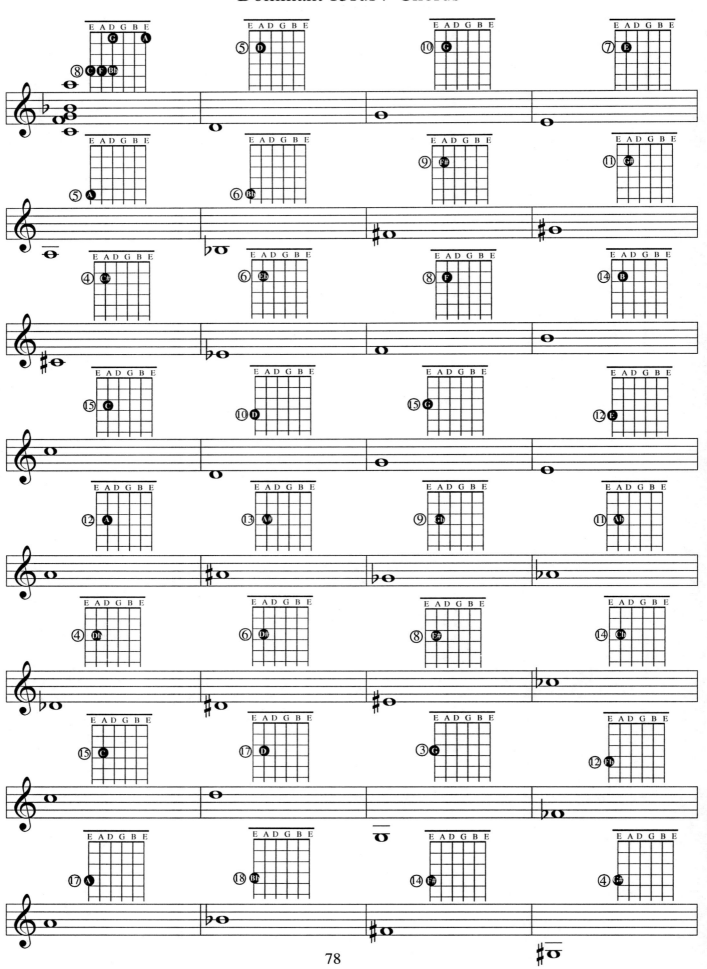

Dominant 7sus4b13 Chords

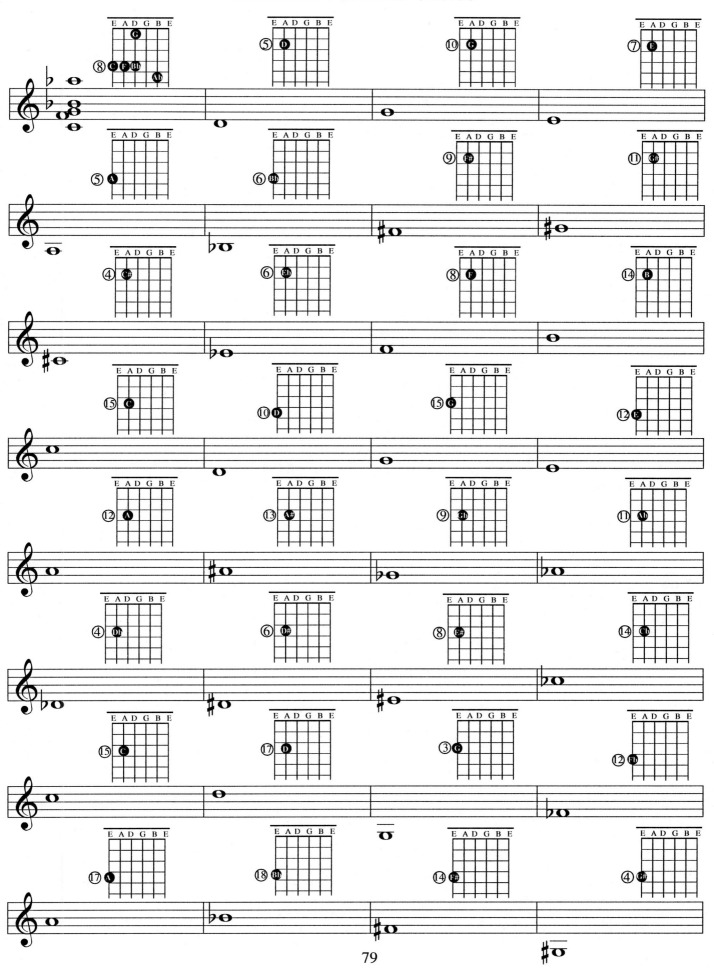

Dominant 9sus4 13 Chords

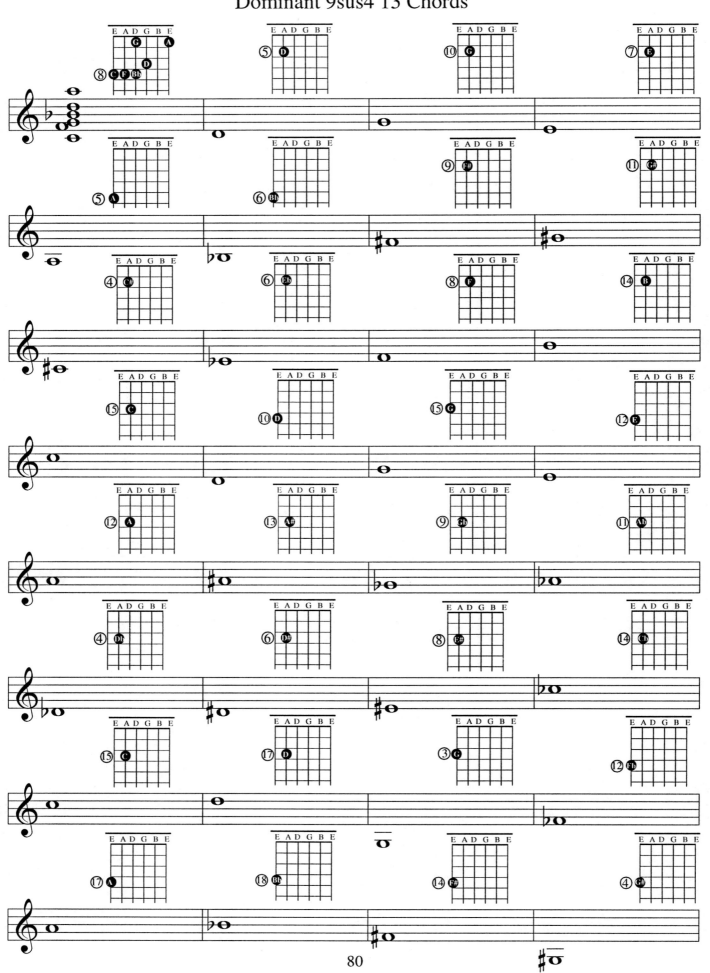

Dominant 9sus4 b13 Chords

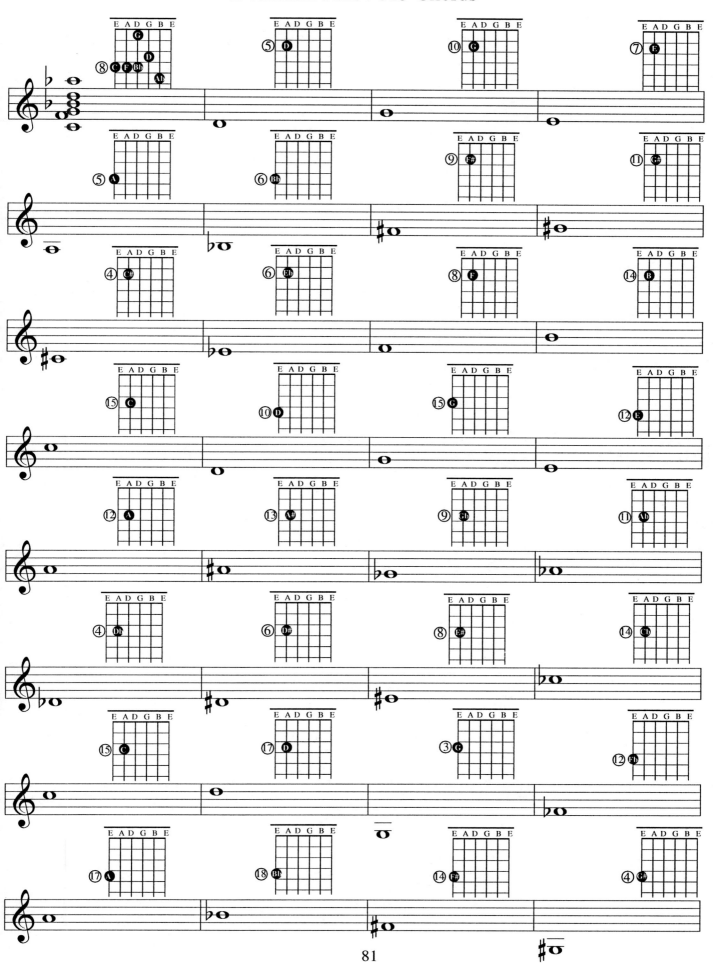

Dominant 7sus4 b9 13 Chords

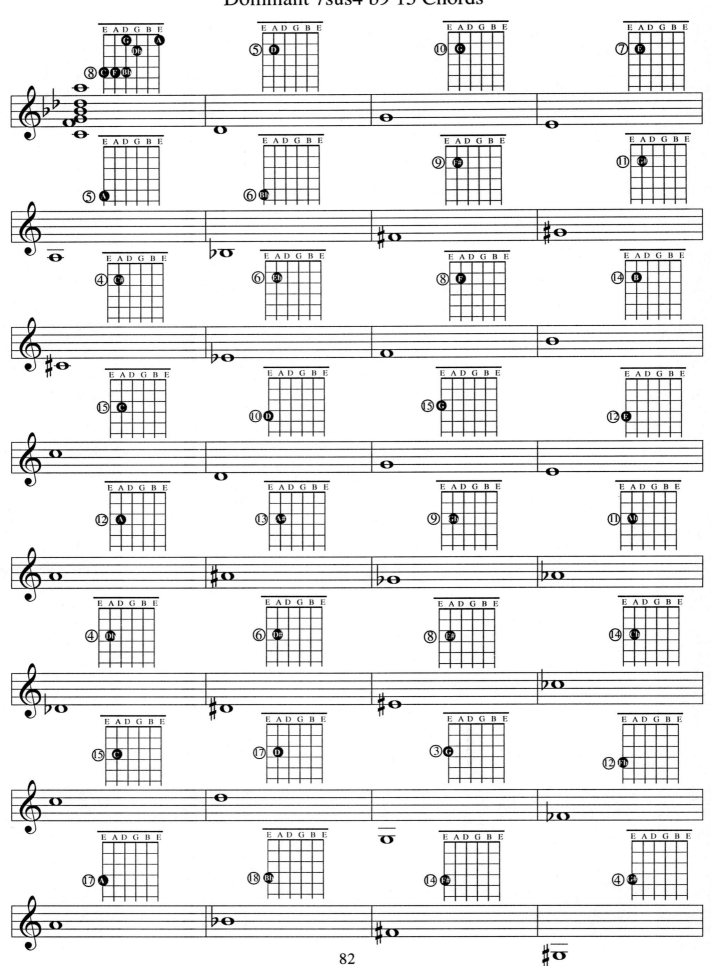

Dominant 7sus4 #9 13 Chords

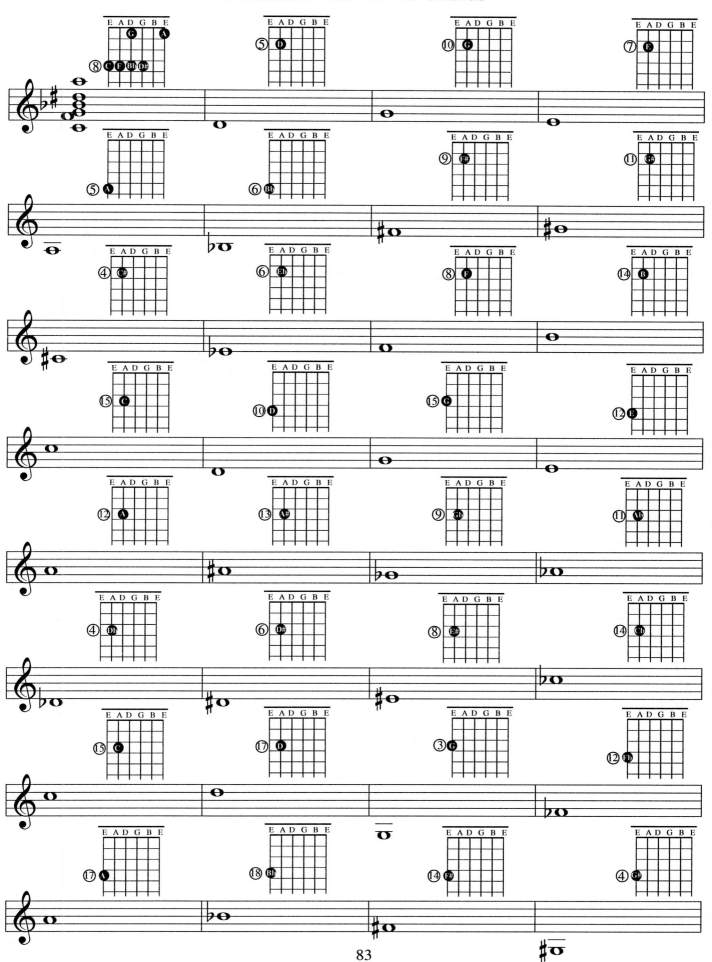

Dominant 7sus4 b9 b13 Chords

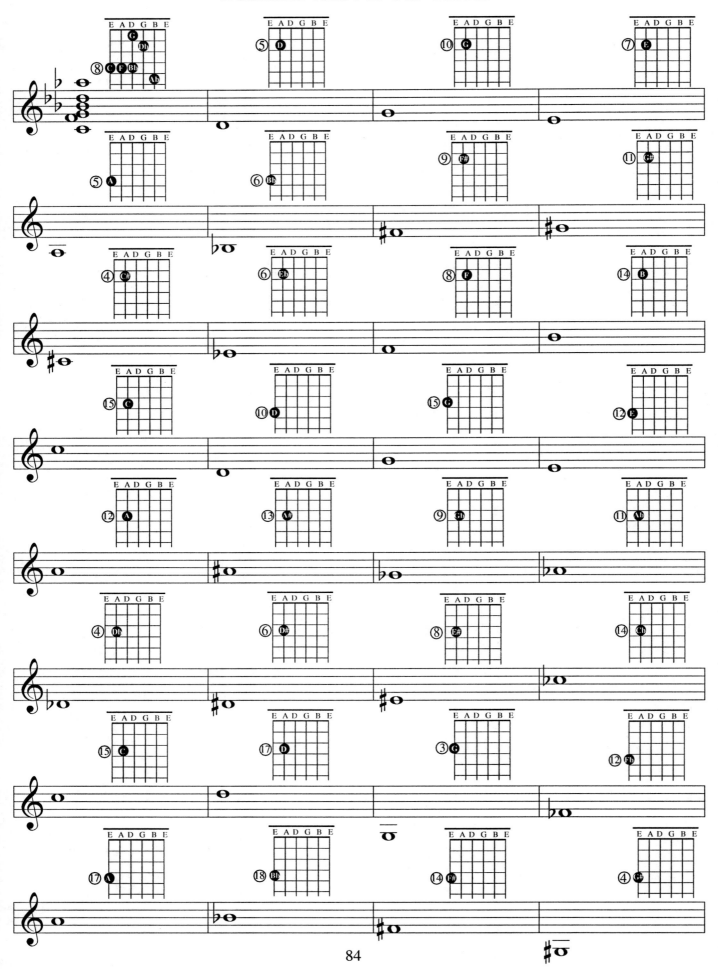

Dominant 7sus4 #9 b13 Chords

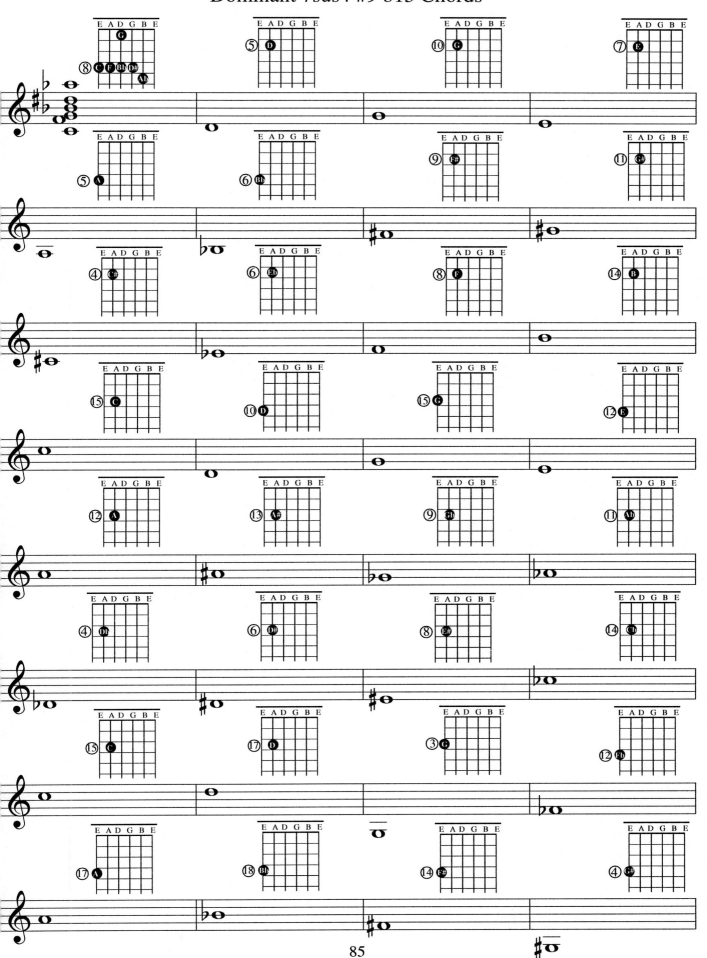

Dominant 13sus4 add10 Chords

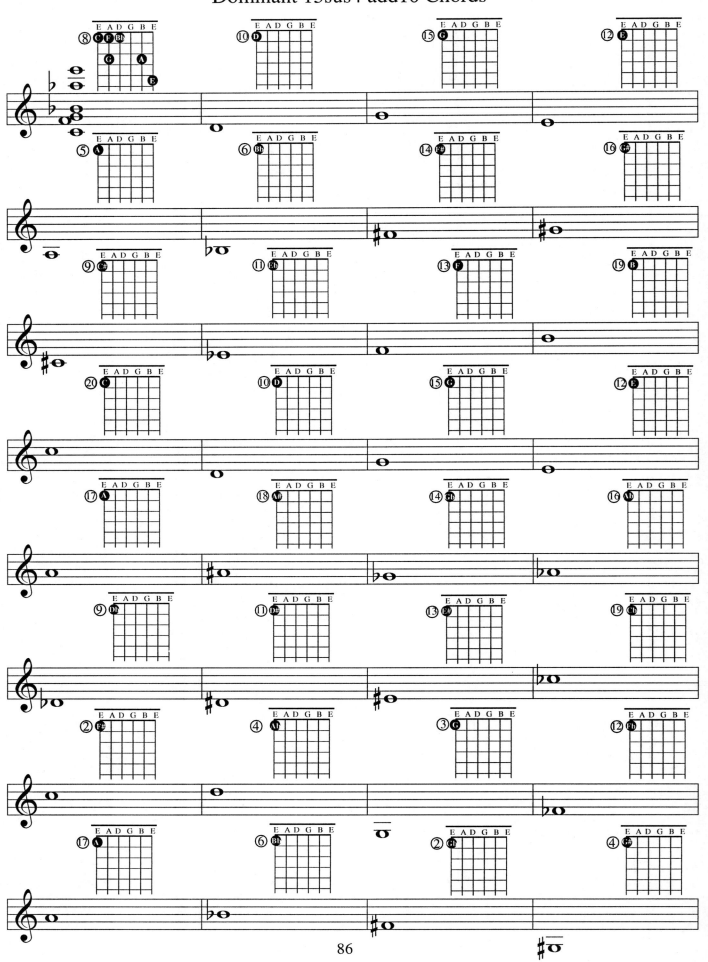

Chord Tones and Tensions
Minor 7th flat 5
-7b5
Chord Tones 1 b3 b5 b7
Tensions 9 11 b13

Chords with Tensions

Below is a list of the chord tones and tensions for a minor 7b5 chord. Minor 7b5 is commonly found in jazz as a II chord in a II V I of minor. For example, D-7b5 to G7b9 to C-7. Like the minor 7th chord the -7b5 chord can sound fine if it is used without tensions. Because of the fingering difficulty associated with adding tensions to a -7b5 chord, guitarists frequently don't add in tensions when playing this chord. The tensions do create a great sound when the situation allows, so don't be afraid to experiment.

The chord tones and tensions for -7b5 are as follows:

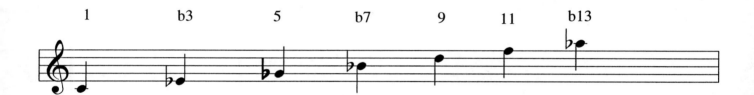

Minor 7b5 add 9 Chords

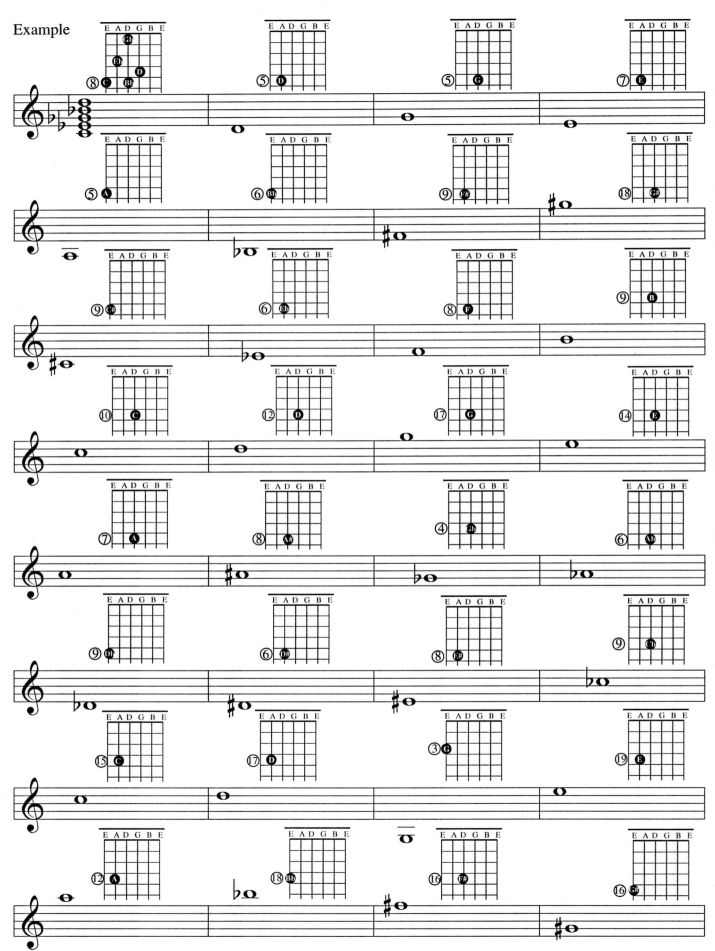

Minor 7b5 add b13 Chords

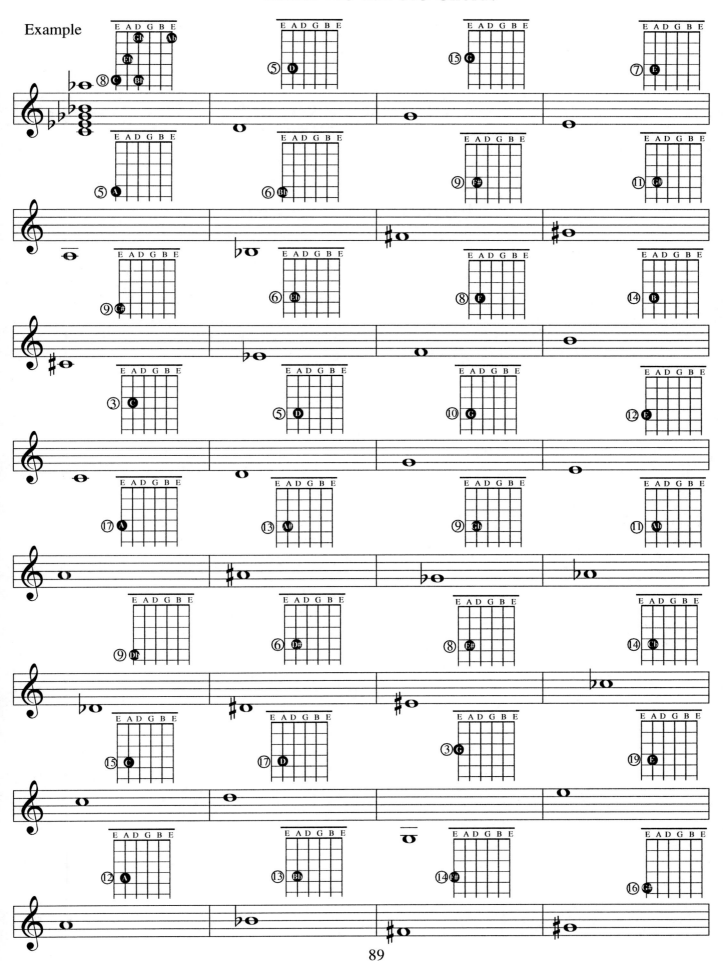

Chord Tones and Tensions
Diminished 7th
°7
Chord Tones 1 b3 b5 bb7
Tensions 9 11 b13 b15

Chords with Tensions

Below is a list of the chord tones and tensions for a diminished 7th chord. °7 is commonly found in jazz as a passing chord. For example, CΔ7 to C#°7 to D-7. You will also find the °7 as a I diminished chord. For example, CΔ7 to C°7 to CΔ7. Like the minor 7th chord the °7 chord can sound fine if it is used without tensions. Because of the fingering difficulty associated with adding tensions to a °7 chord guitarist frequently don't add them in when playing this chord. Tensions do create a great sound when the situation allows, so don't be afraid to experiment.

The chord tones and tensions for °7 are as follows:

Diminished 7th add 9 Chords

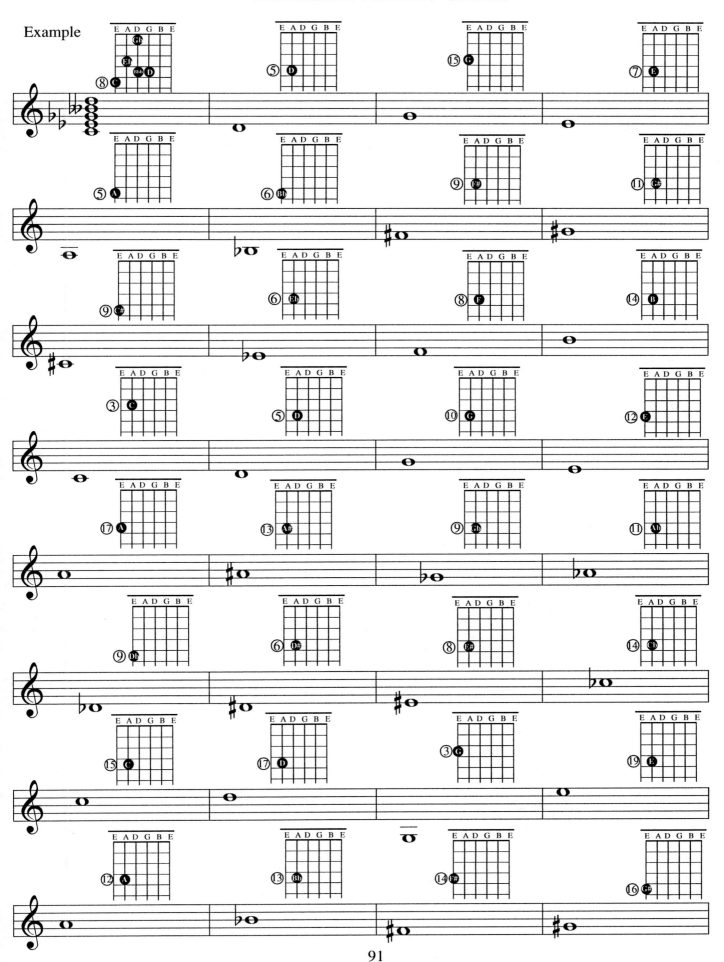

Diminished 7th add 11 Chords

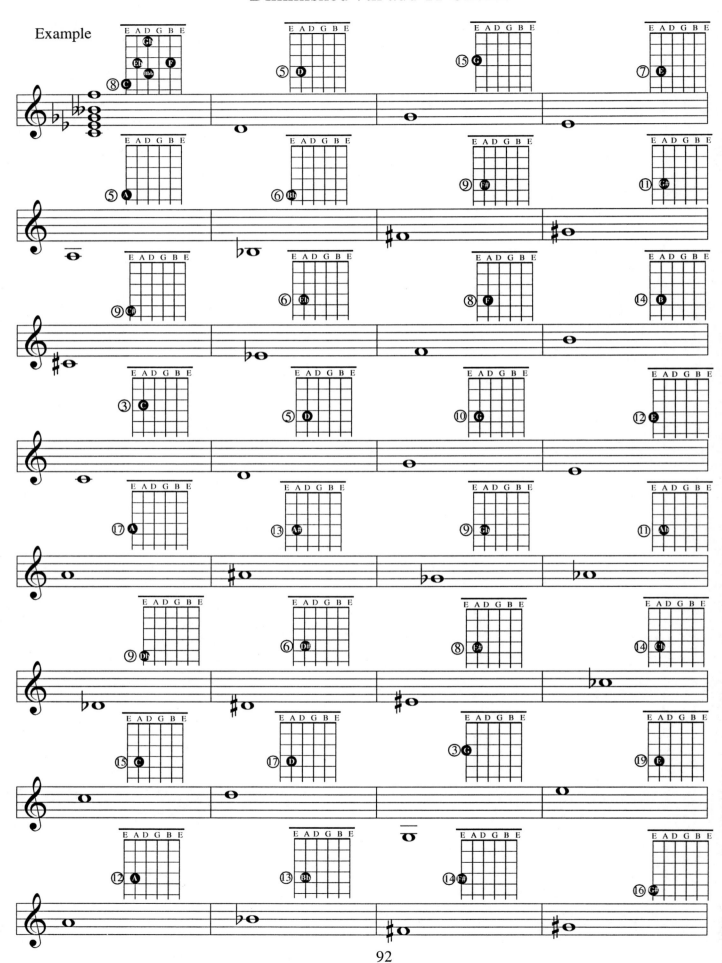

Diminished 7th add b13 Chords

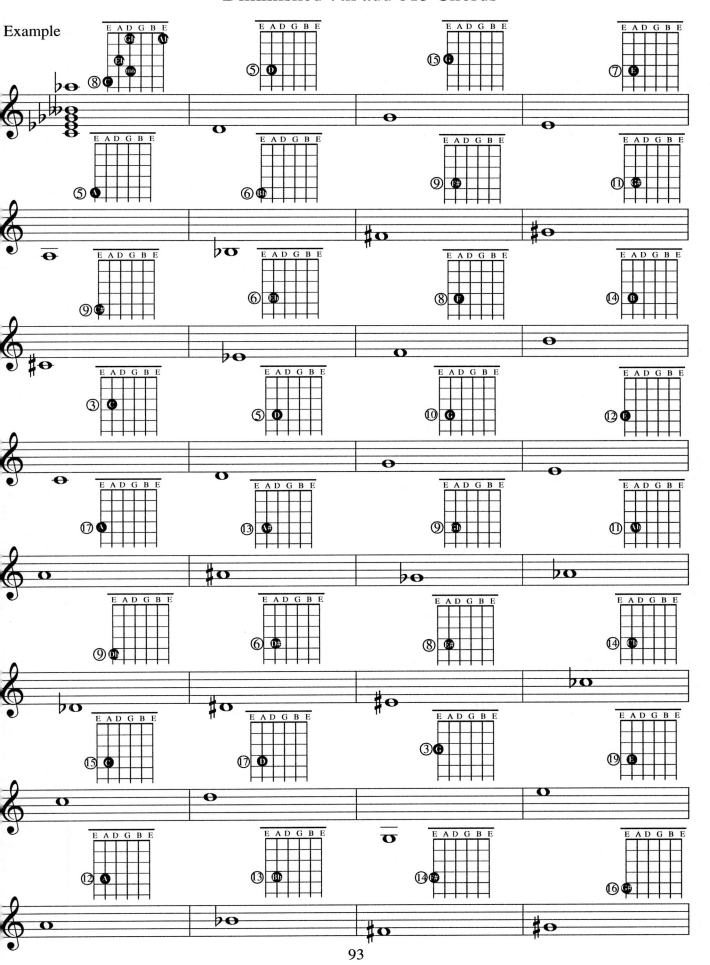

Diminished 7th add Major 7th Chords

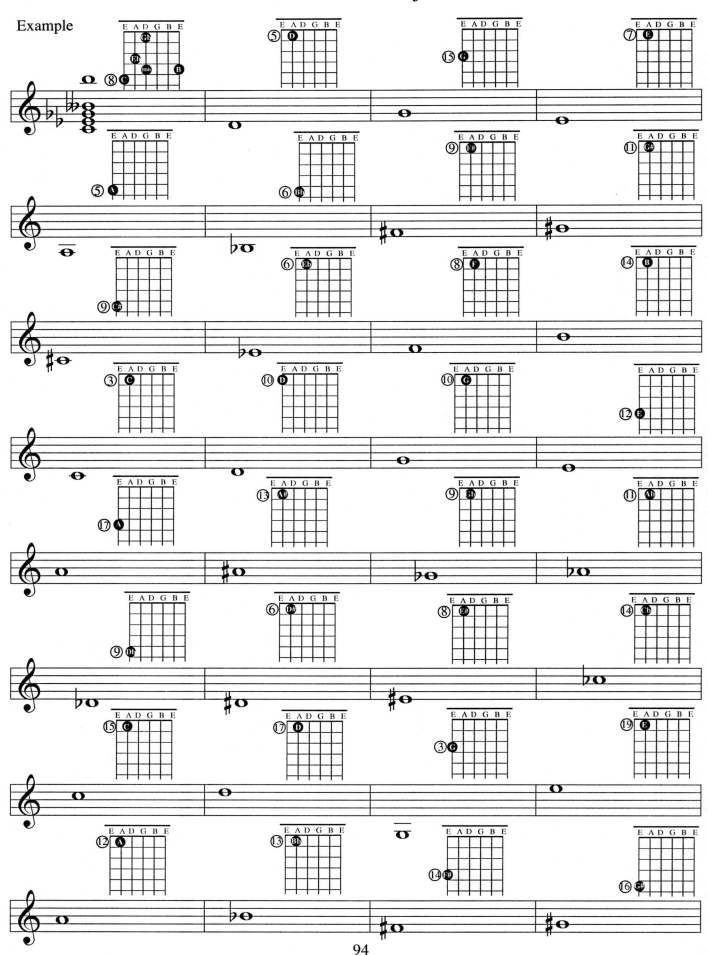

Chord Tones and Tensions
Minor Major 7th
-Δ7
Chord Tones 1 b3 5 7
Tensions 9 11 #11 13

Chords with Tensions

Below is a list of the chord tones and tensions for a -Δ7 chord. -Δ7 is commonly used in jazz as a substitute chord for a minor 7th. For example, rather than D-7b5 to G7b9 to C-7, you would use D-7b5 to G7b9 to C-Δ7. When a -7 chord is the last chord of a song the -Δ7 is a commonly used as a replacement. This creates a sound that really feels like the song has ended . For example if the song ends on a C-7 you could replace it with a C-Δ7. Like the minor 7th chord the -Δ7 chord can sound fine if it is used without tensions. Again, because of the fingering difficulty associated with adding tensions to a -Δ7 chord, guitarists frequently don't add in tensions when playing it. By the way, I highly recommend using the -Δ7b5 chord as an ending chord, it sounds great.

The chord tones and tensions for -Δ7 are as follows:

Minor Major 7 9 Chords

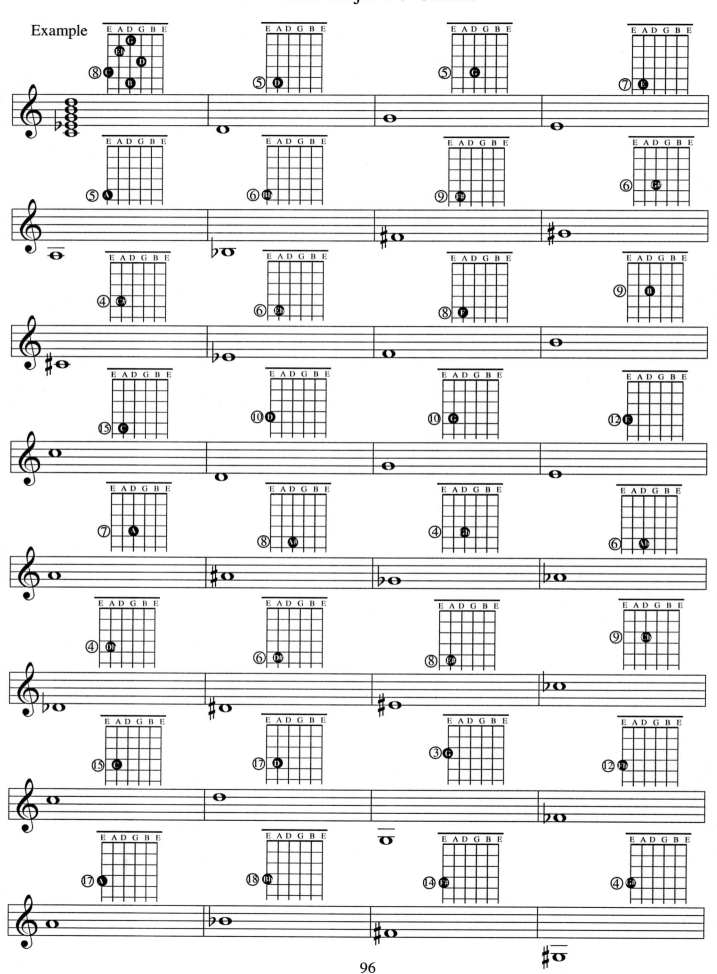

96

Minor Major 7 11 Chords

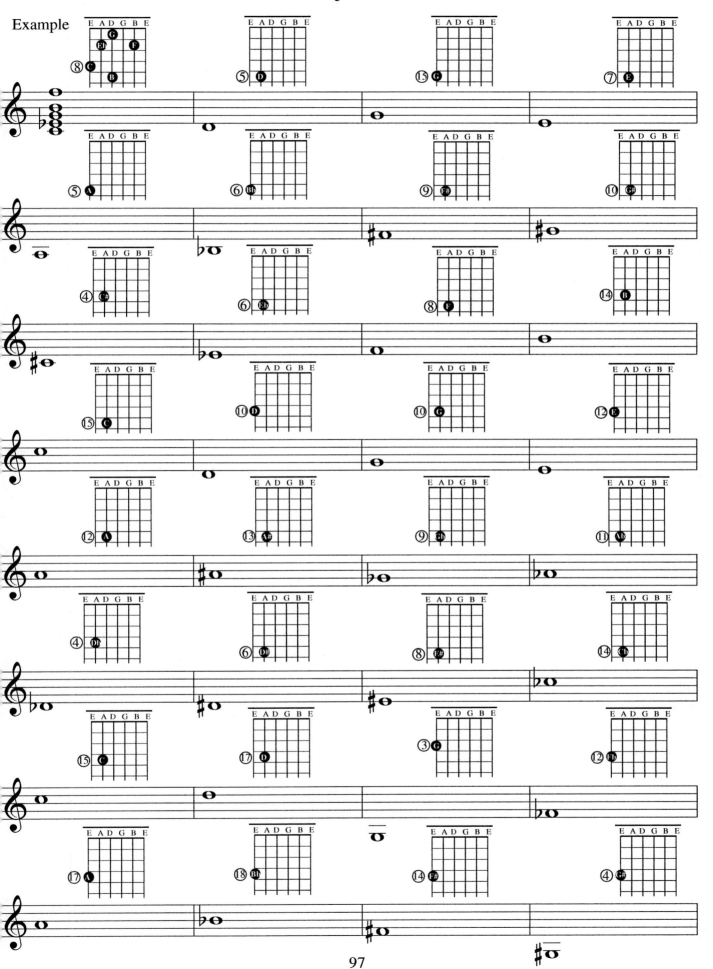

Minor Major 7 6 Chords

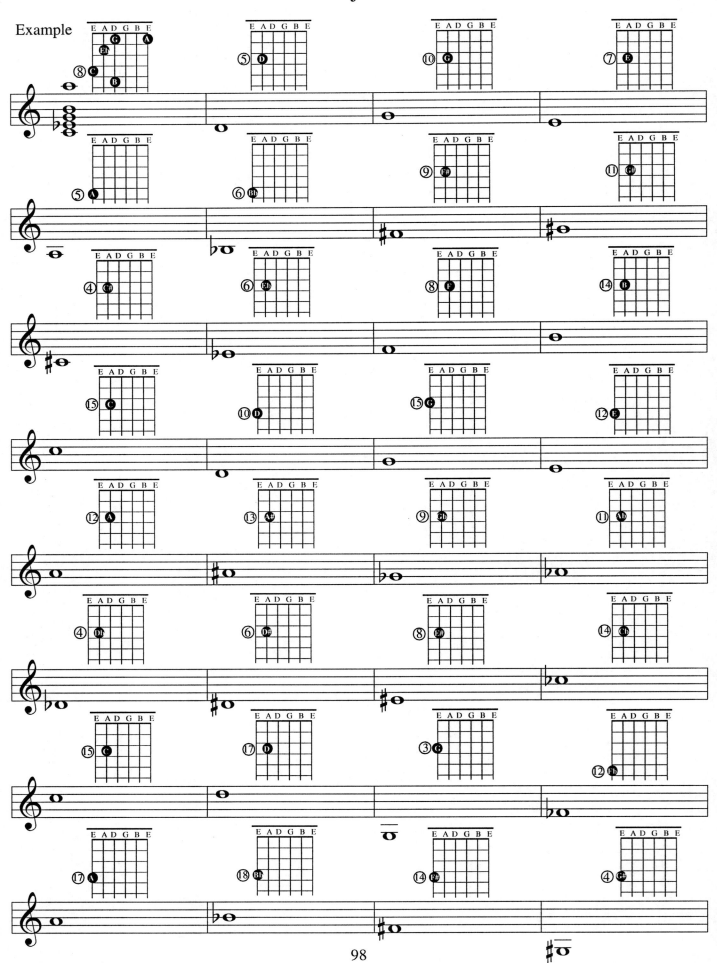

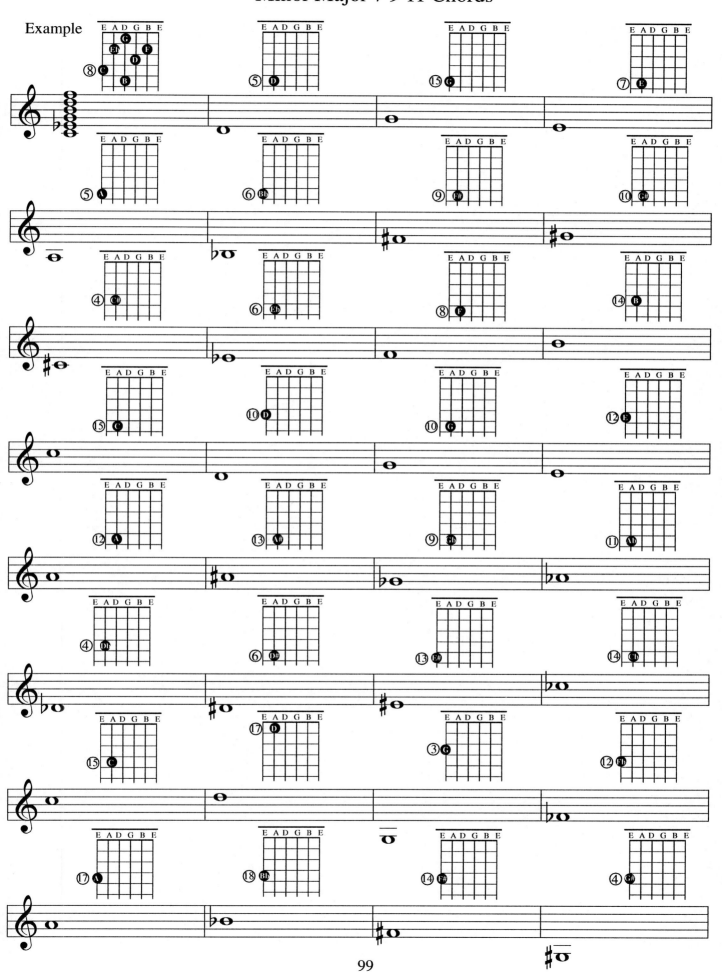

Minor Major 7 6 9 Chords

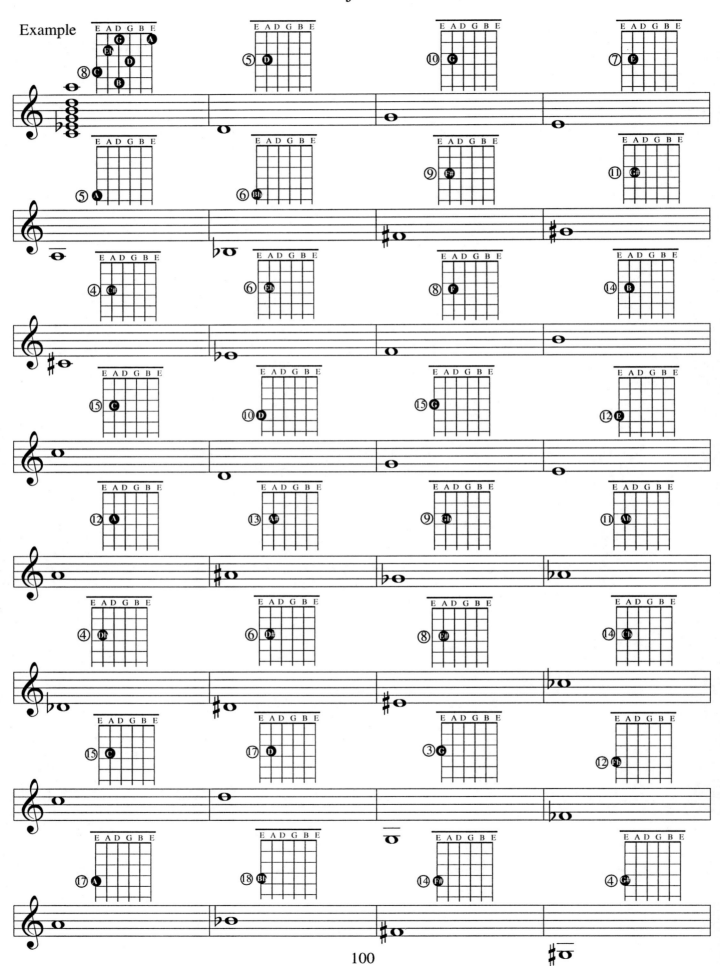

Minor Major 7 6 11 Chords

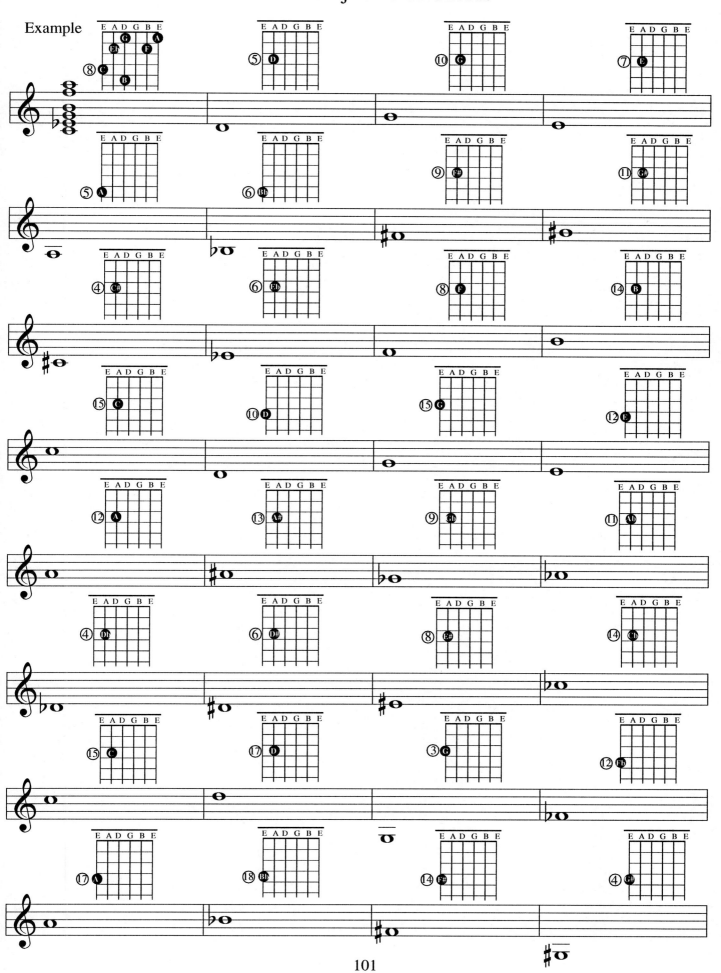

Minor Major 7b5 Chords

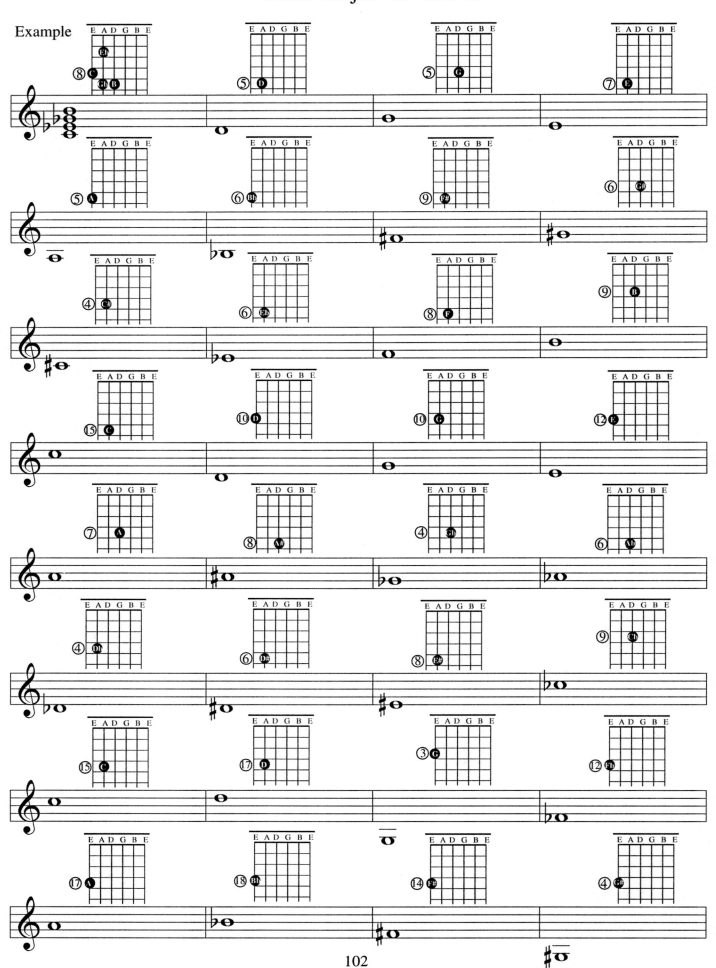

Minor Major 7b5 add9 Chords

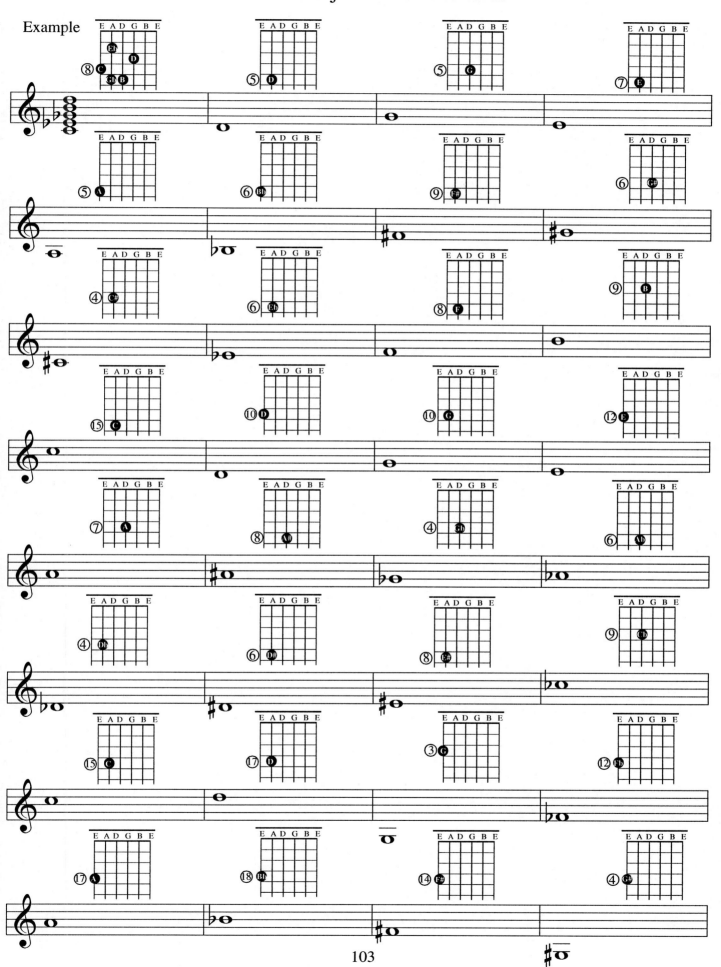

Minor Major 7b5 add11 Chords

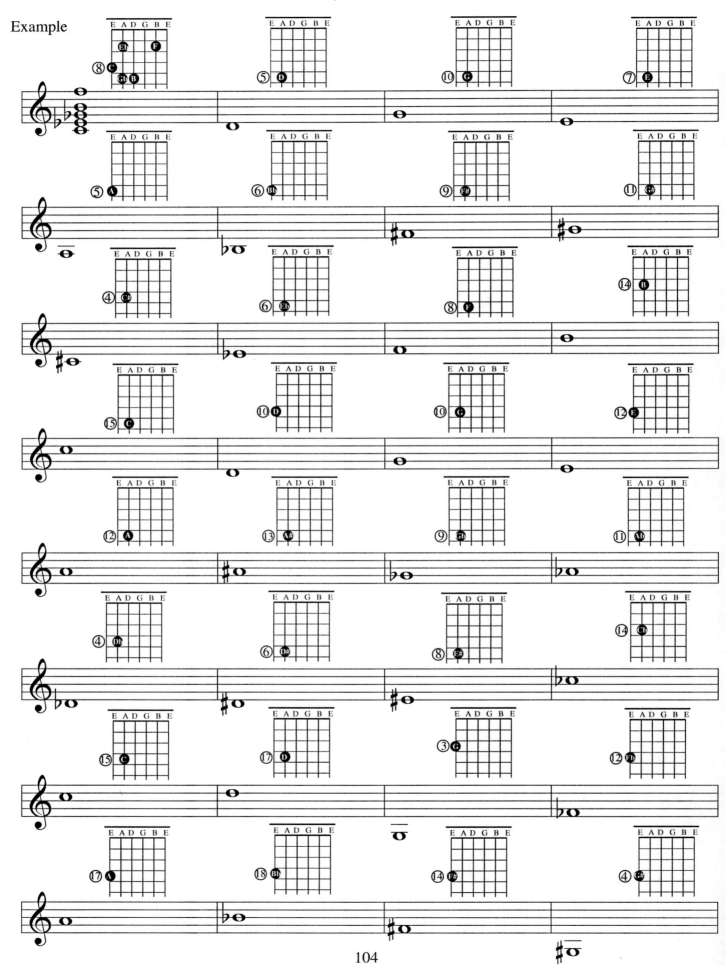

Chord Tones and Tensions
Major 7th sharp 5
Δ7#5
Chord Tones 1 3 #5 7
Tensions 9 #11

Chords with Tensions

Below is a list of the chord tones and tensions for a Δ7#5 chord. Δ7#5 is commonly used in jazz as a substitute chord for a Δ7 chord. For example, rather than D-7 to G7 to CΔ7, you would use D-7 to G7 to CΔ7#5. When a Δ7 chord is the last chord of a song the Δ7#5 is a commonly used as a replacement. This creates a highly colorful sound that really spices up the end of a tune . For example if the song ends on a CΔ7 you could replace it with a CΔ7#5. Like the minor 7th chord, the CΔ7#5 chord can sound fine if it is used without tensions. This is another example of infrequently added tensions due to fingering difficulties. But if you can do it, the rewards are there. I highly recommend using the CΔ7#5 chord as an ending chord, it works beautifully.

The chord tones and tensions for CΔ7#5 are as follows:

Major 7#5 add 9 Chords

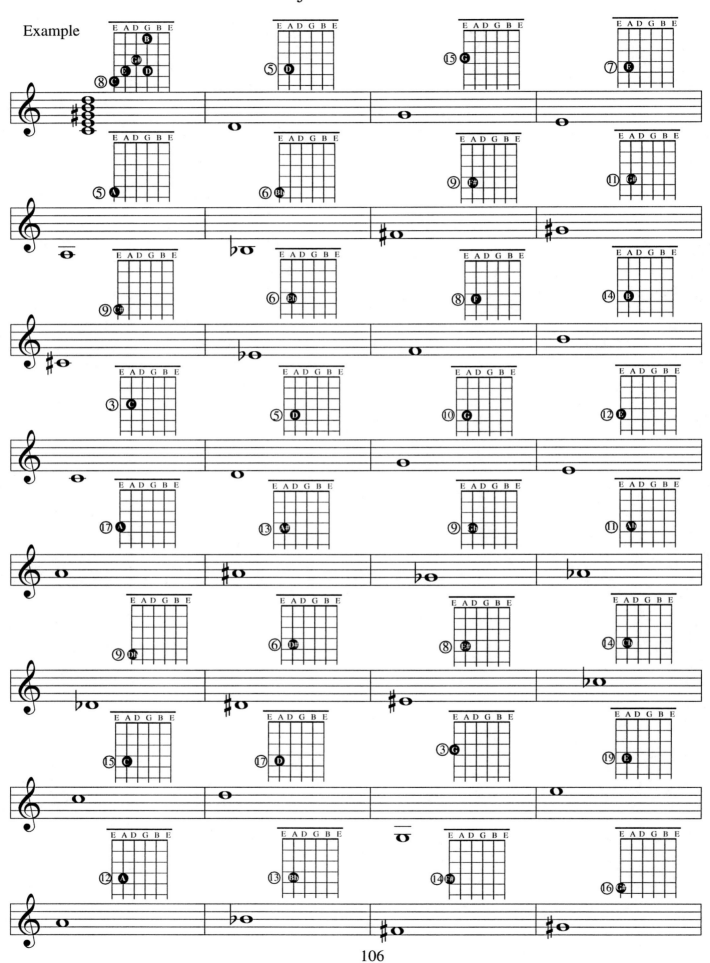

Major 7#5 add #11 Chords

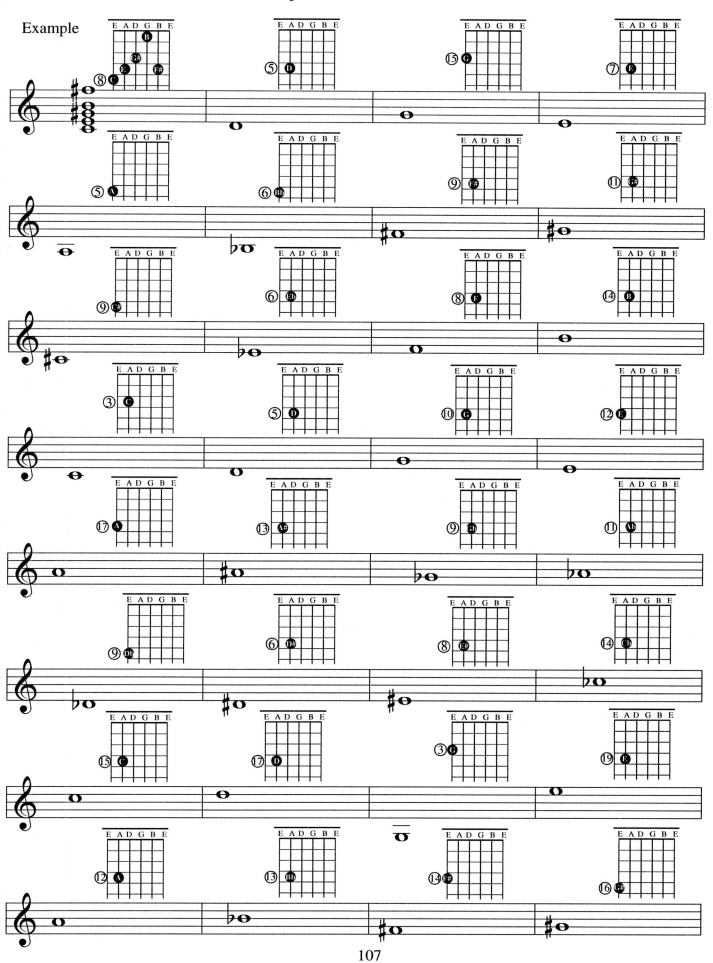

ANSWER PAGES

The following pages contain the answers to all the exercises presented in this book. Keep in mind that because the same note can appear in many different places on the guitar neck, there can be more than one correct answer to each exercise. If you would like a complete list of answers for each exercise you can download the alternative answers at www.muse-eek.com The answers found on the following pages and on the alternative answer pages on the muse-eek website limit the range to five frets on the guitar fretboard. Five frets in the most comfortable and practical range for most guitarist's hands. There are of course even more possible answers but they would use uncomfortably large stretches or totally unplayable combinations.

Muse Eek hosts a secure area of their website for customers who own their books. This secure area provides additional resources for the serious student. At this time there is no additional charge for this information; just register and receive a password to enter it. This secure section is an ongoing project provided by Muse Eek, containing extra help files, video clips, and other educational information.

Our goal at Muse Eek is to provide the best distance learning resource for music, and any suggestions to augment or improve the site are welcomed. Please e-mail us at info@muse-eek.com

Also keep in mind that the 6 pages of fretboard charts found in the back of this book will give you all the different places each pitch can be found on the guitar and its corresponding placement on the music staff.

Basic Intervals Answers

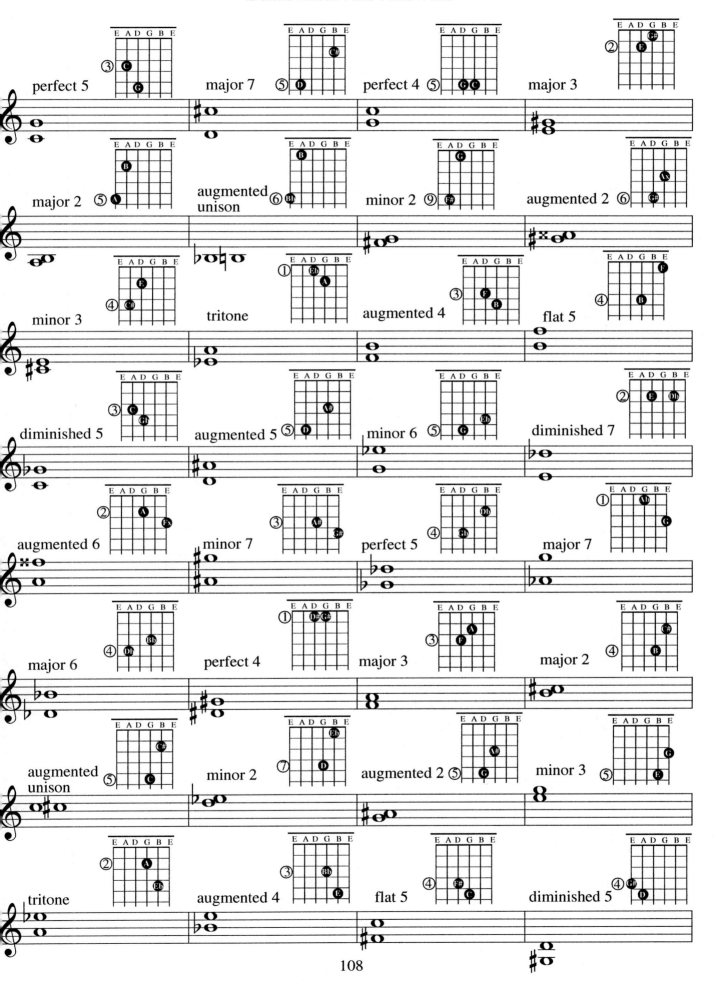

Larger Intervals Answers

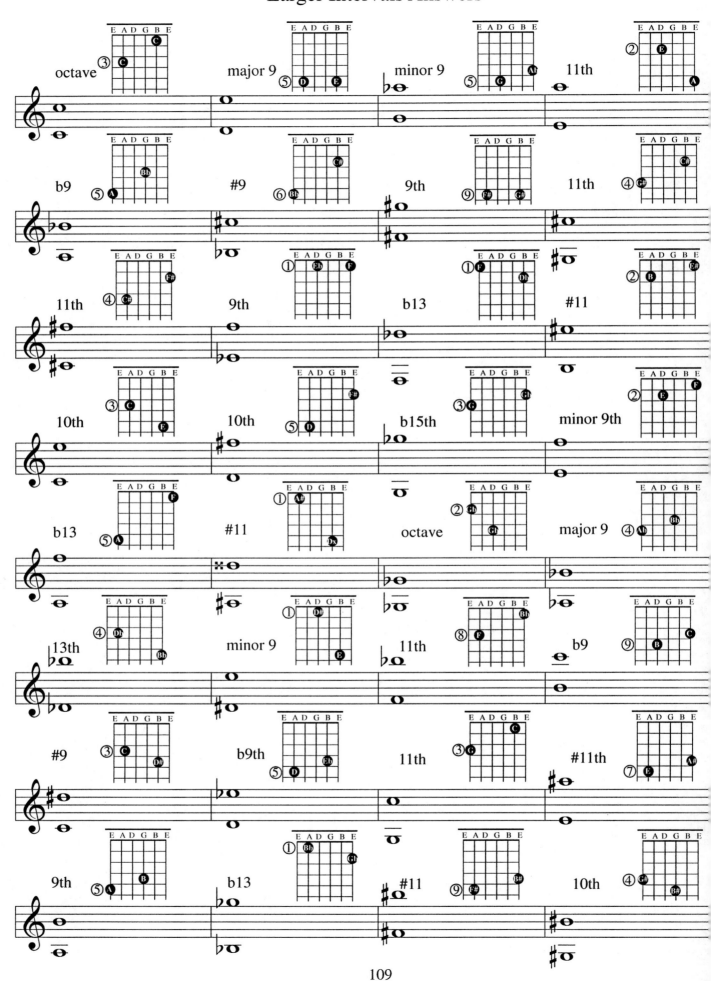

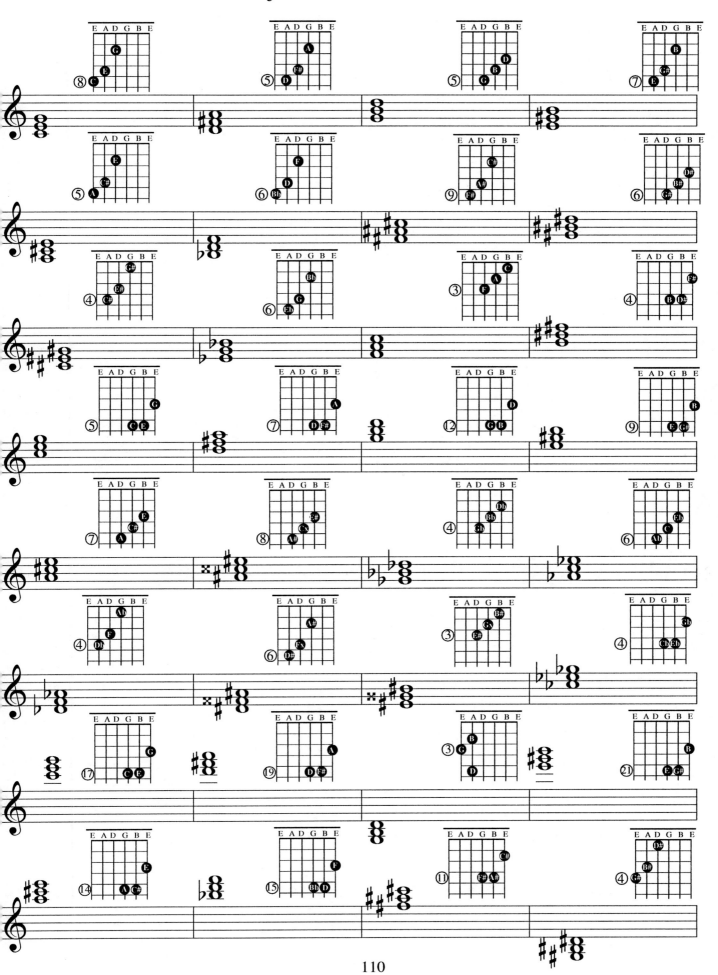

Minor Triads Answers

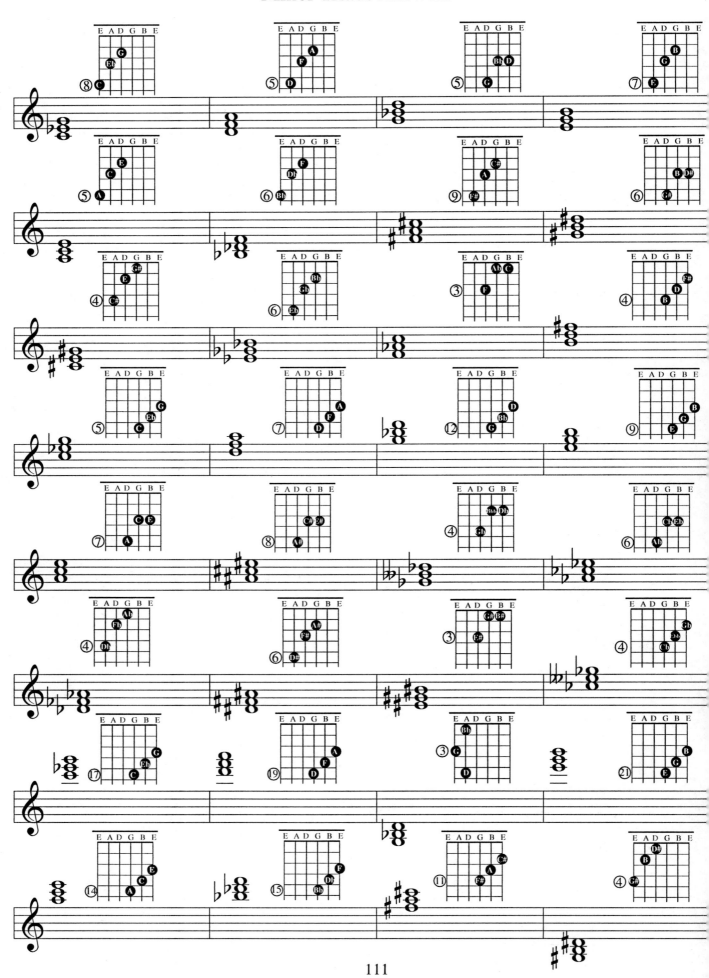

Diminished Triads Answers

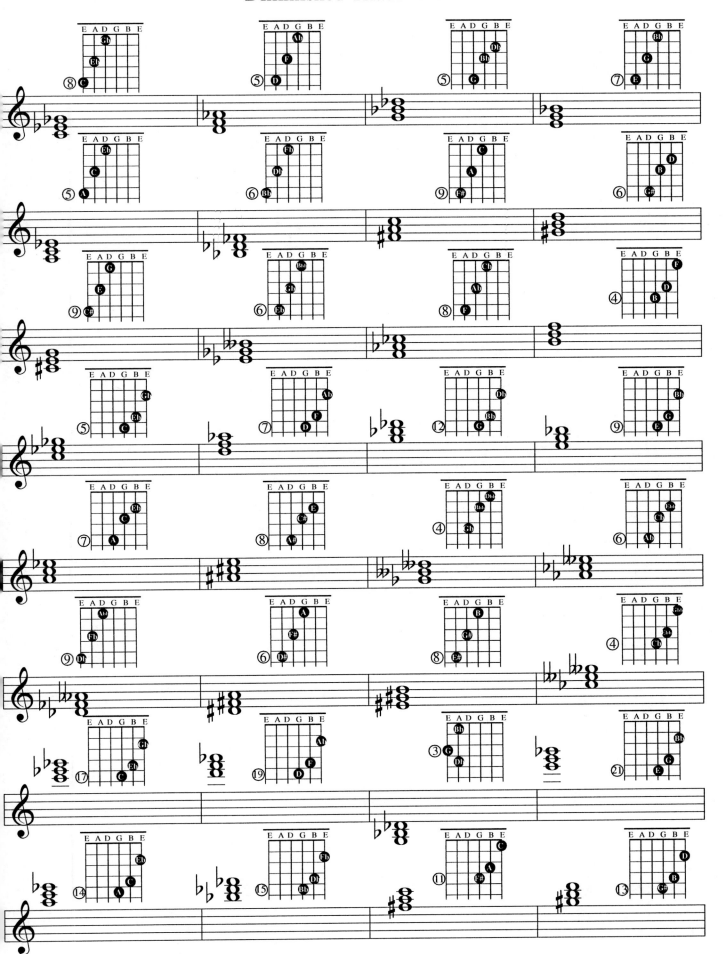

Augmented Triads Answers

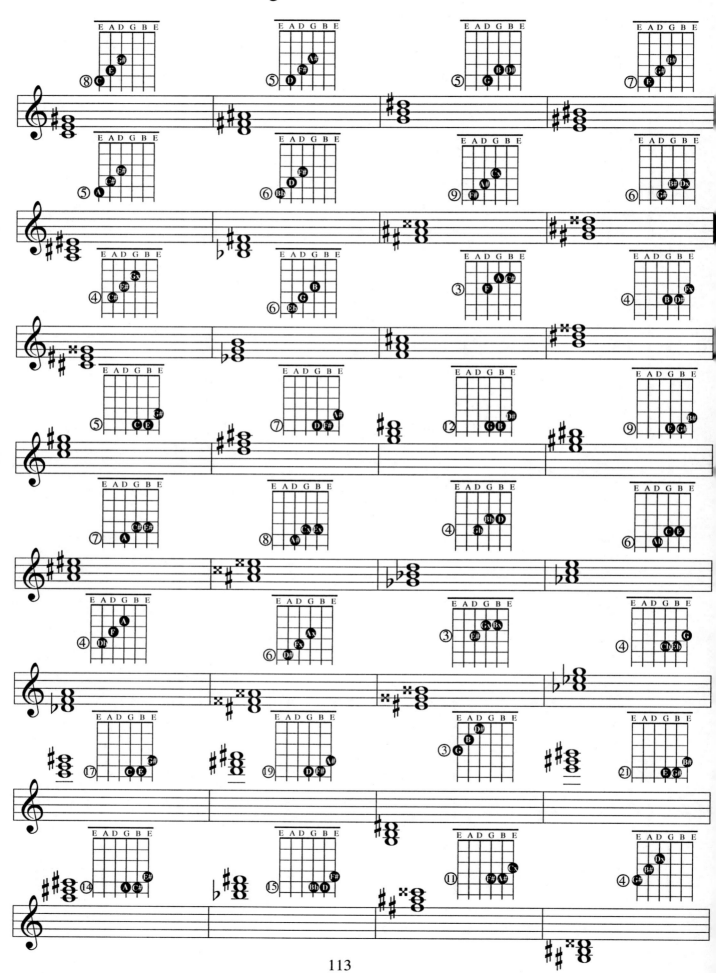

Suspended 4th Triads Answers

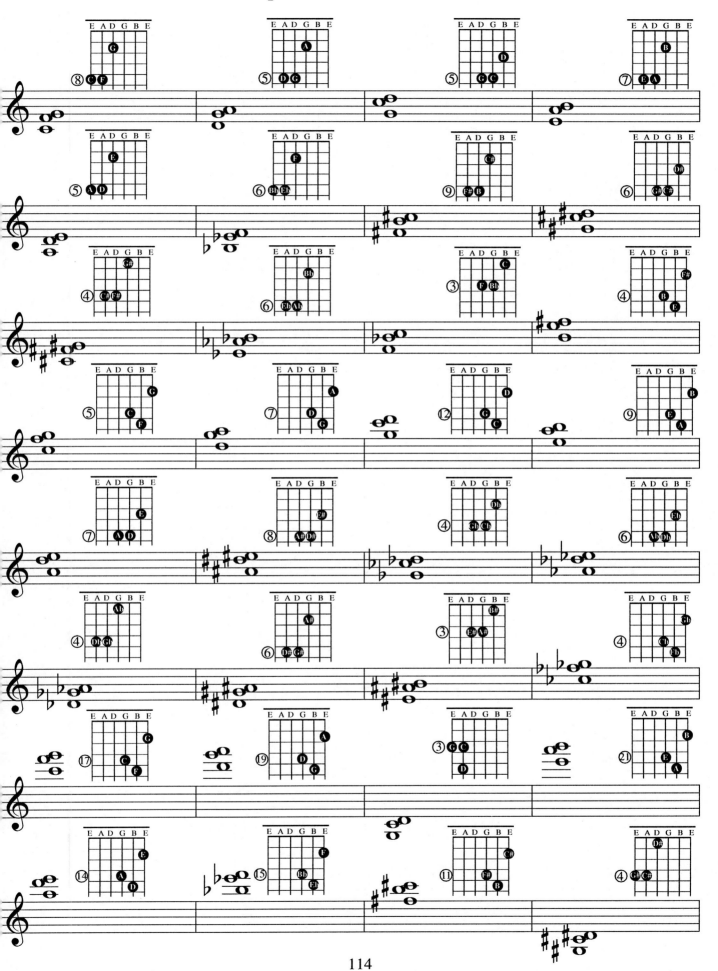

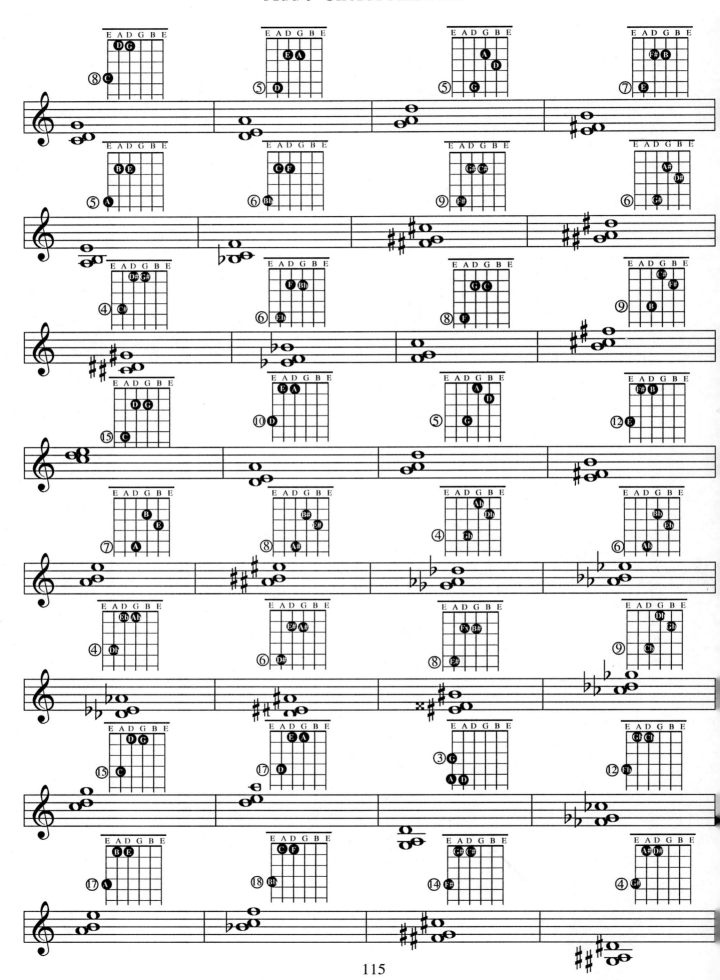

Major Seventh Chords Answers

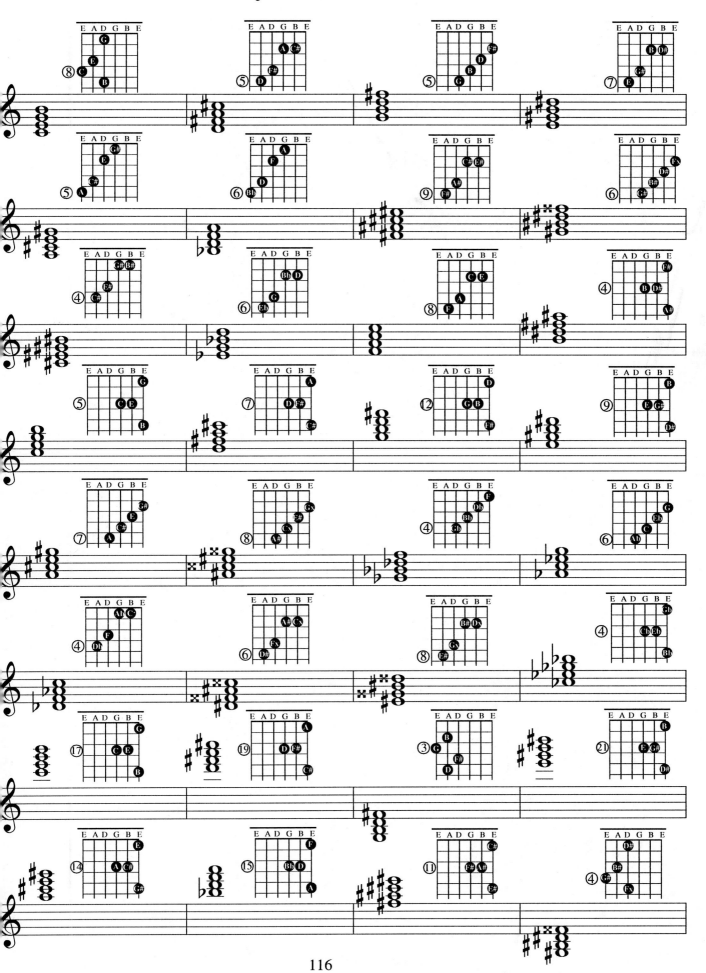

Minor Seventh Chords Answers

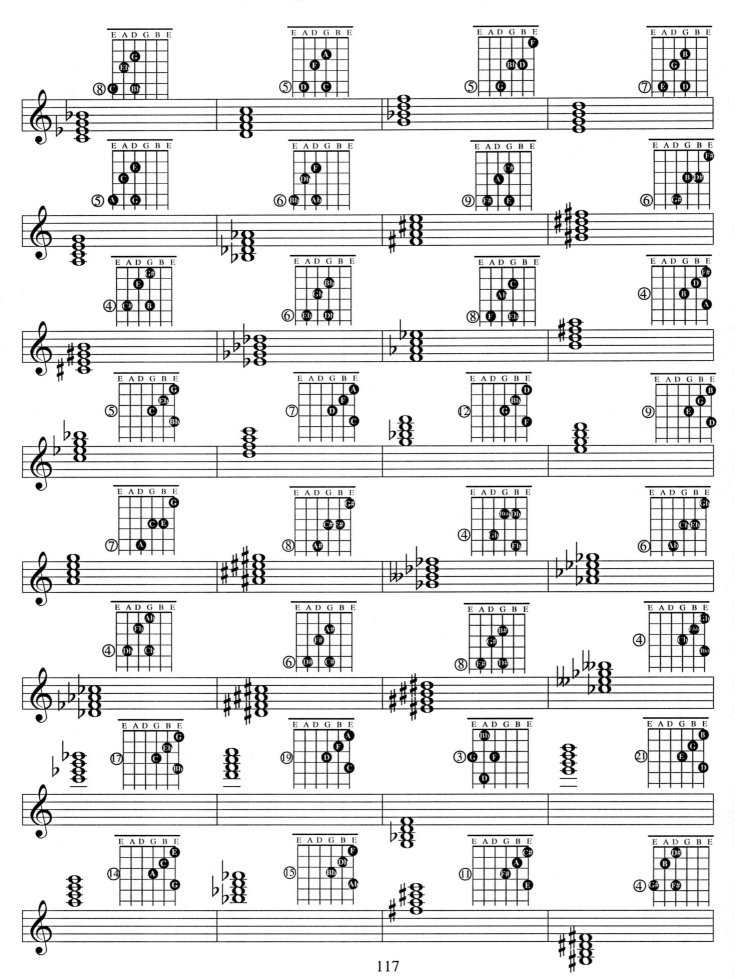

Dominant Seventh Chords Answers

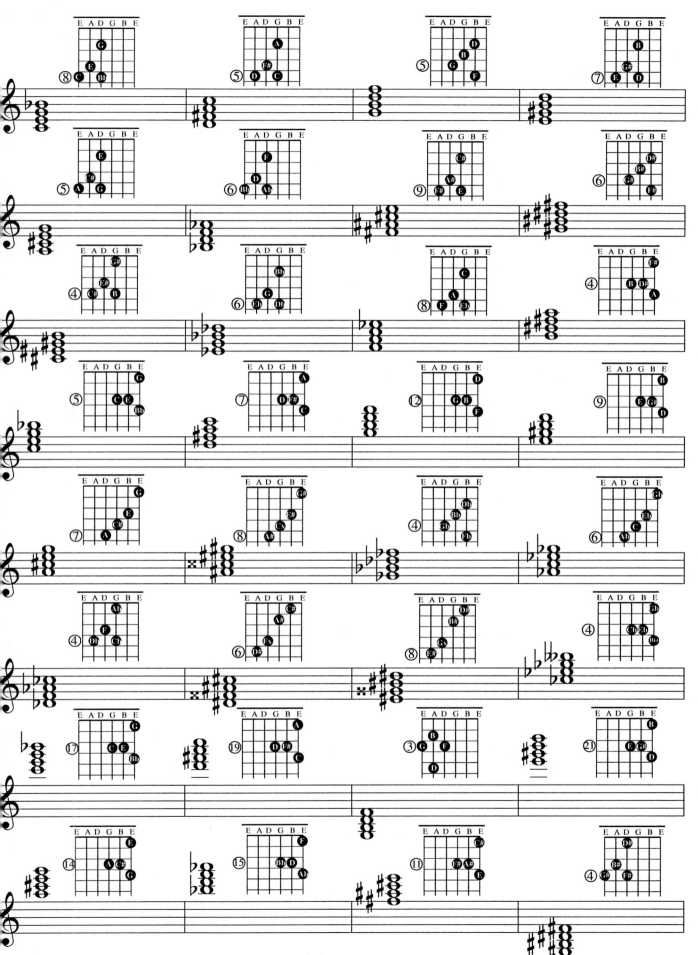

Dominant 7sus4 Chords Answers

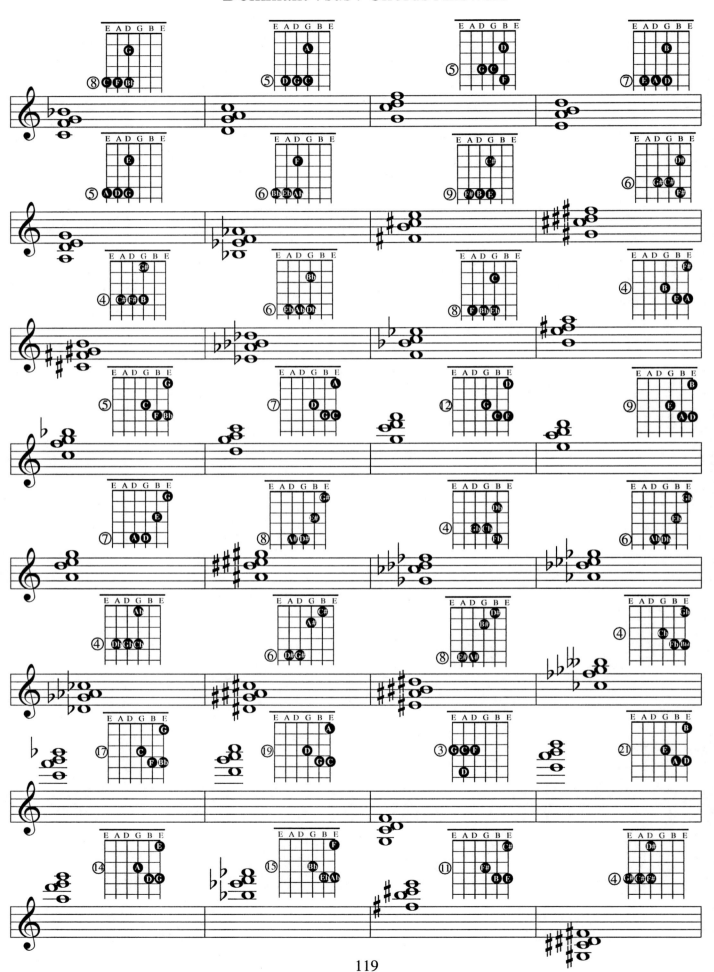

119

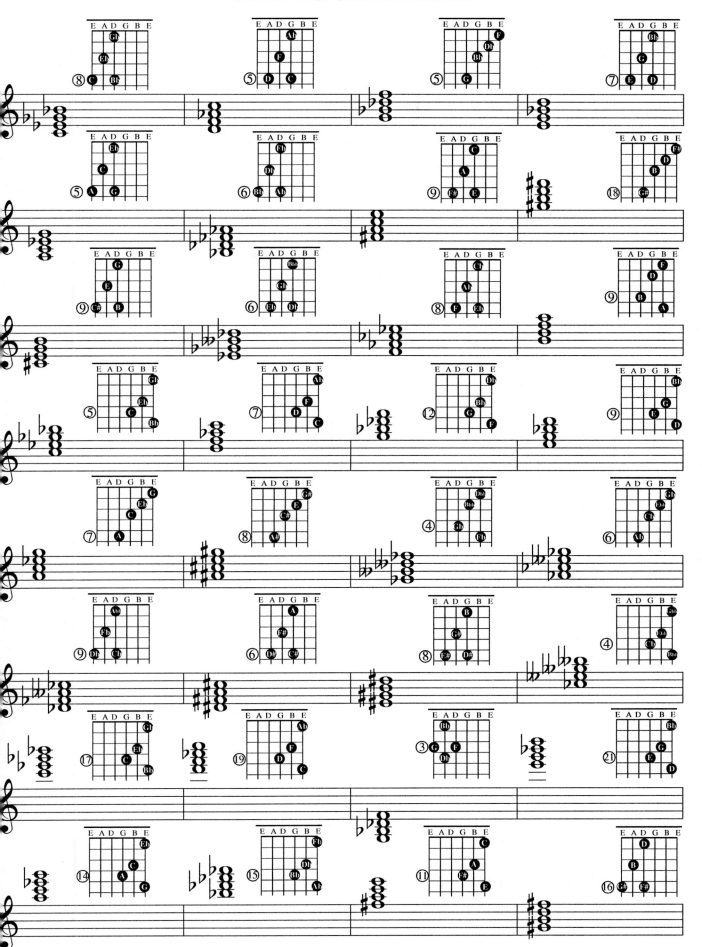

Diminished 7th Chords Answers

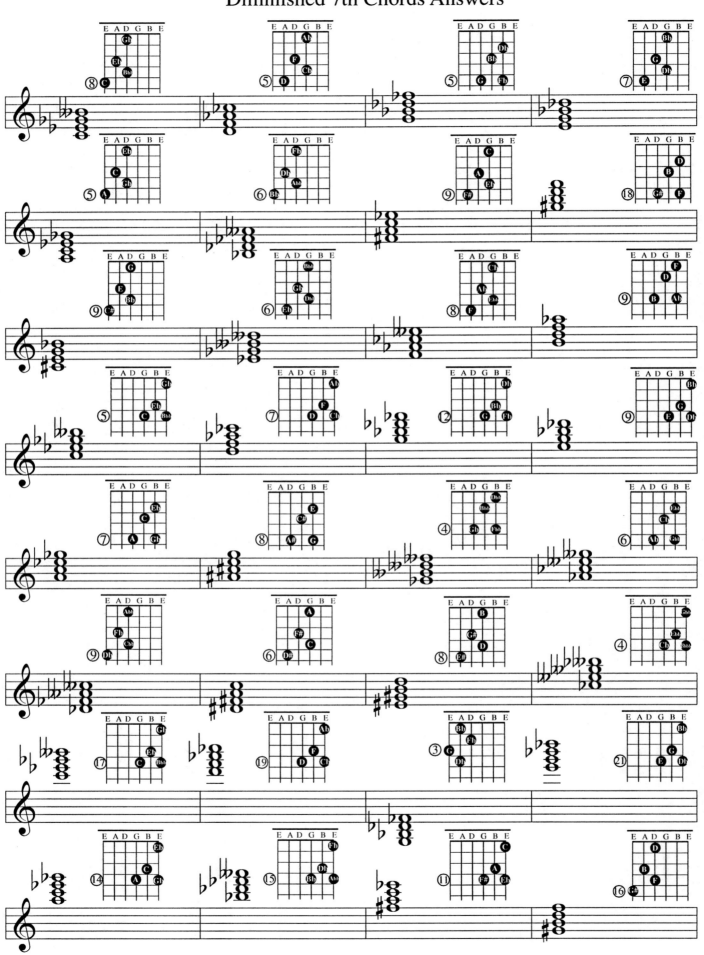

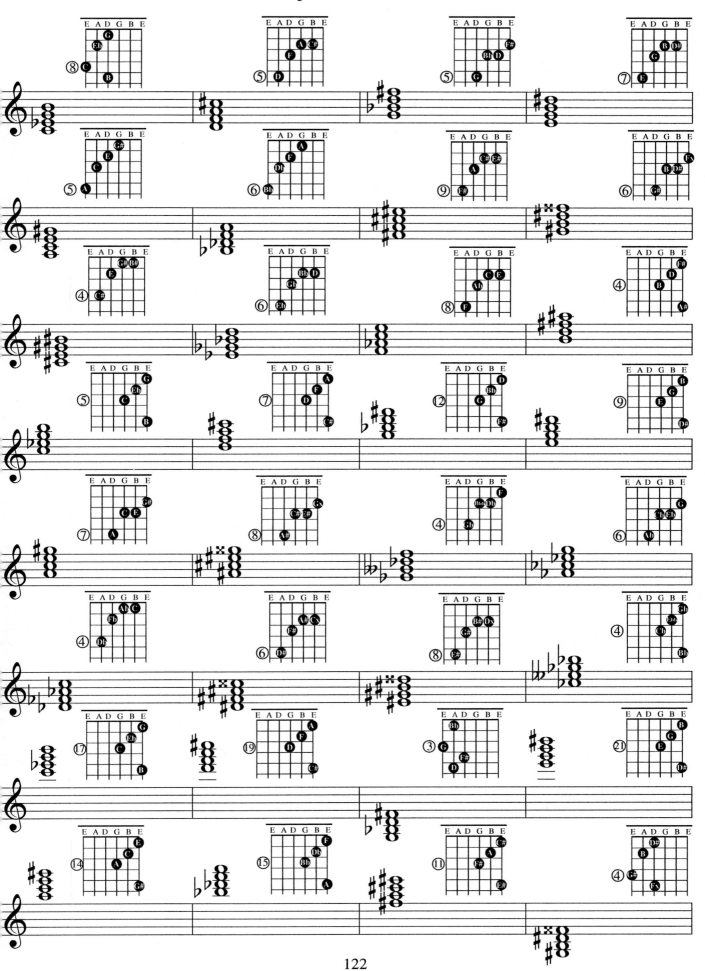

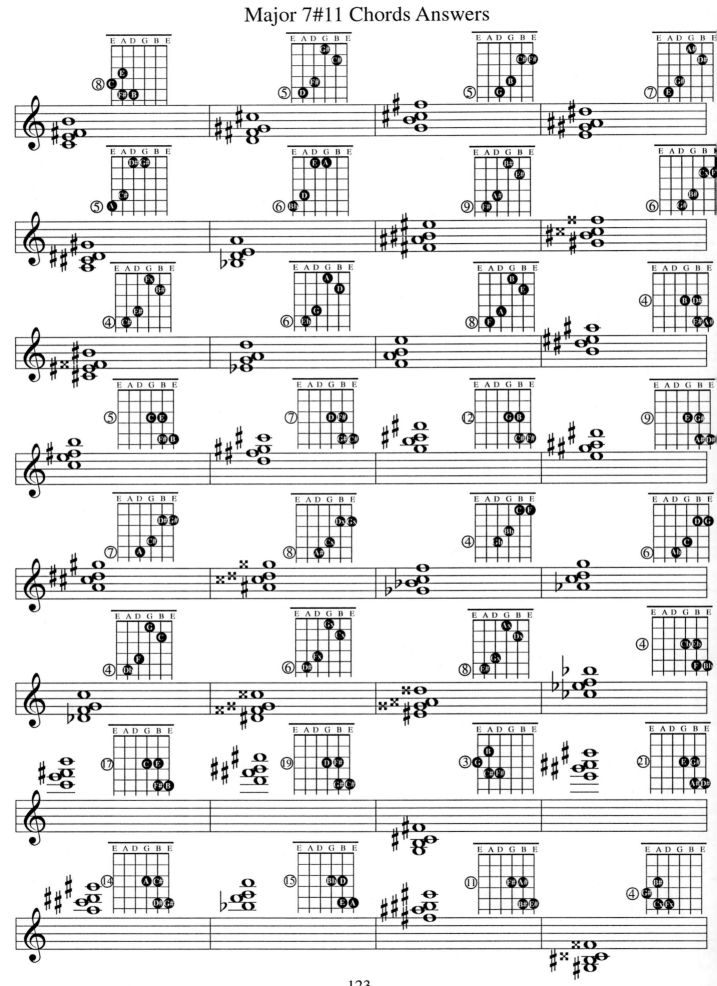

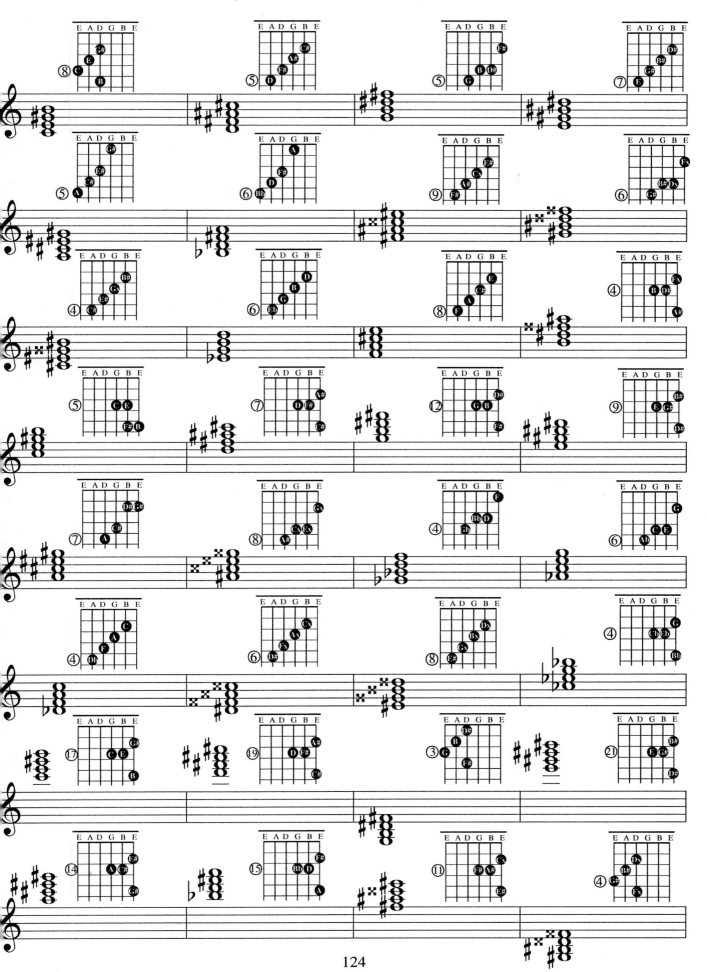

Dominant 7b5 Chords Answers

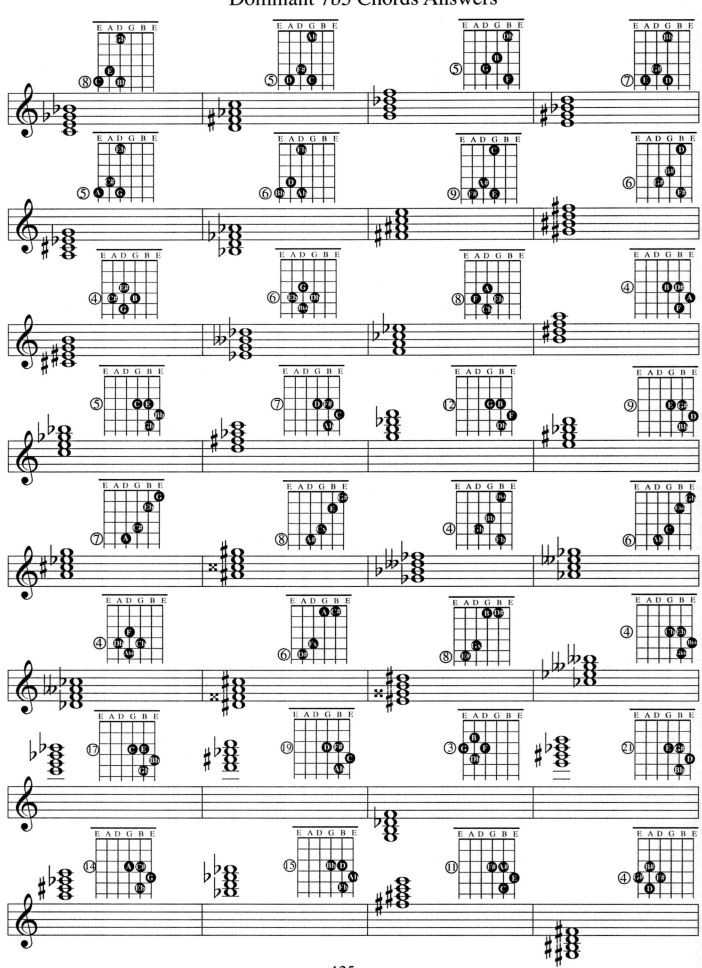

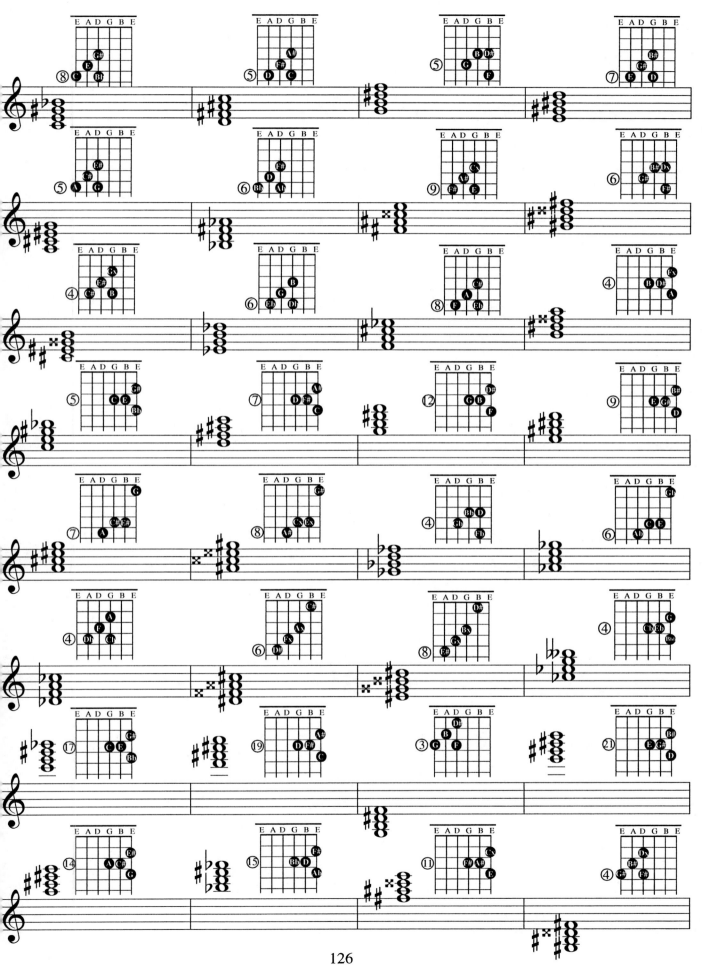

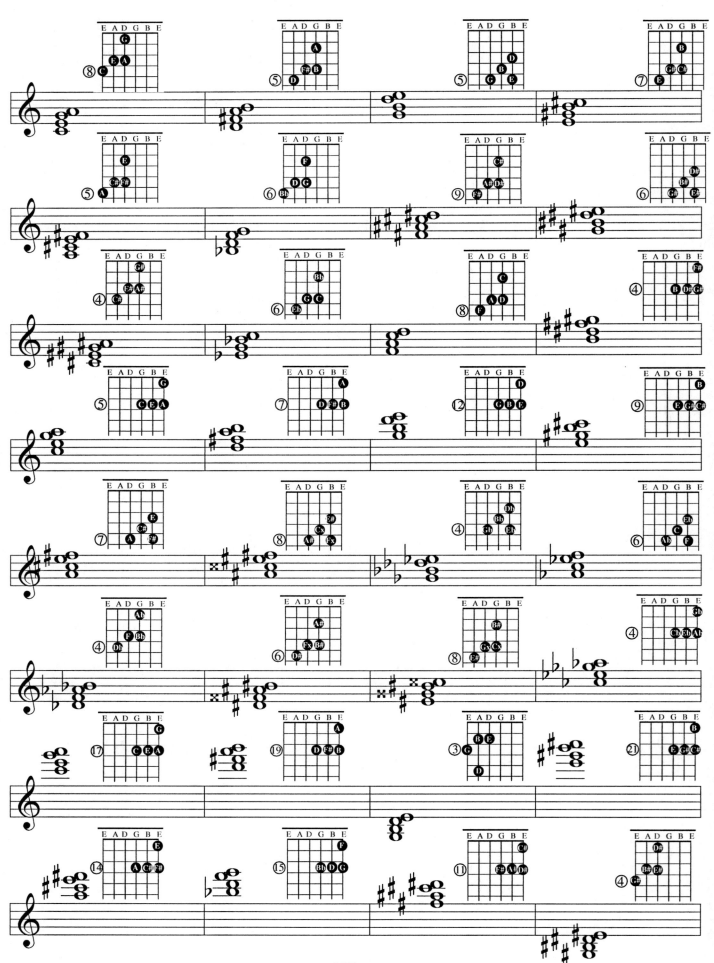

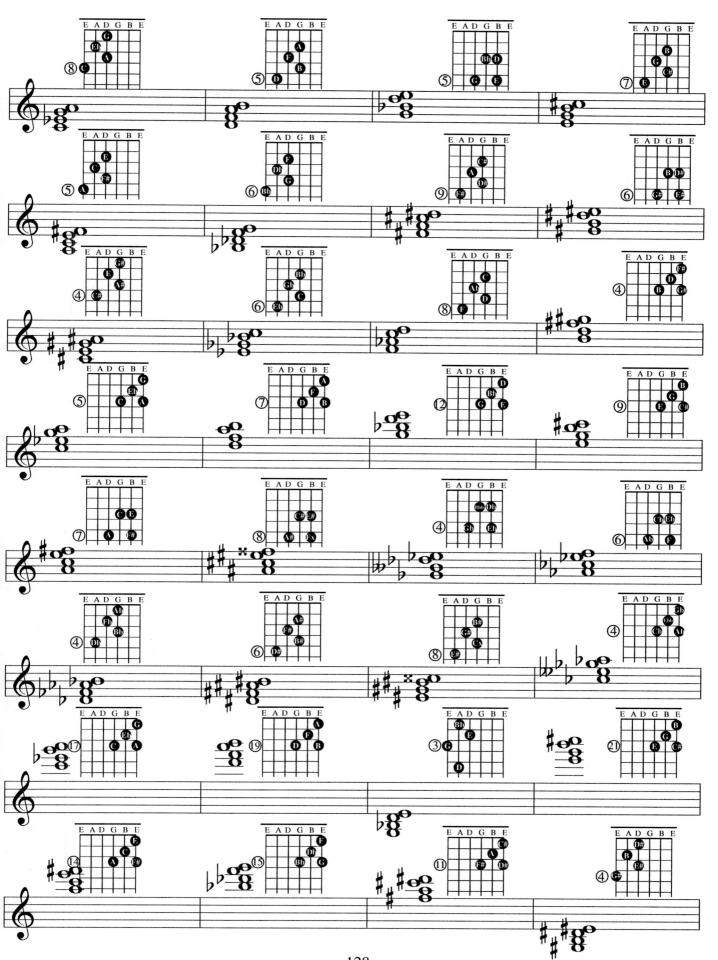

Major 7 9 Chords Answers

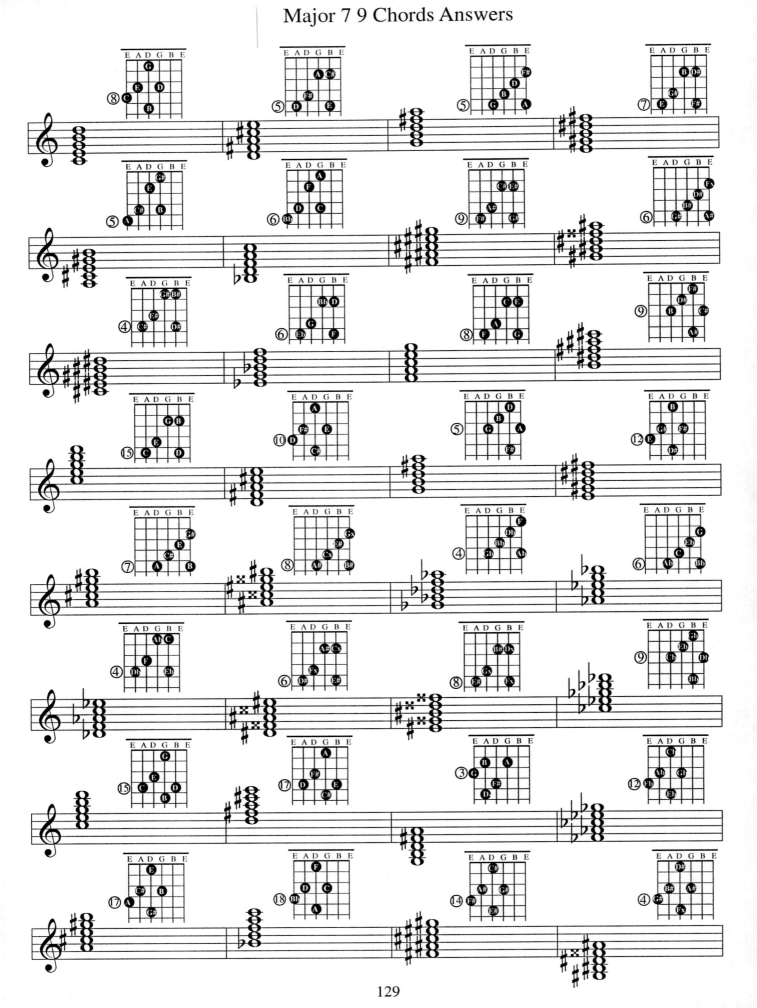

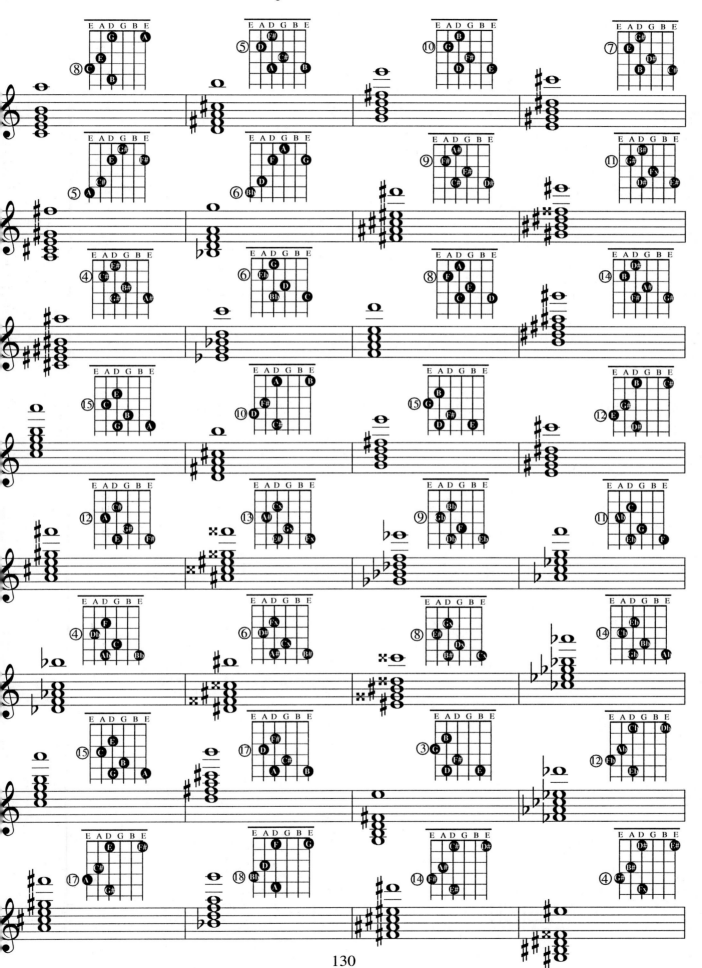

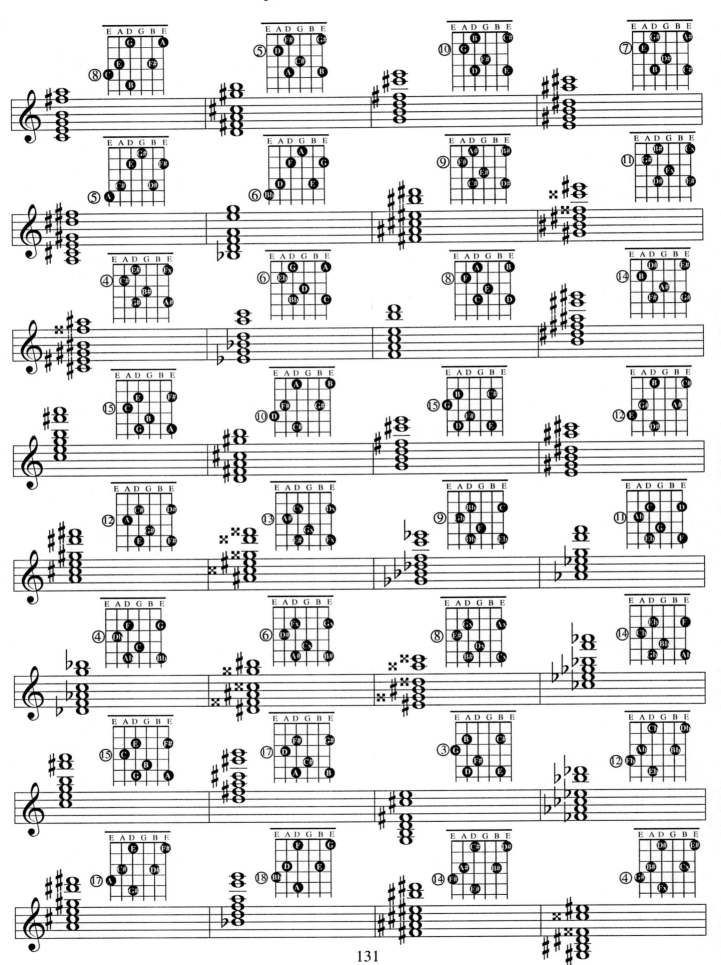

Major 7 9 #11 Chords Answers

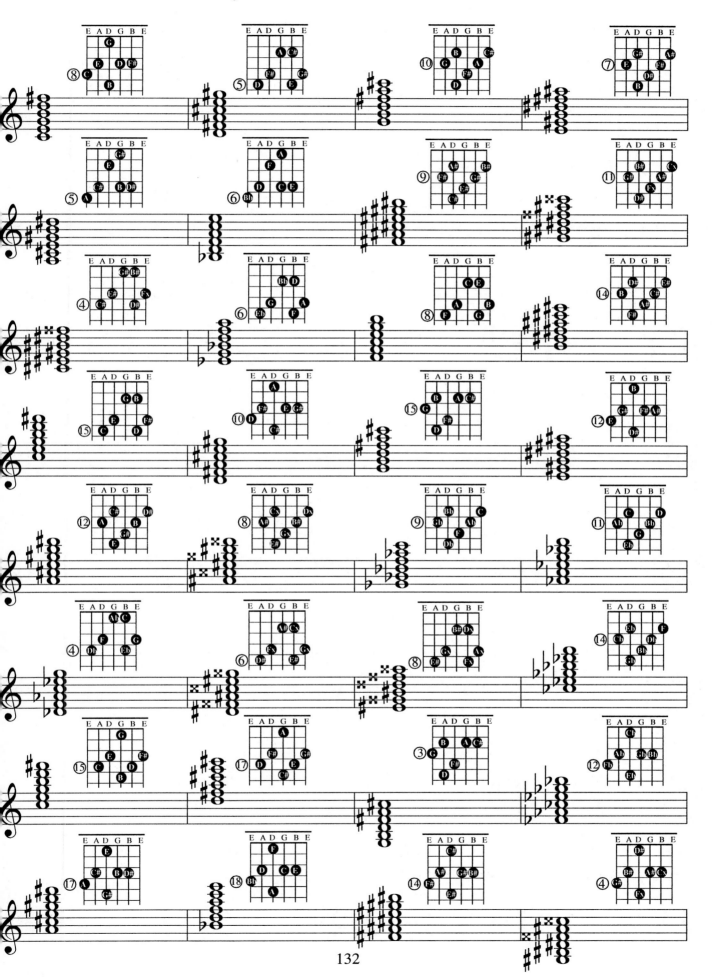

Major 7 6 9 Chords Answers

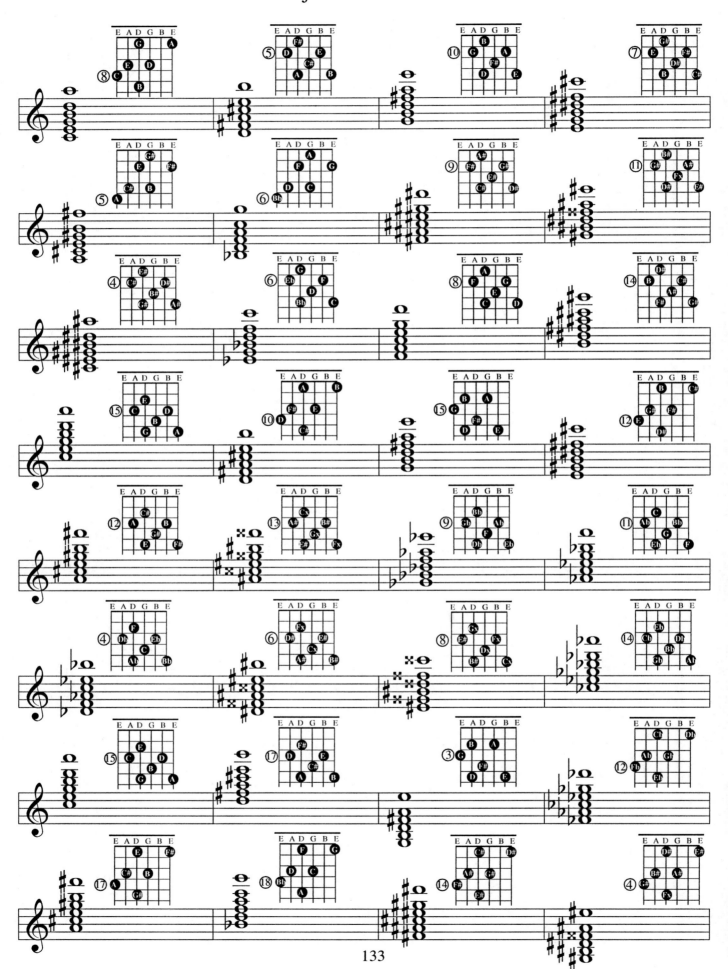

133

Major 6 9 Chords Answers

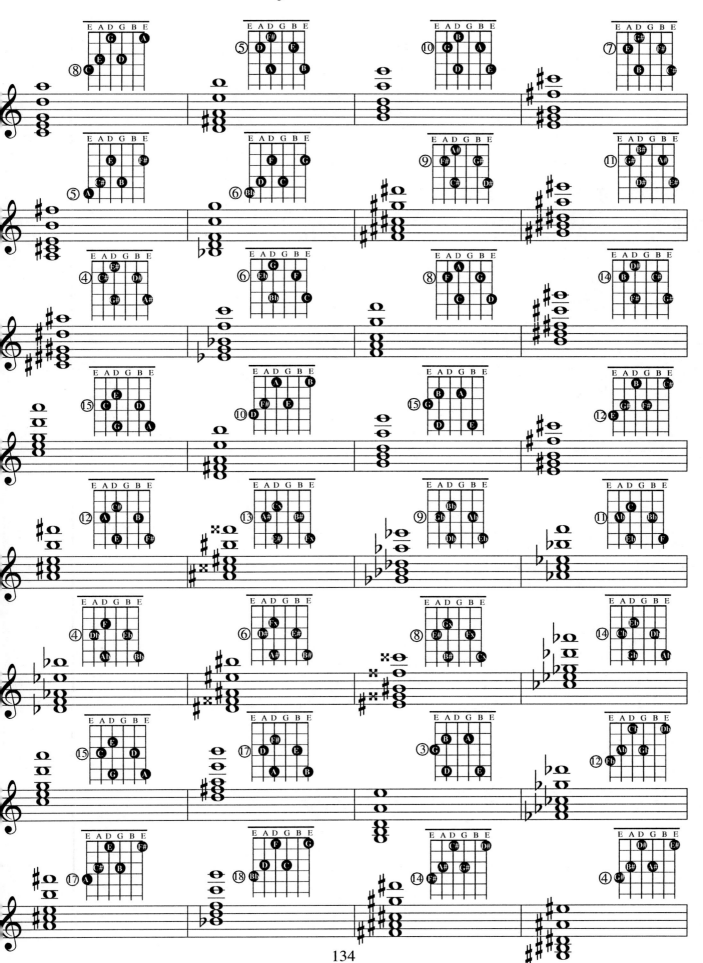

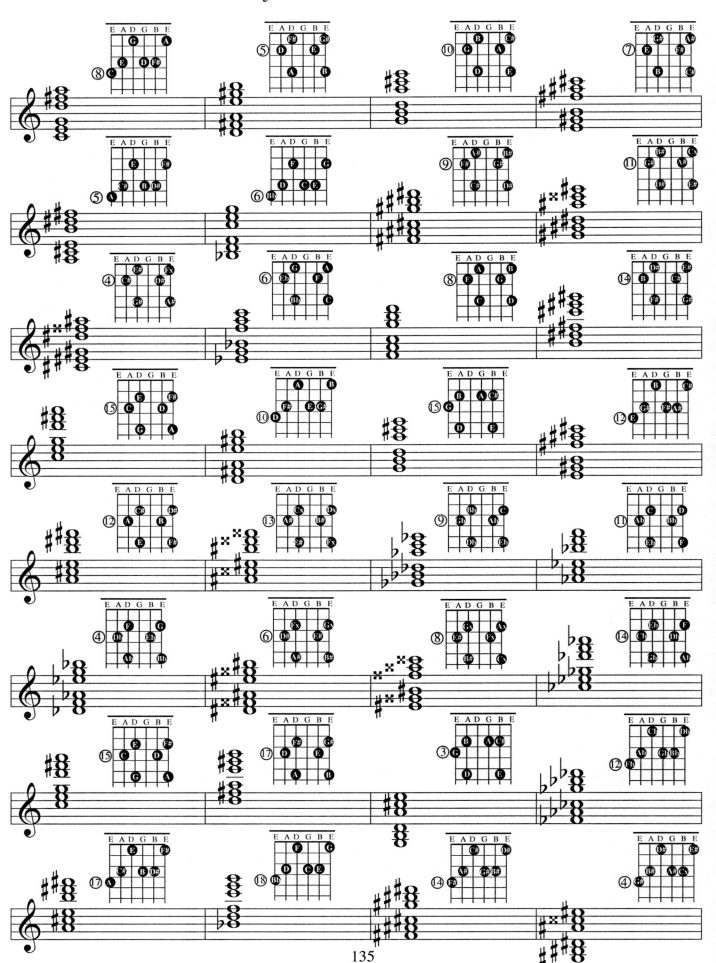

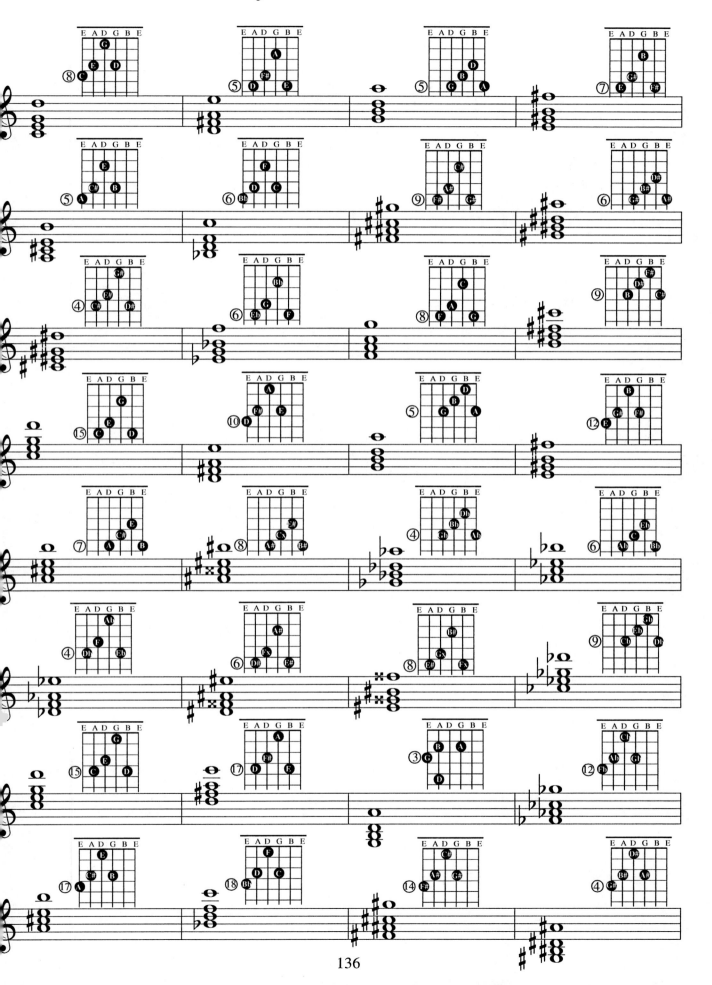

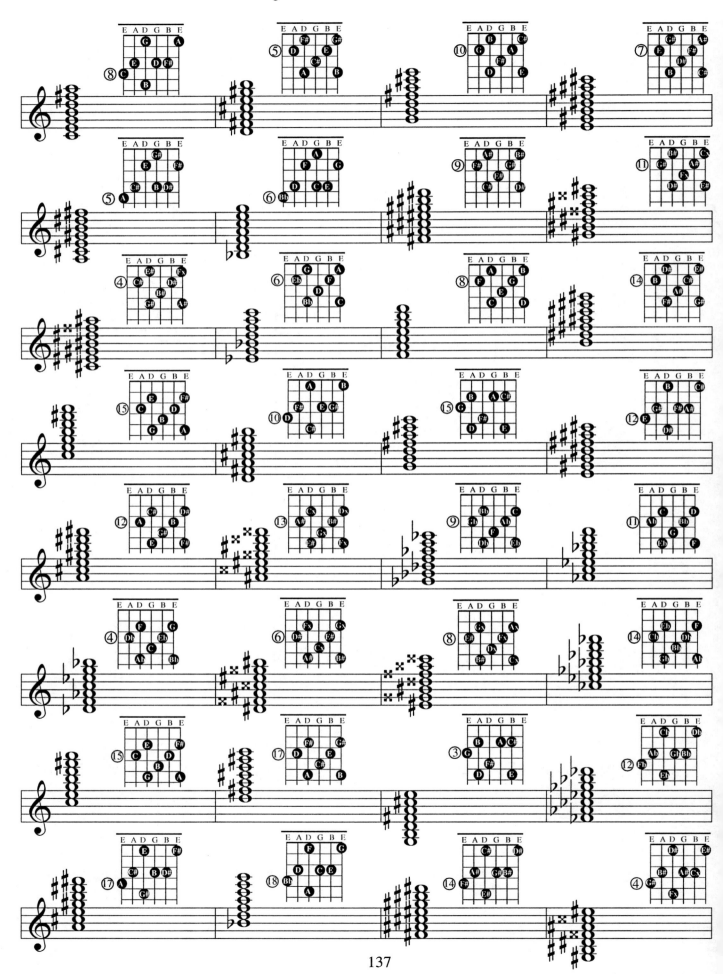

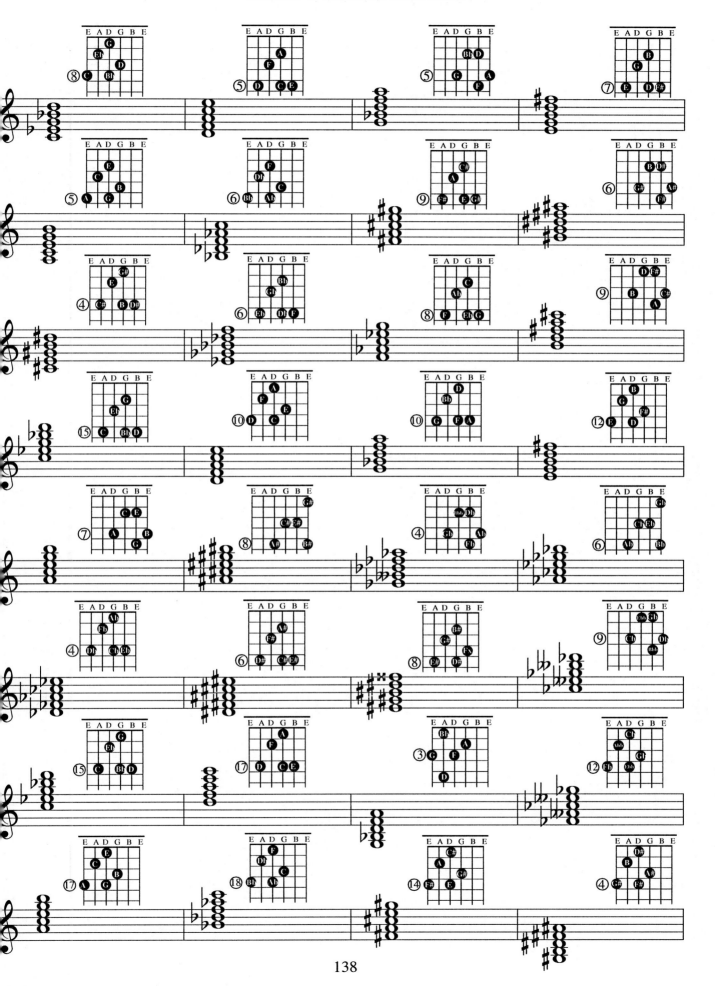

Minor 911 Chords Answers

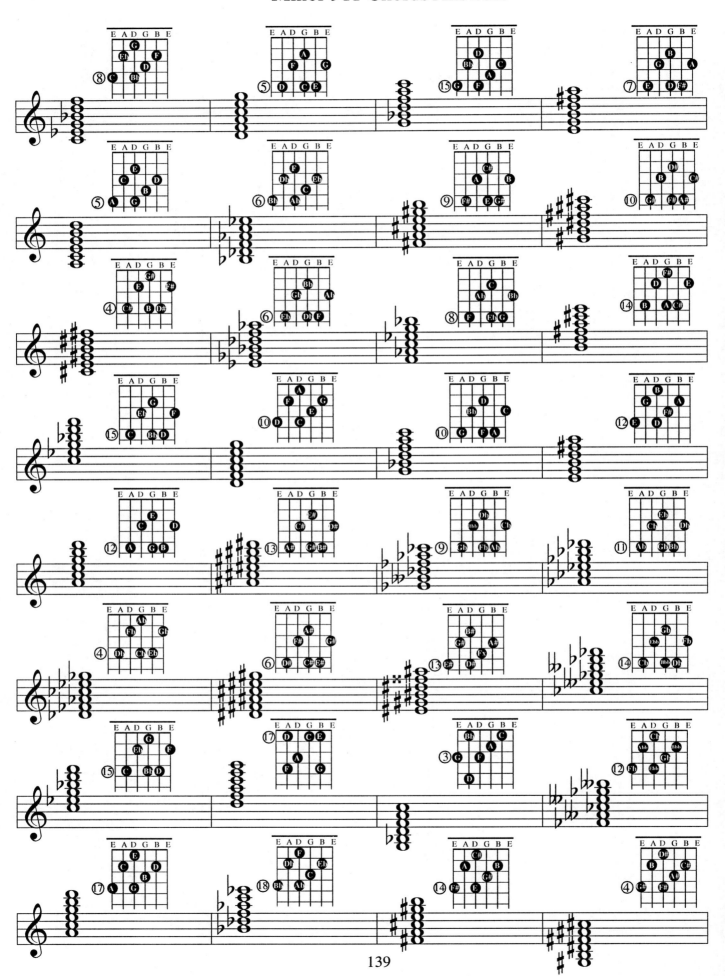

139

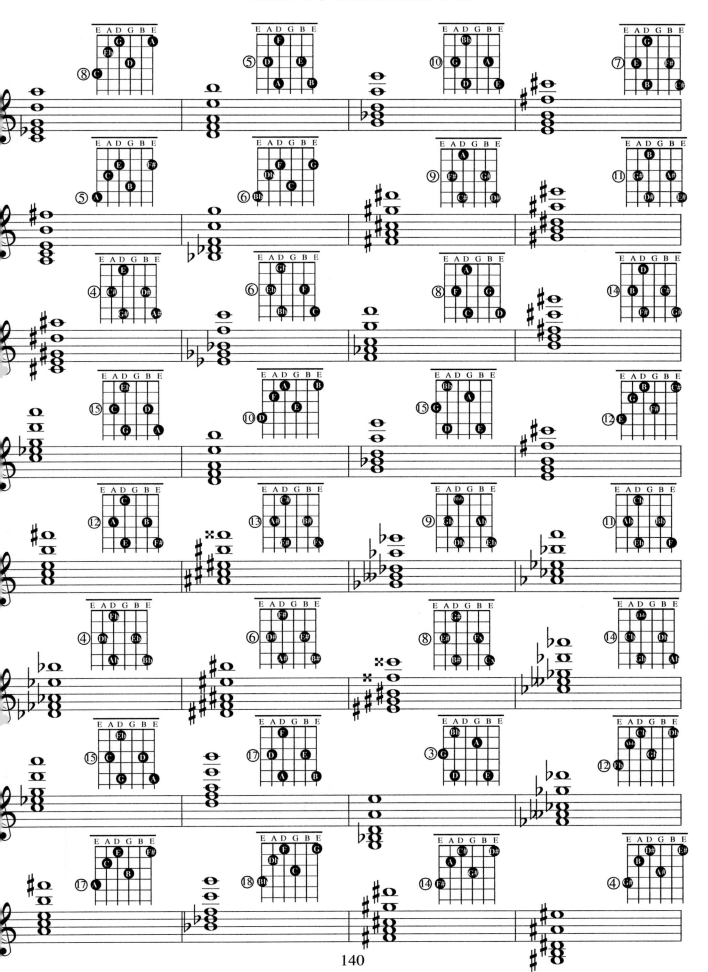

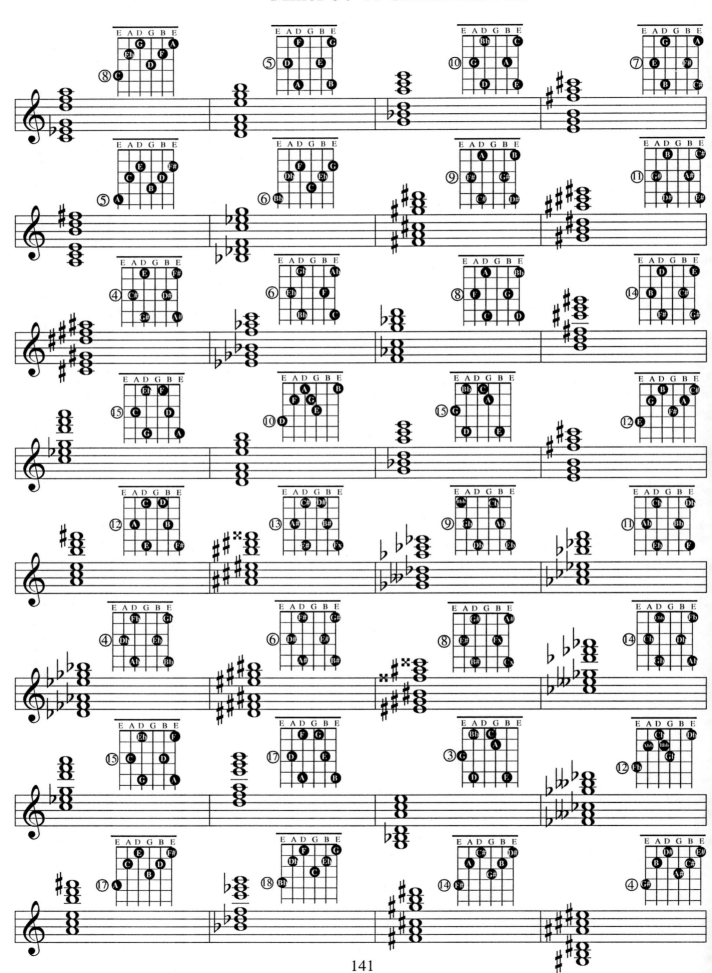

Minor 11 Chords Answers

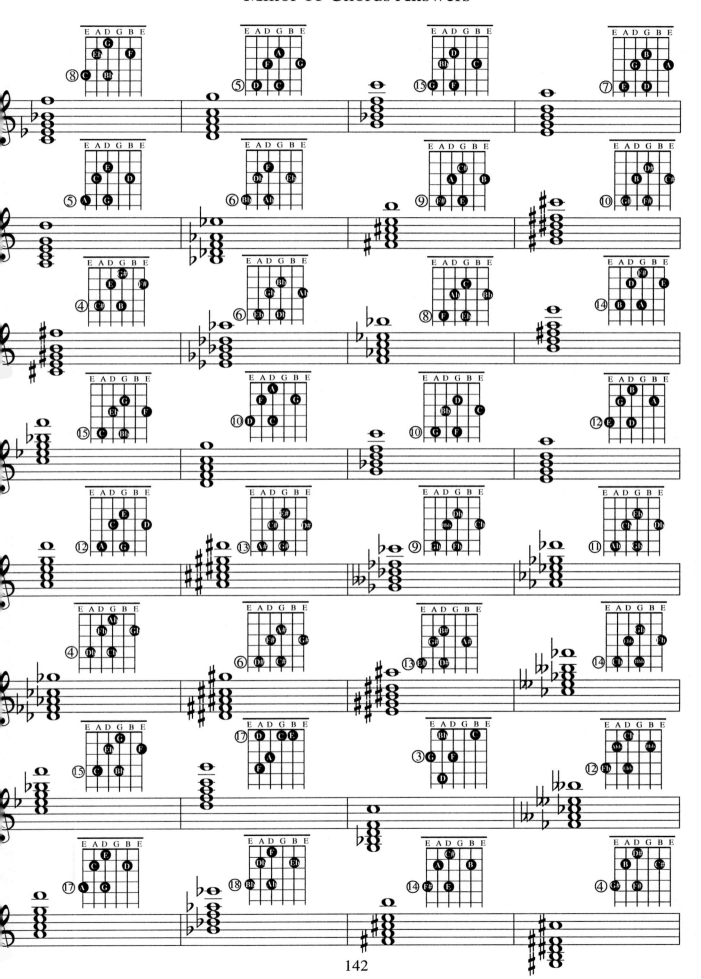

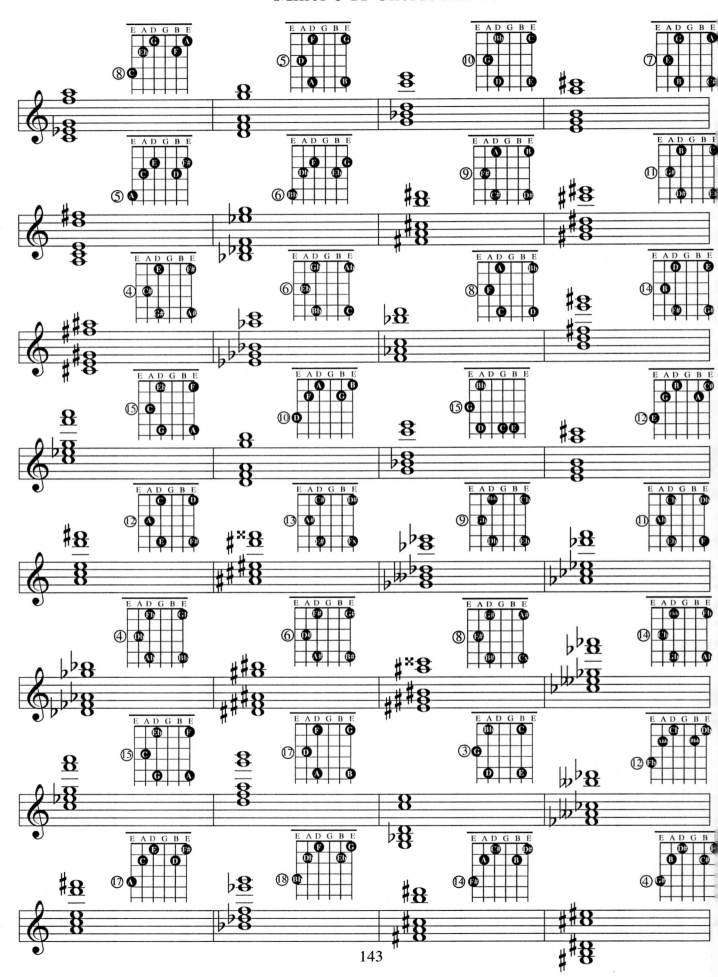

Minor 6 7 Chords Answers

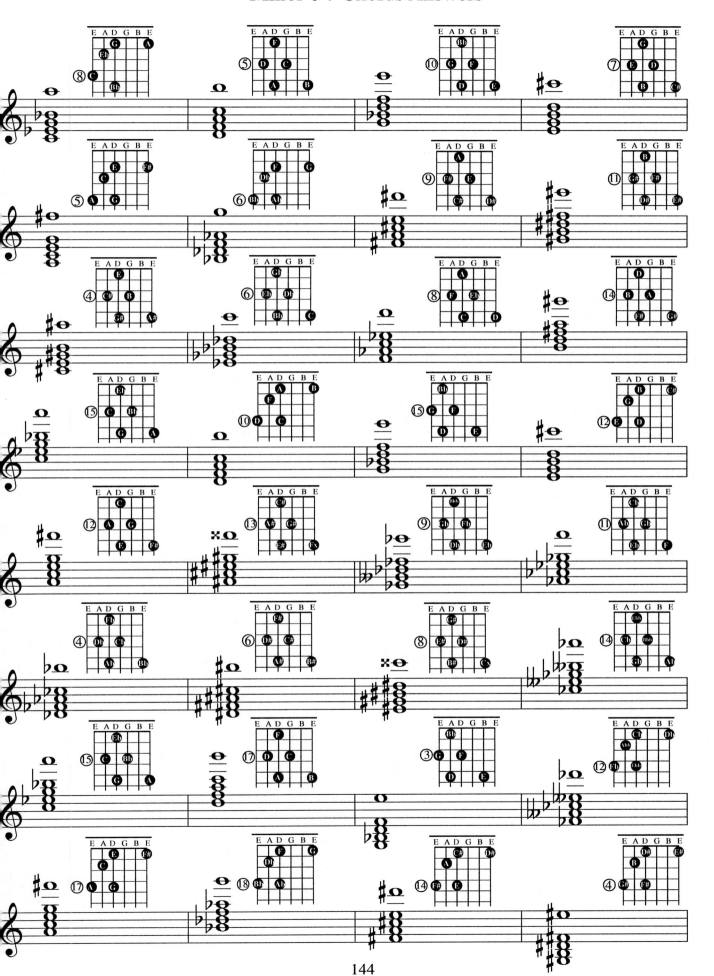

144

Minor 7 6 9 Chords Answers

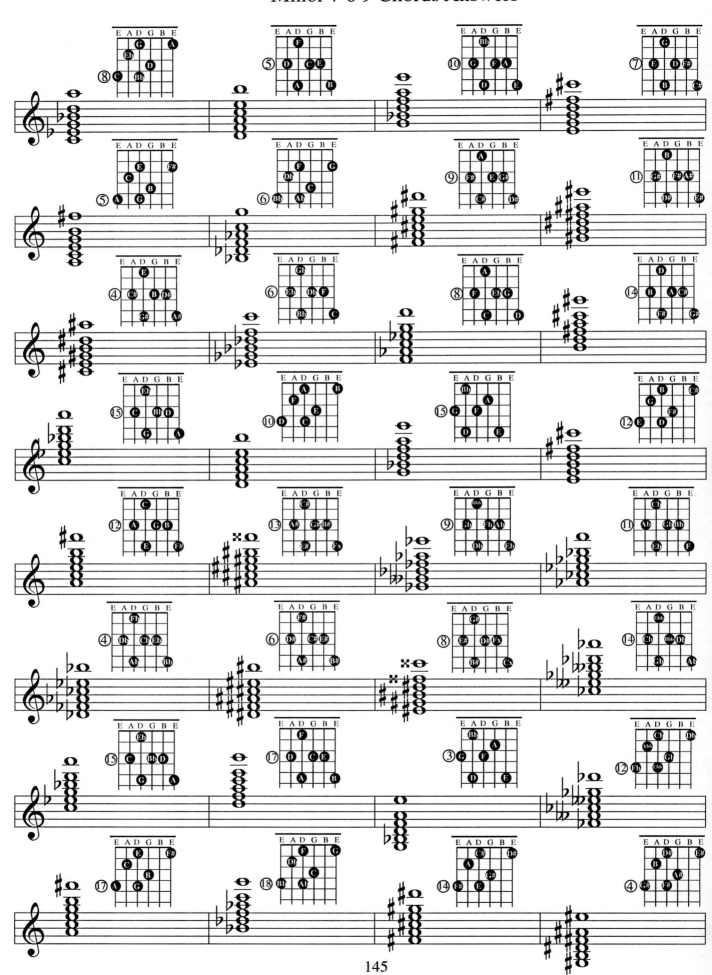

Dominant 9th Chords Answers

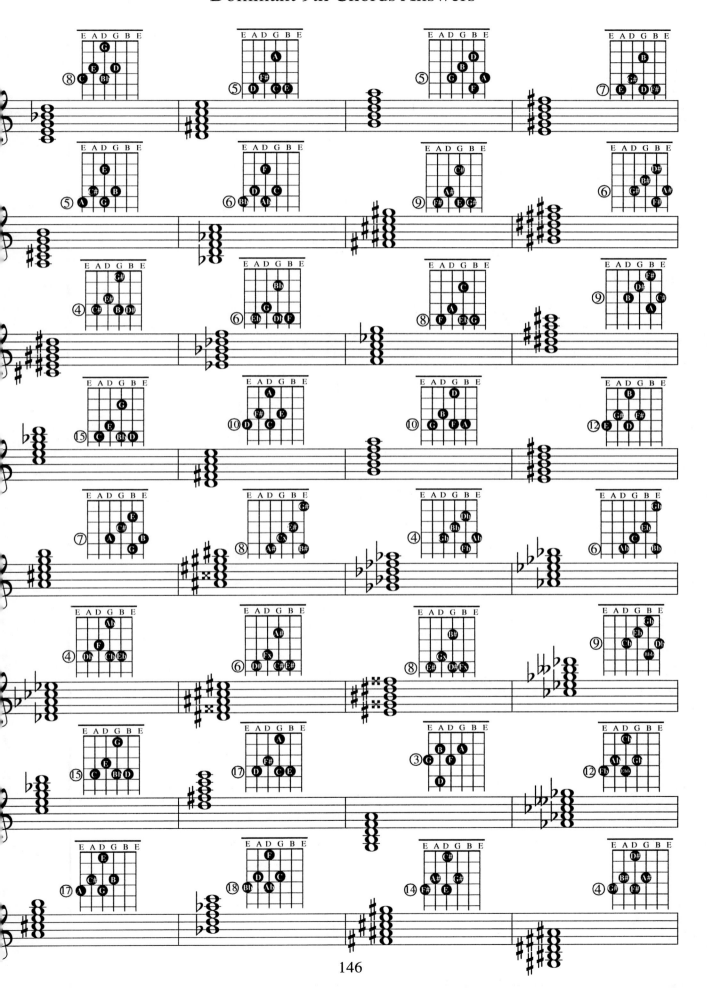

Dominant 7b9 Chords Answers

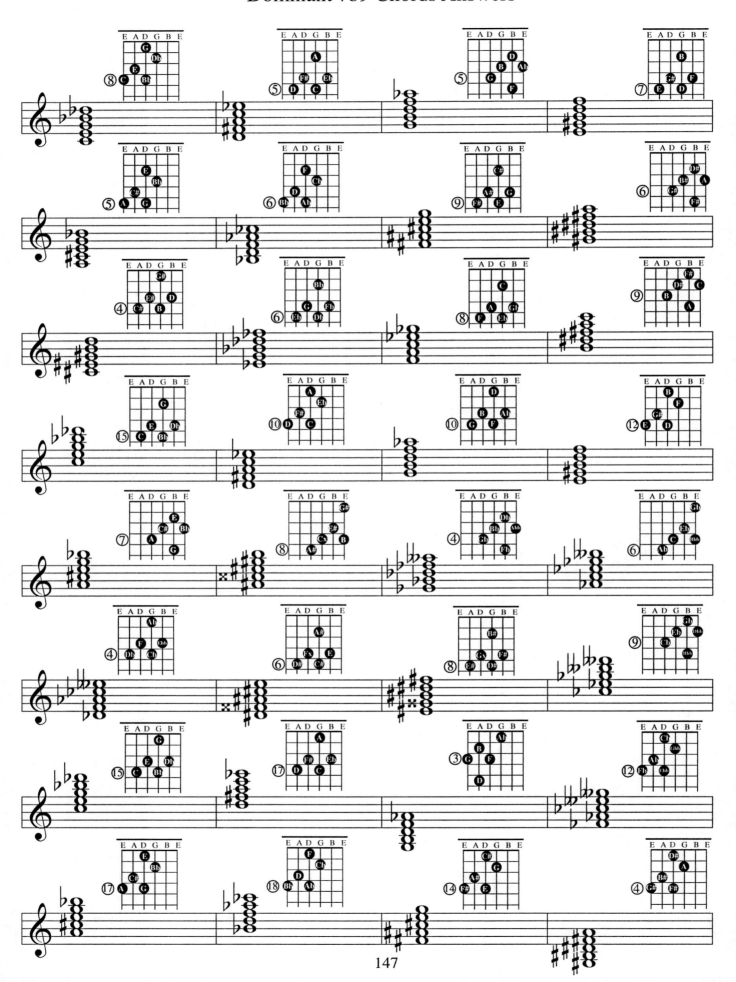

Dominant 7#9 Chords Answers

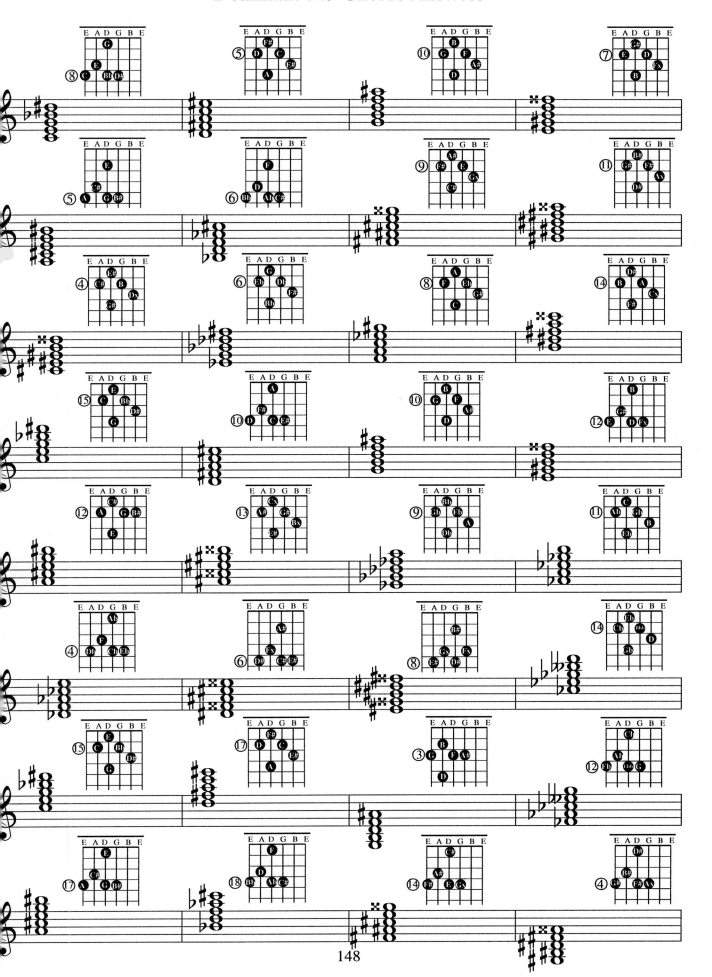

Dominant 13th Chords Answers

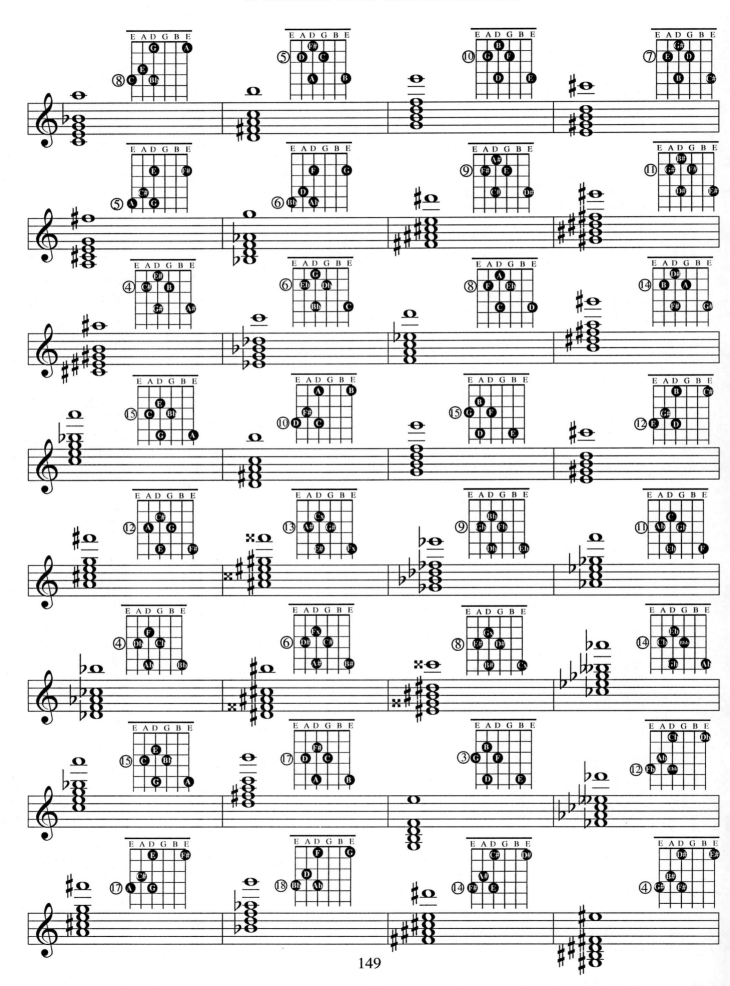

149

Dominant 7 b13 Chords Answers

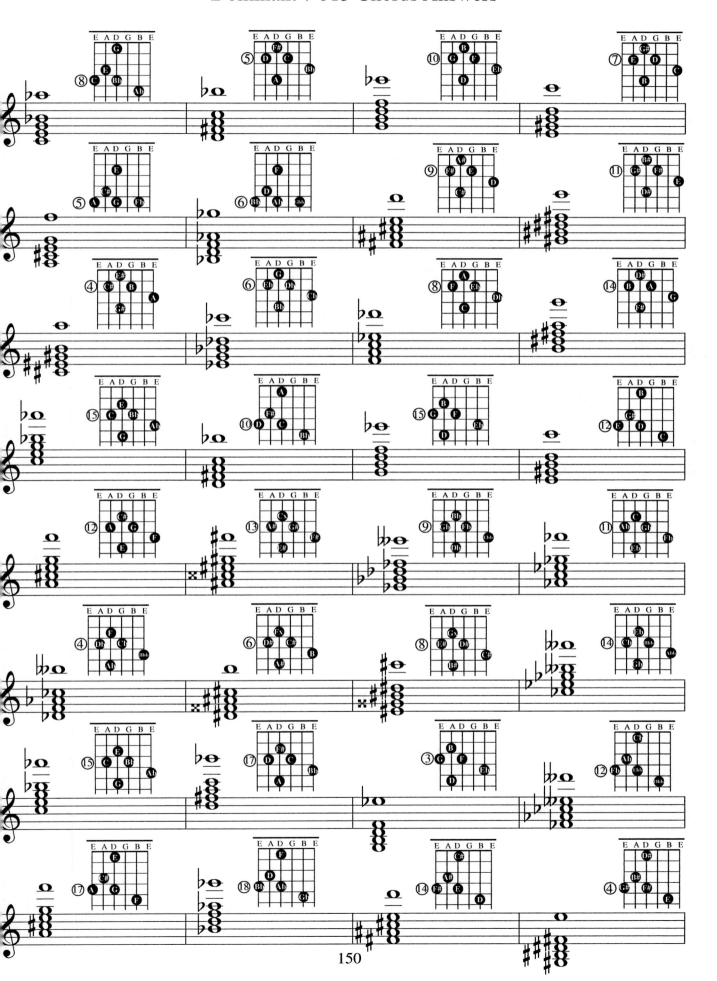

150

Dominant 9 13th Chords Answers

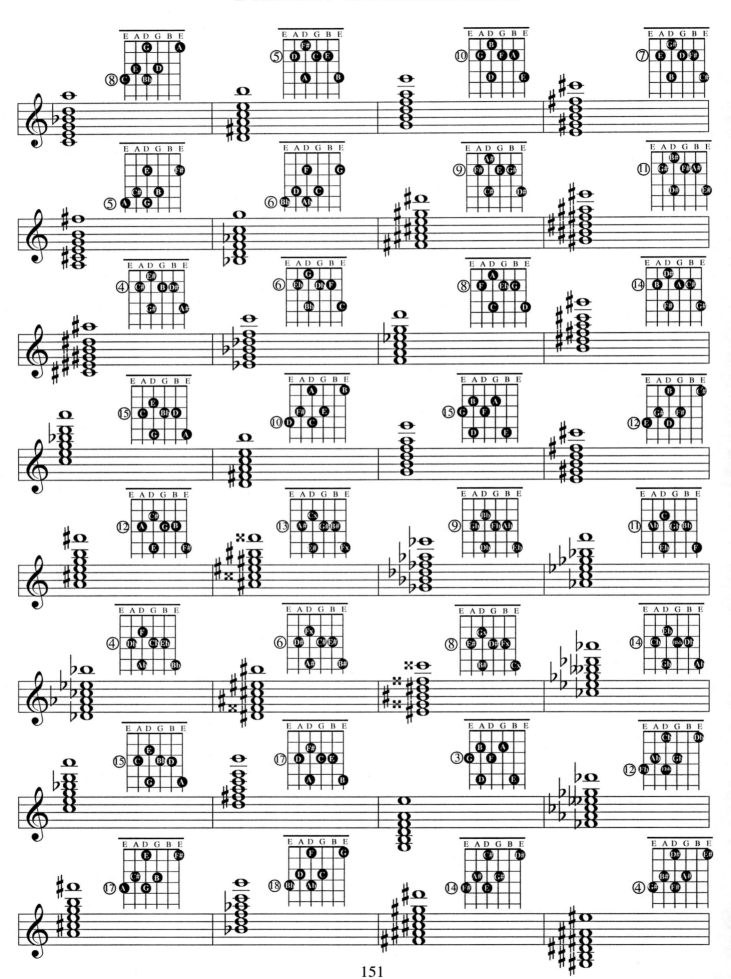

151

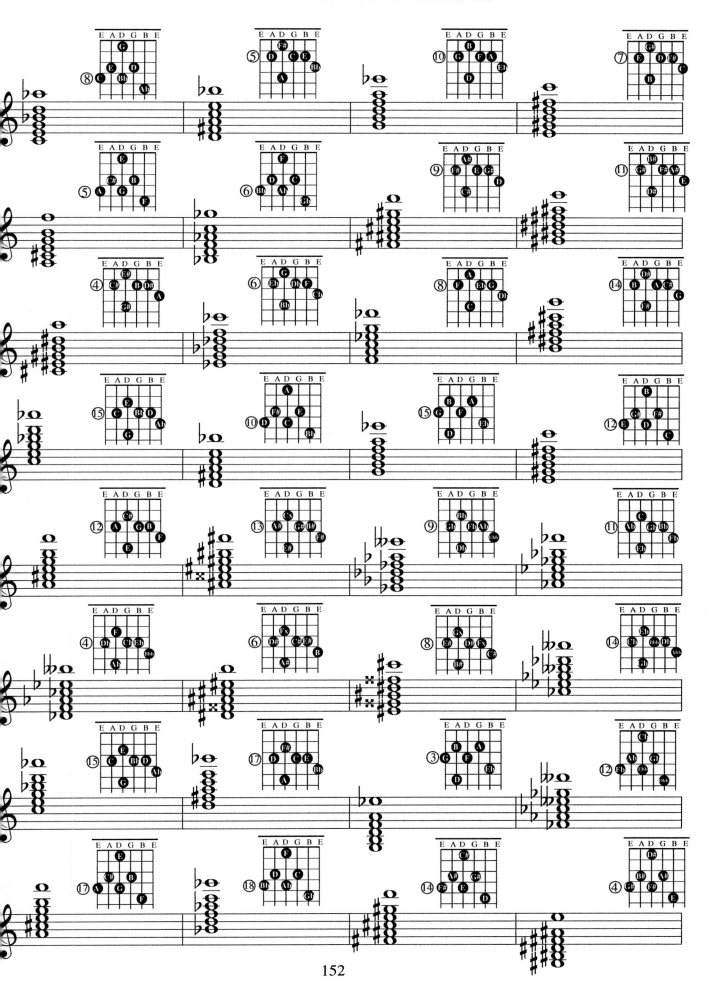

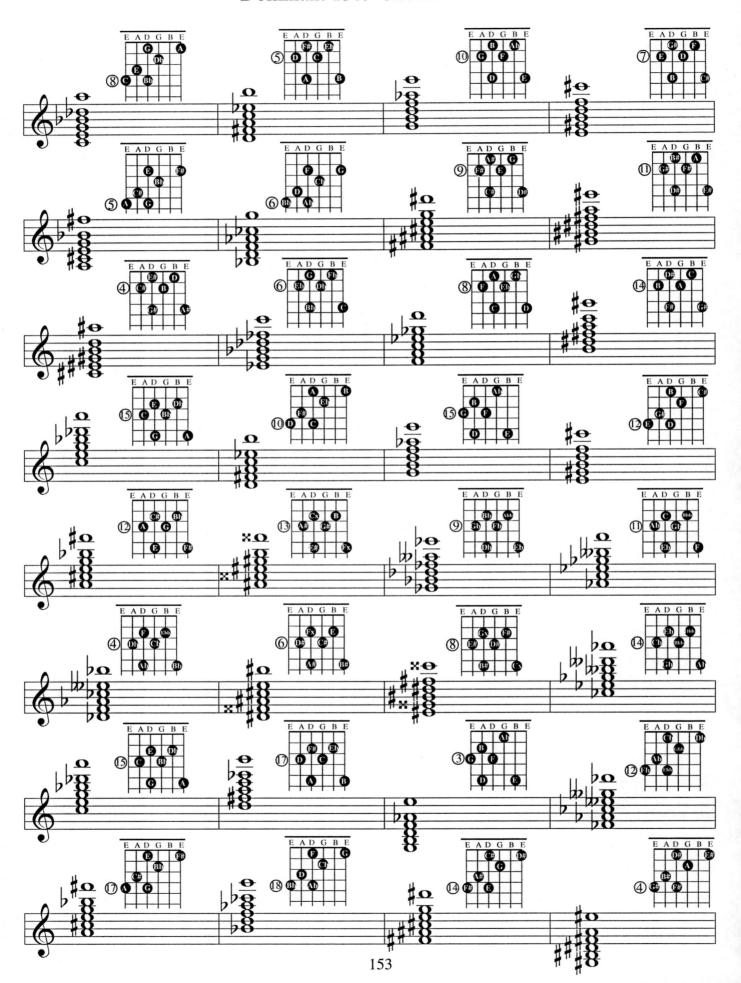

Dominant 13#9 Chords Answers

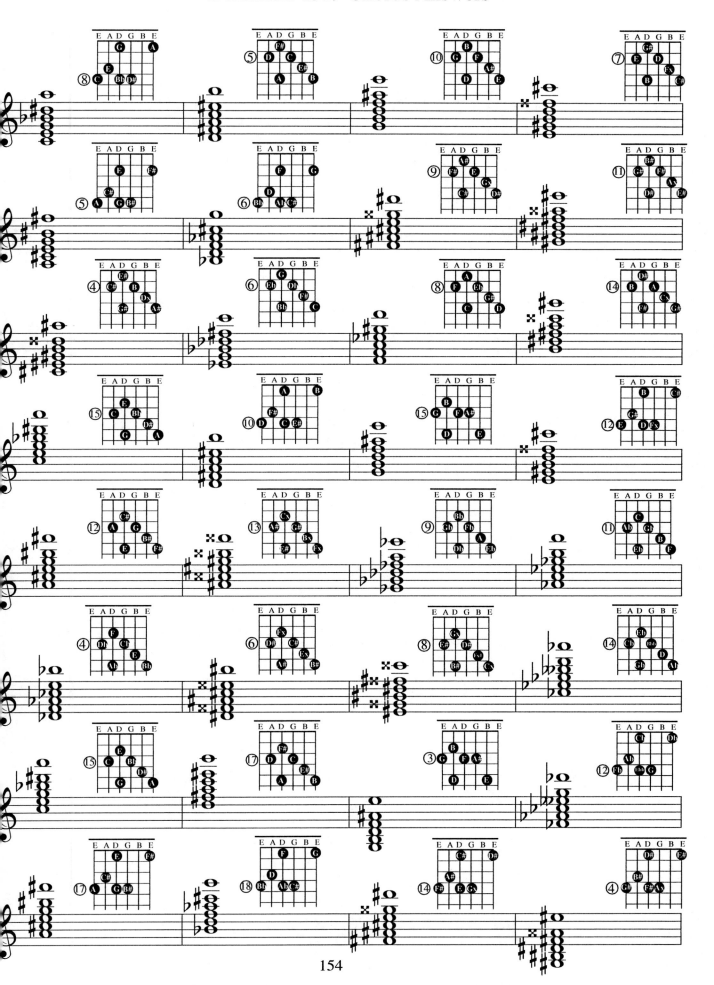

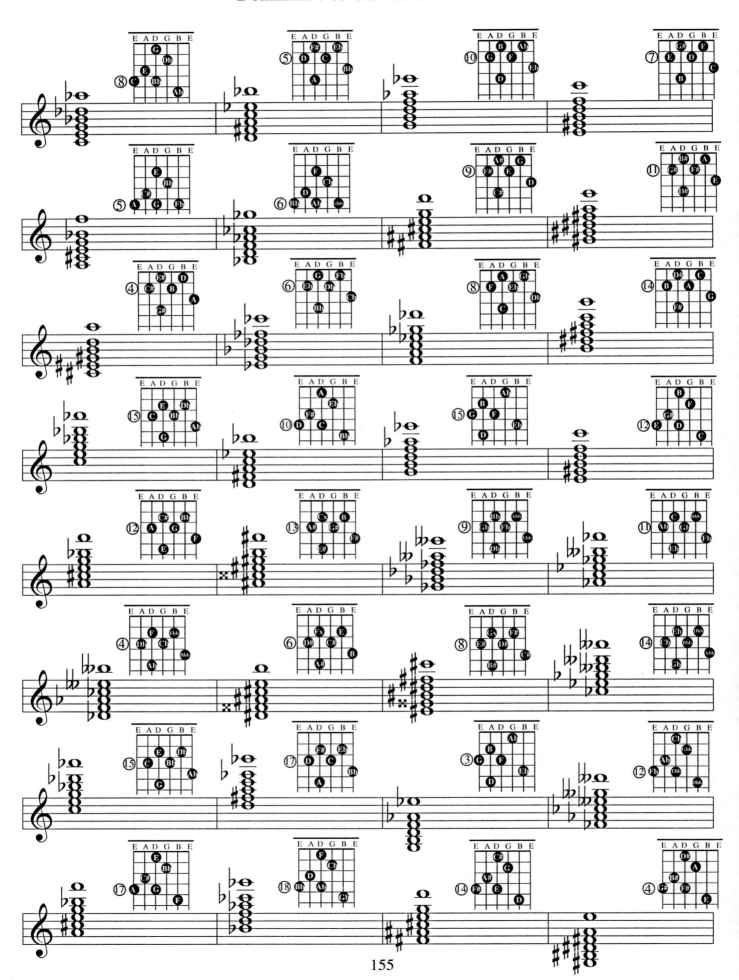

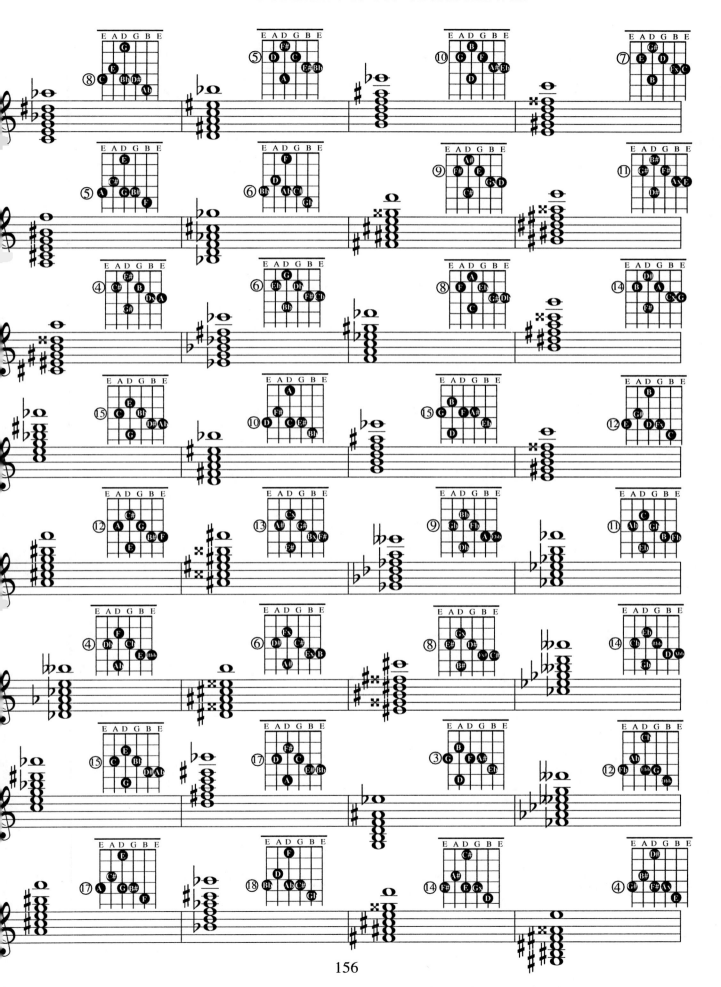

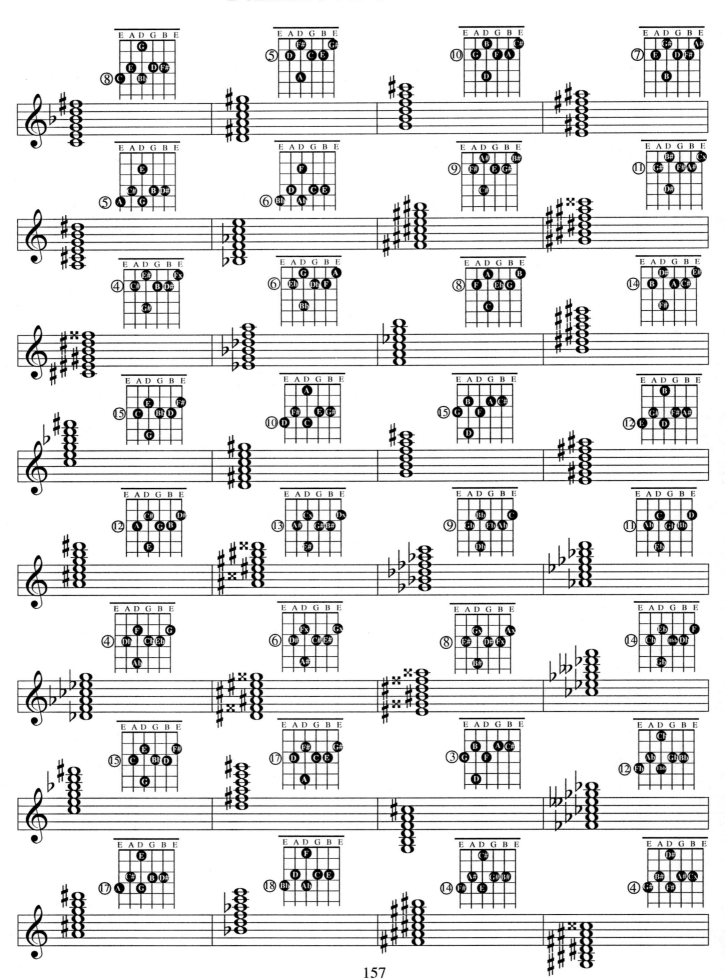

Dominant 7 b9 #11 Chords Answers

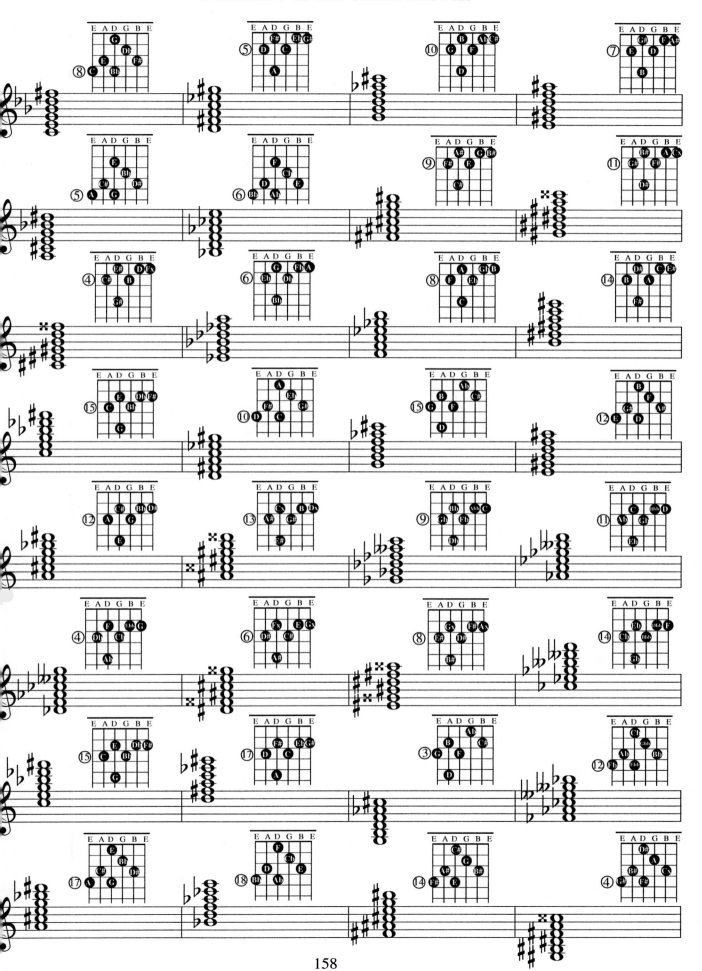

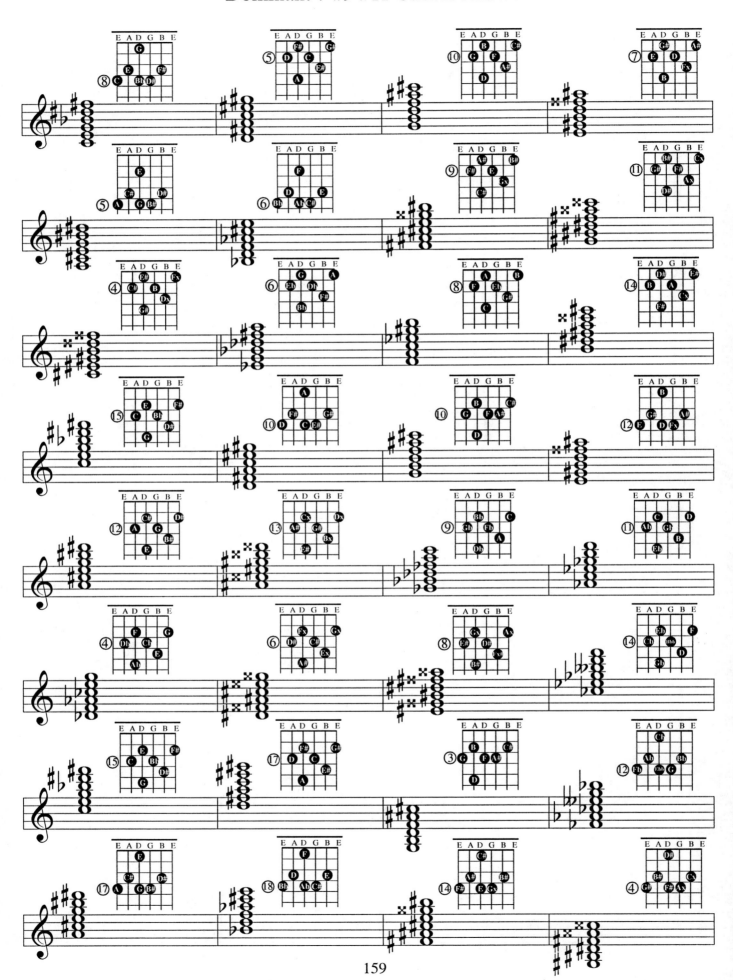

Dominant 13 #11 Chords Answers

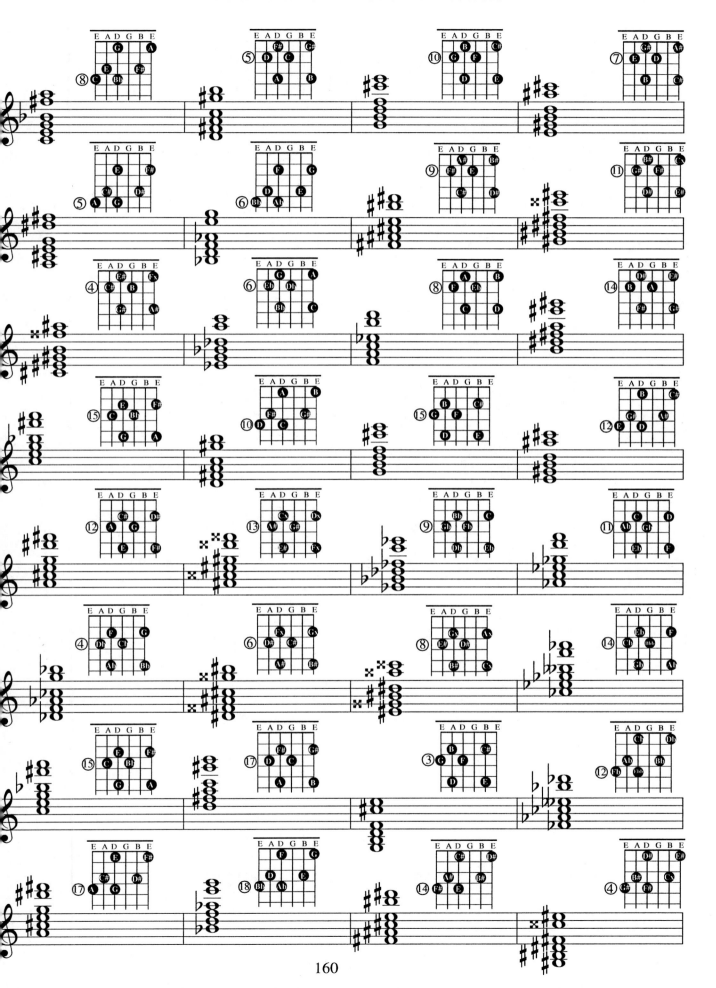

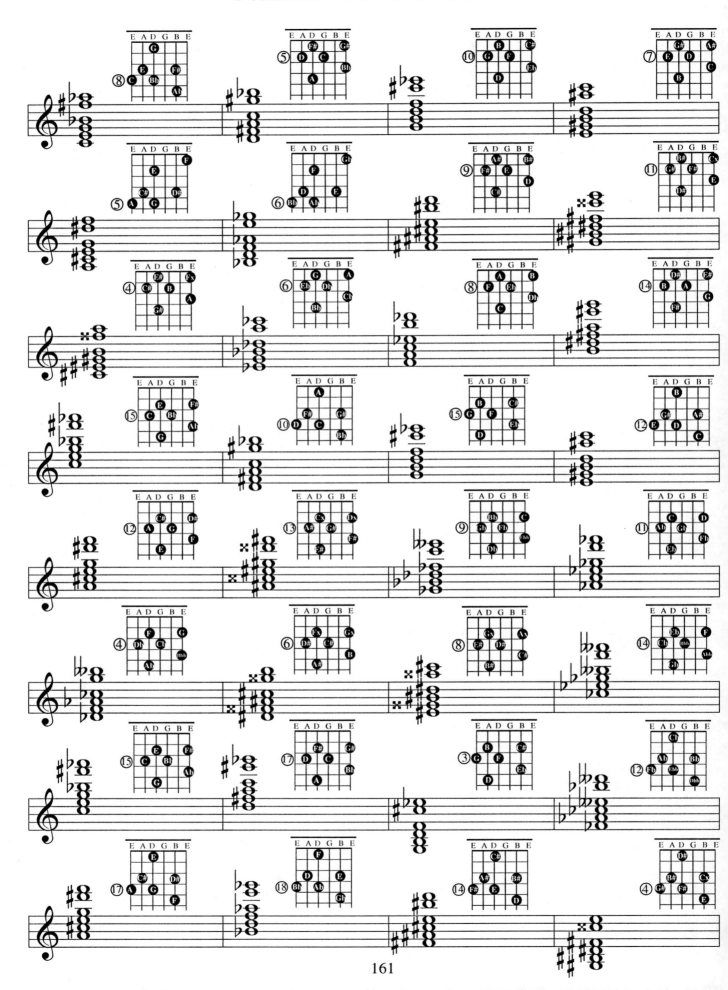

Dominant 9sus4 Chords Answers

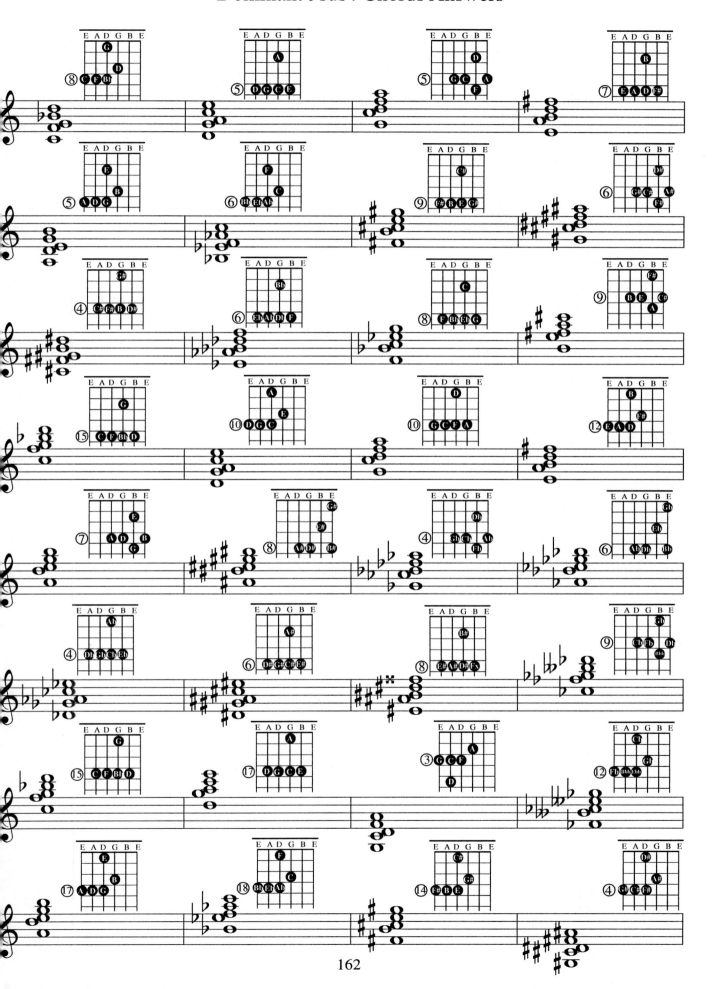

Dominant 7 sus4 b9 Chords Answers

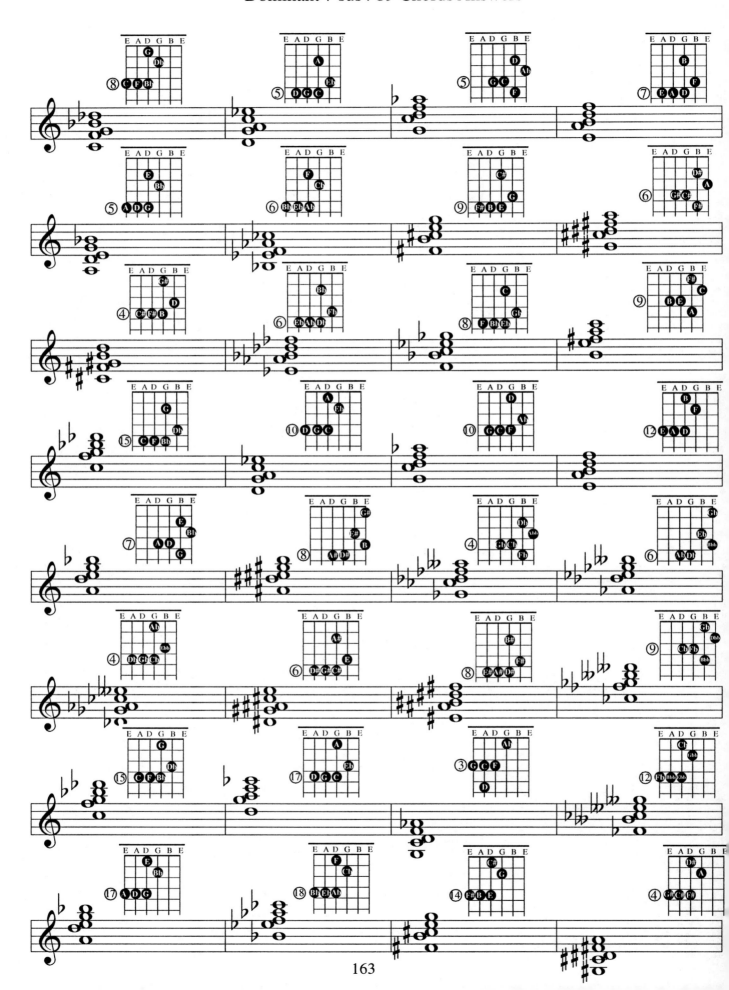

Dominant 7sus4#9 Chords Answers

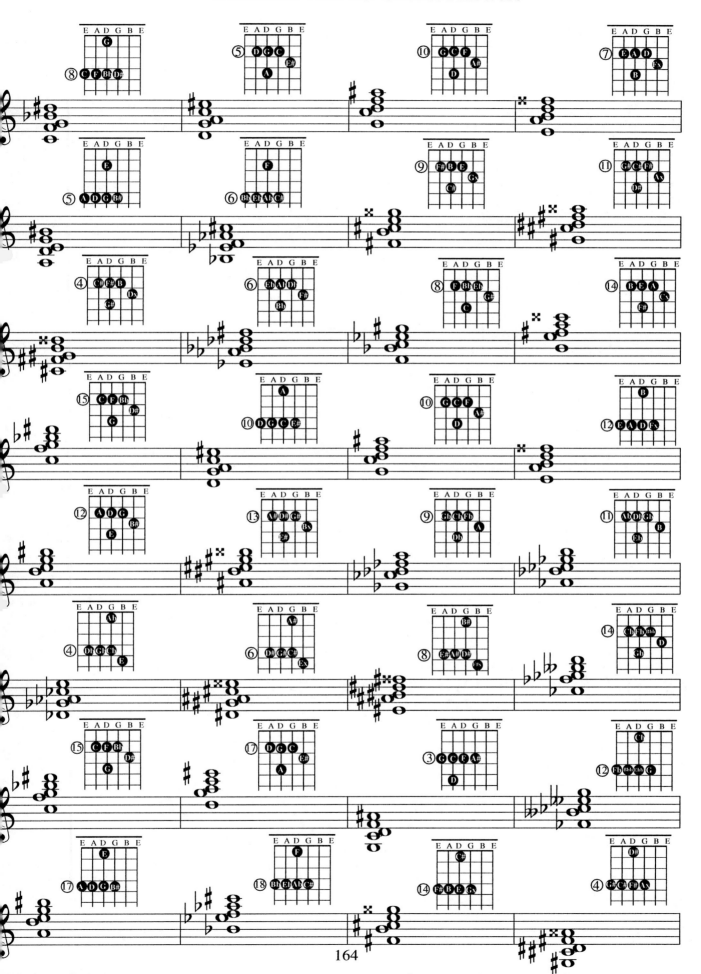

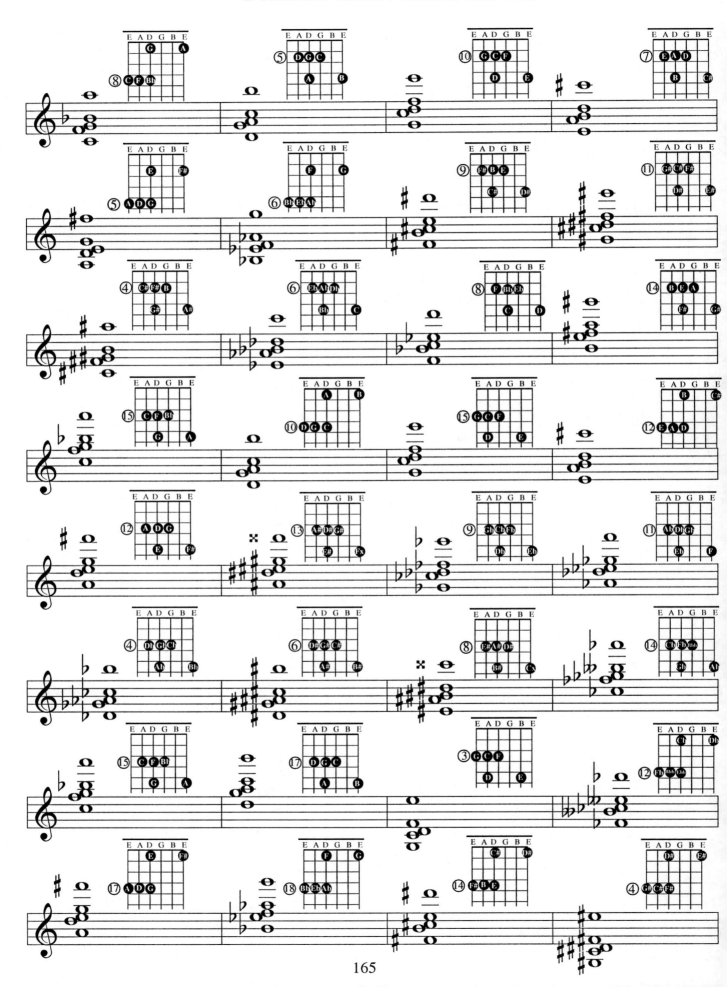

Dominant 7 sus4 b13 Chords Answers

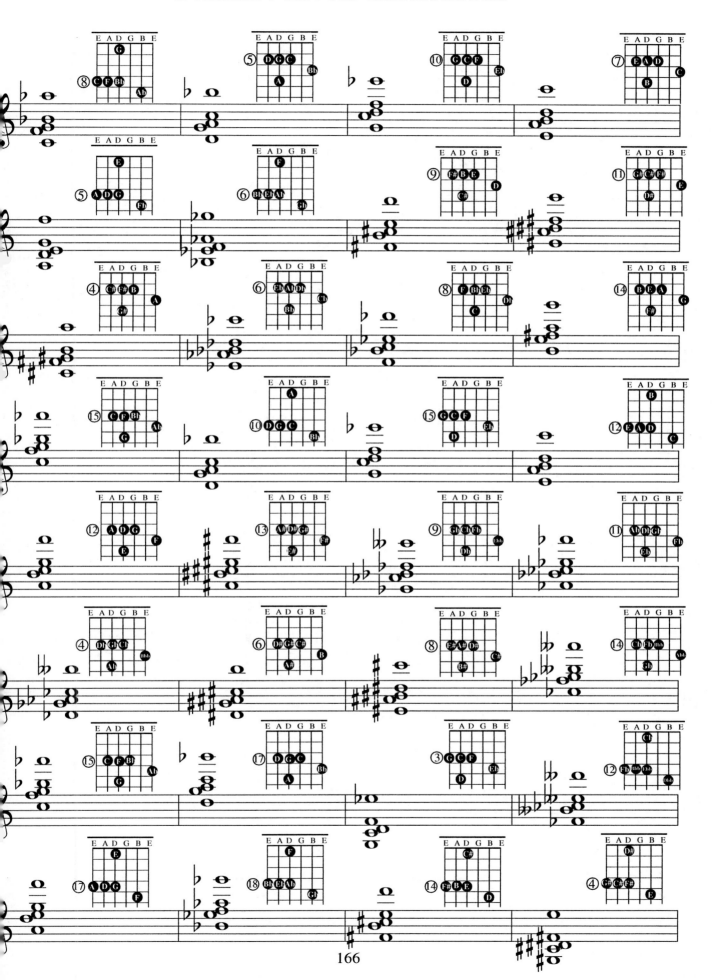

Dominant 9sus4 add 13 Chords Answers

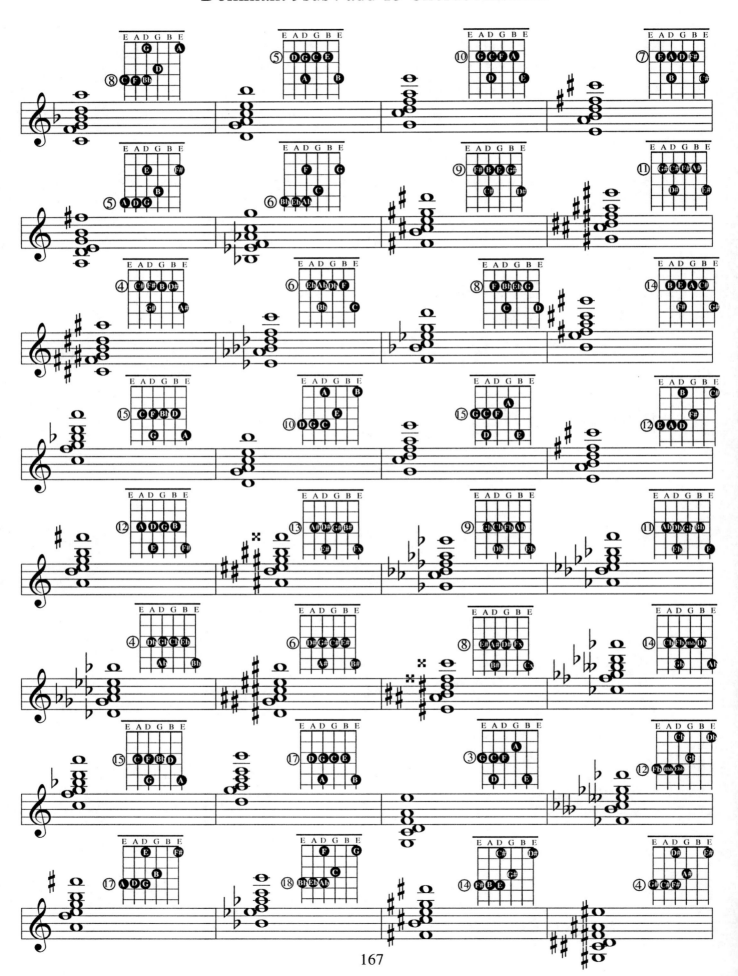

Dominant 9sus4 b13 Chords Answers

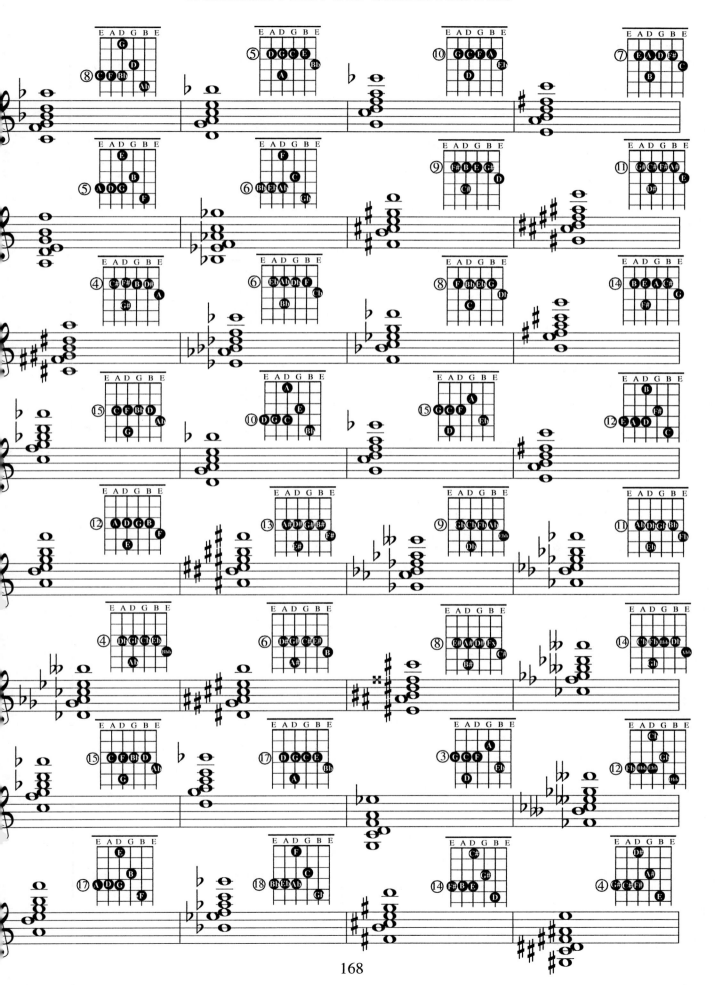

Dominant 13sus4b9 Chords Answers

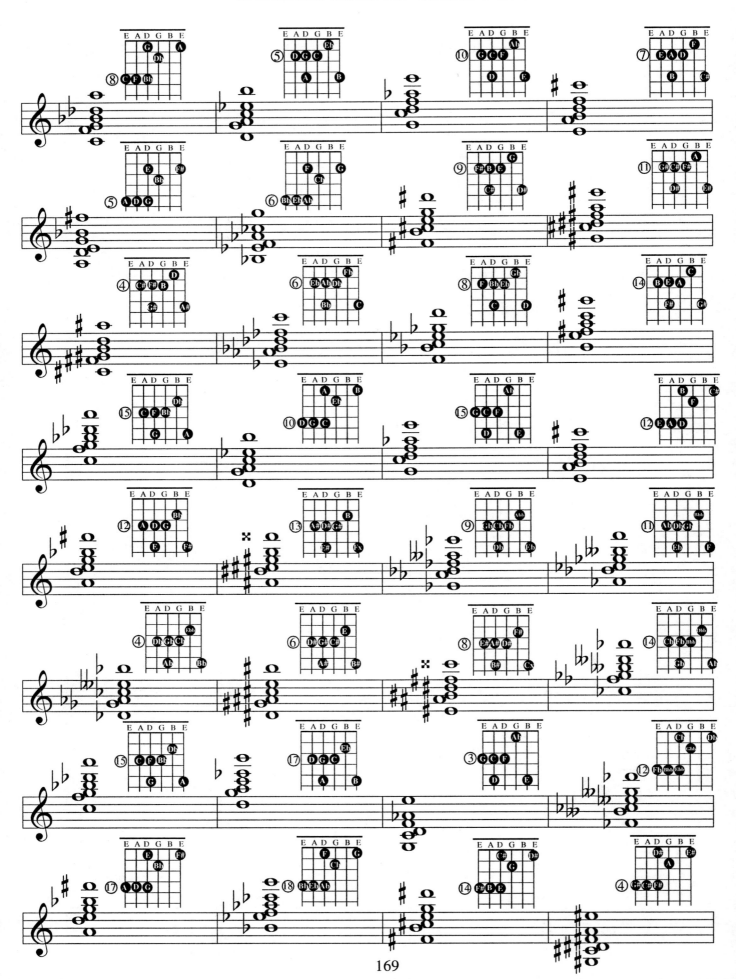

169

Dominant 13sus4#9 Chords Answers

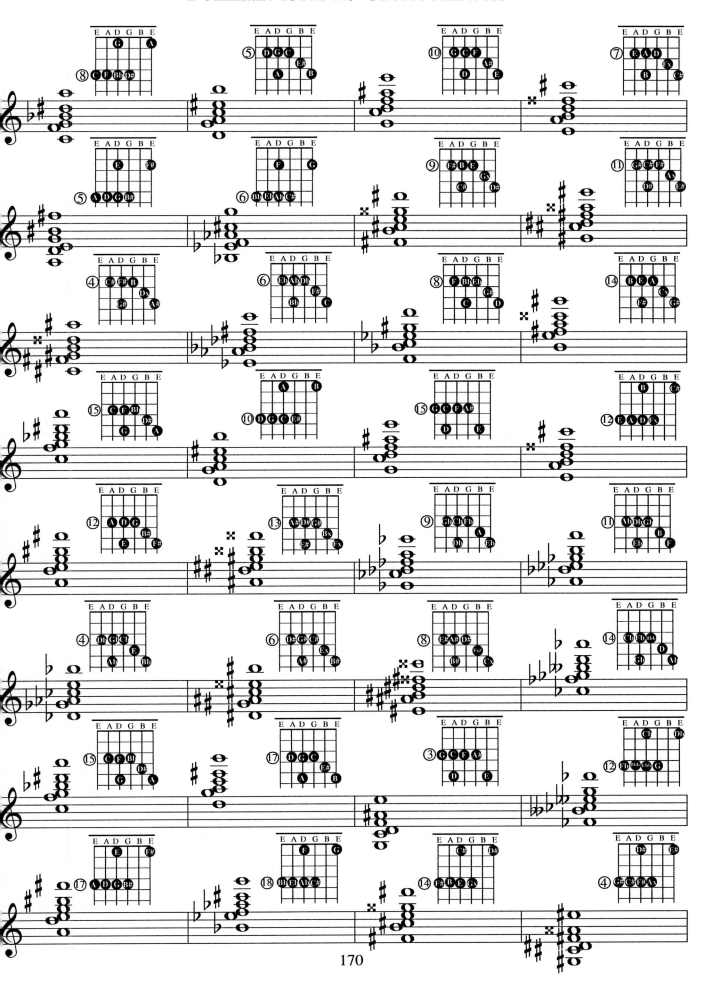

Dominant 7sus4 b9 b13 Chords Answers

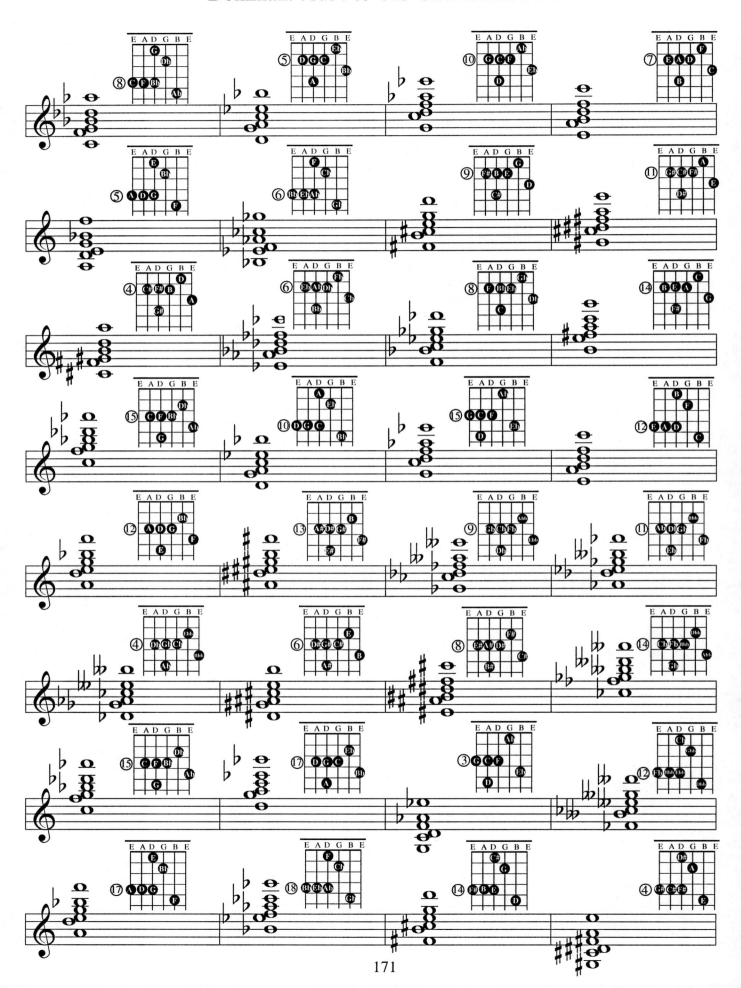

171

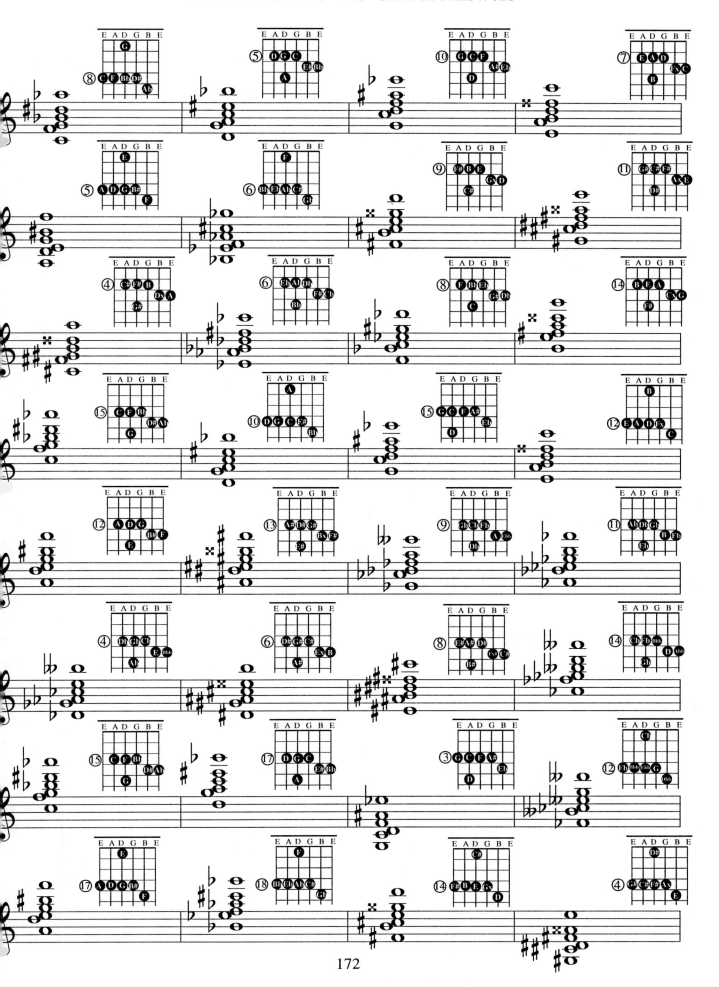

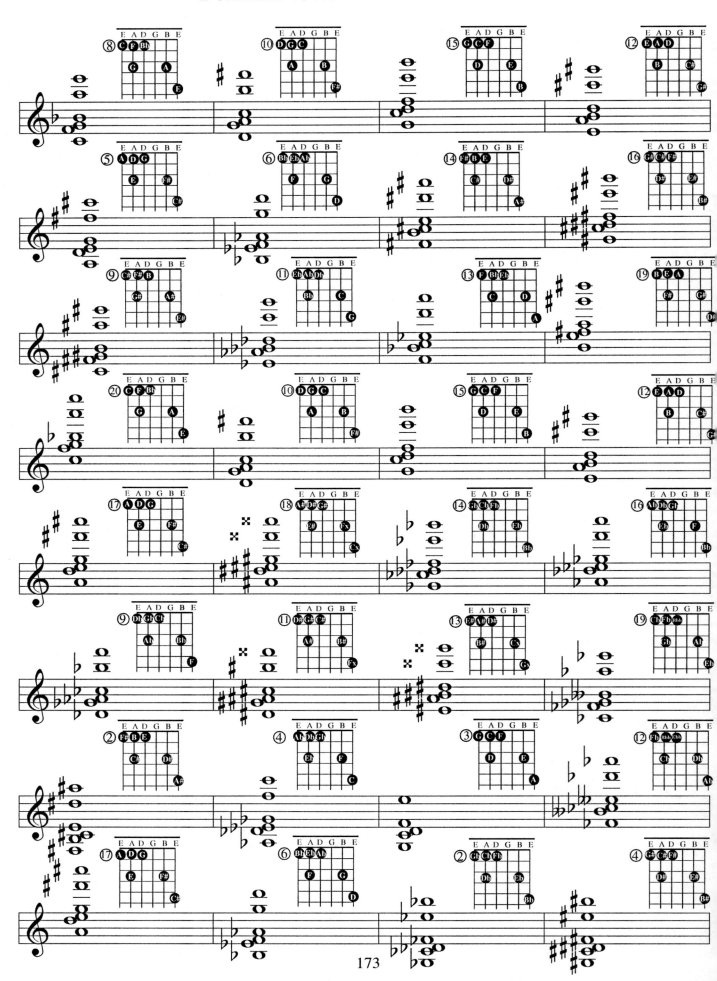

Minor 7b5 add 9 Chords Answers

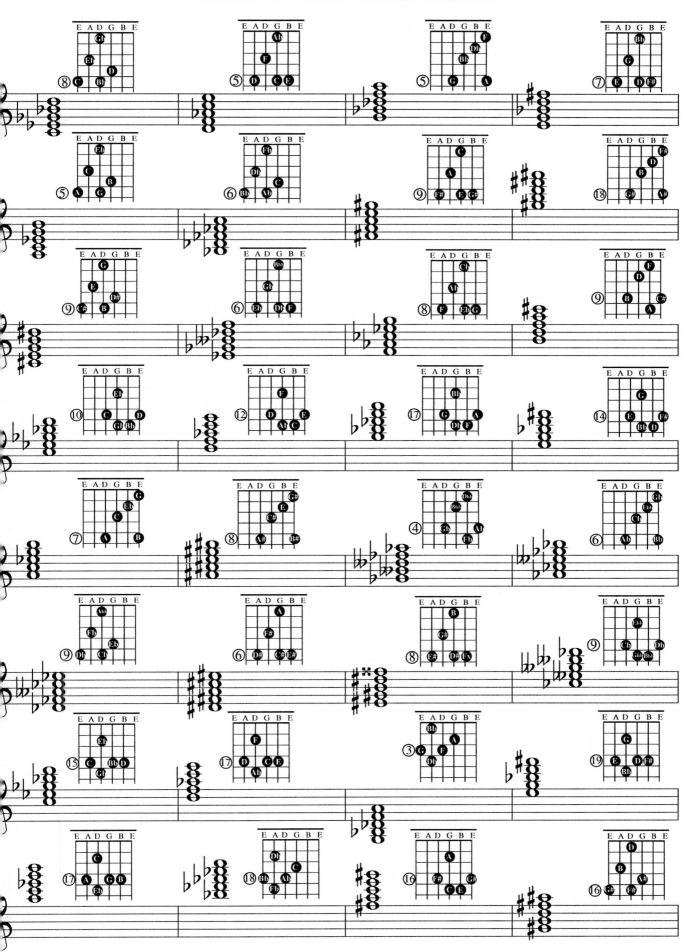

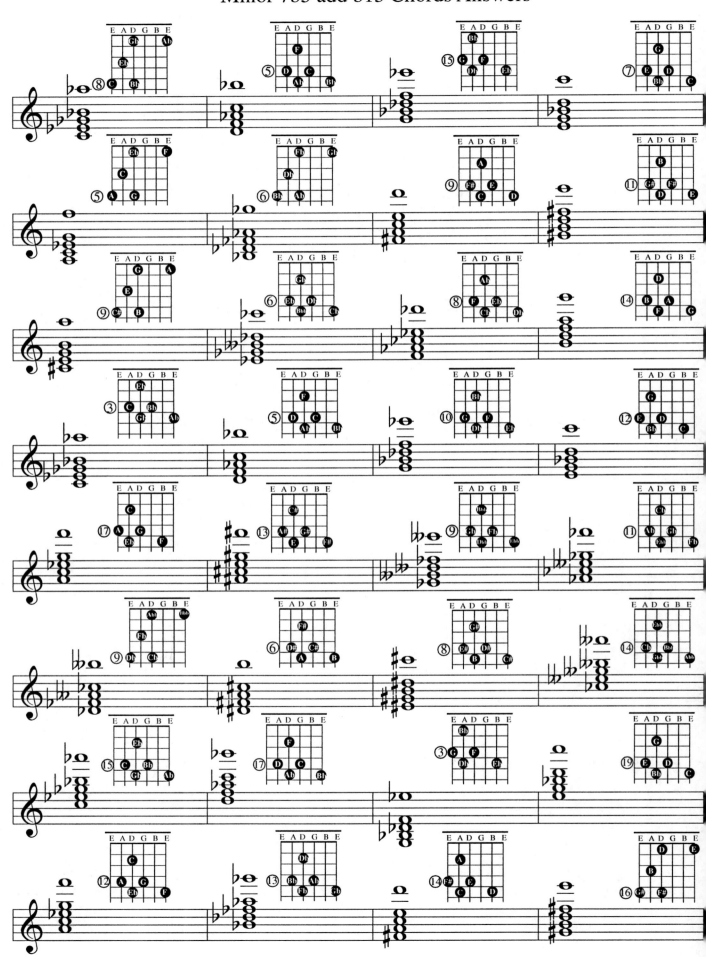

Diminished 7th add 9 Chords Answers

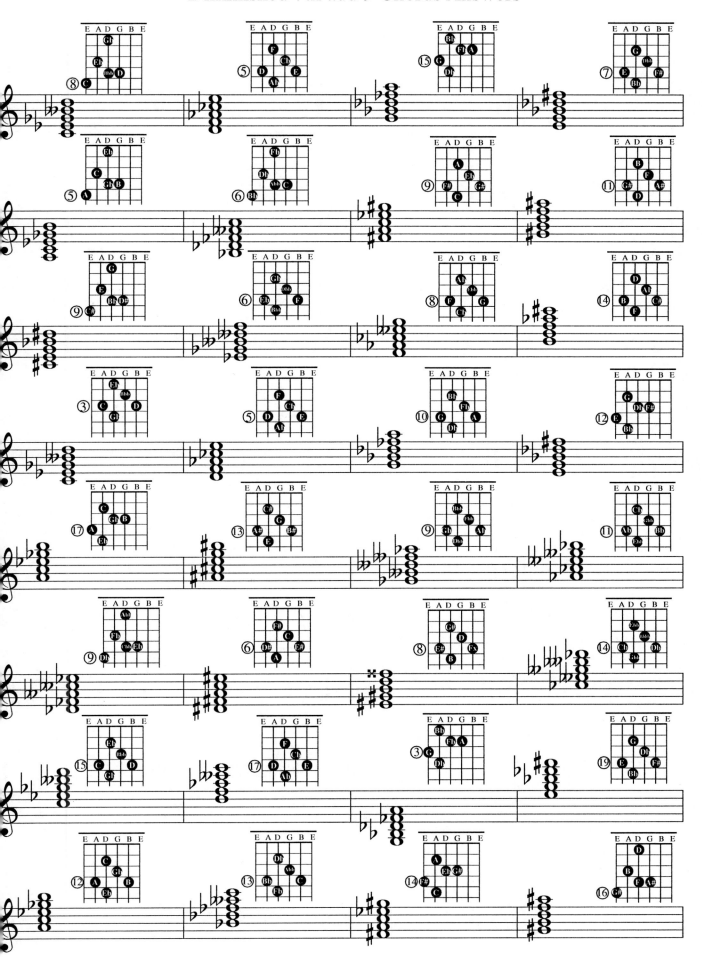

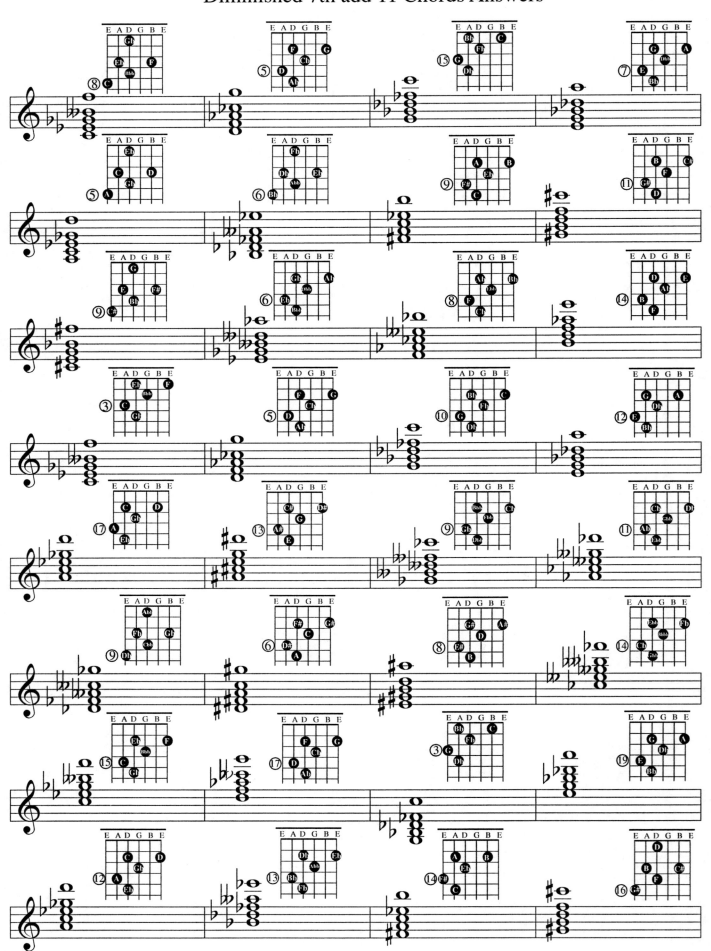

Diminished 7th add b13 Chords Answers

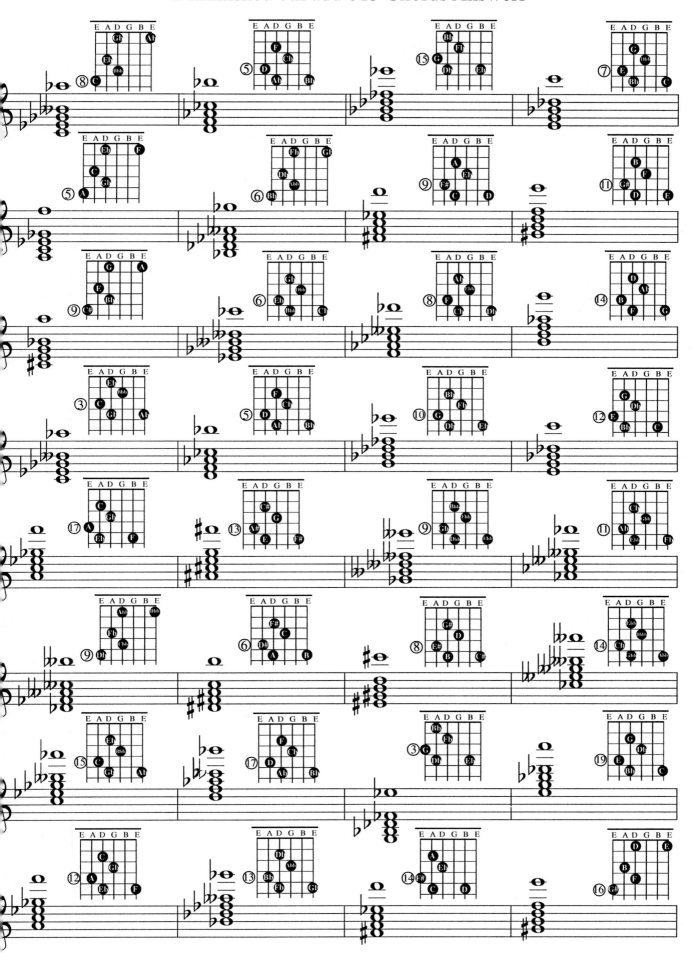

178

Diminished 7th add Major 7 Chords Answers

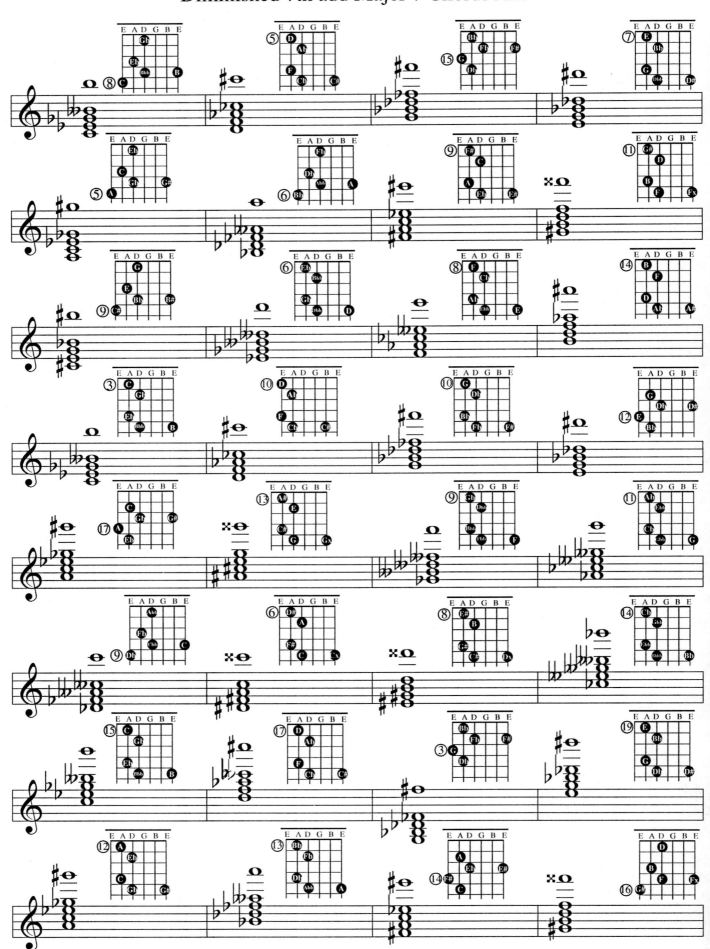

Minor Major 79 Chords Answers

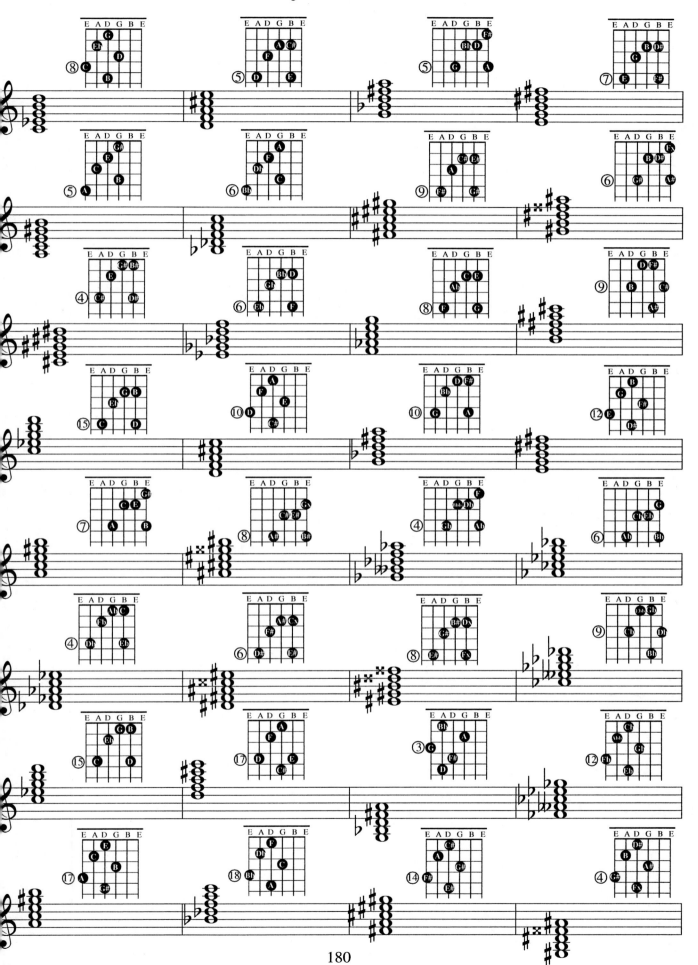

180

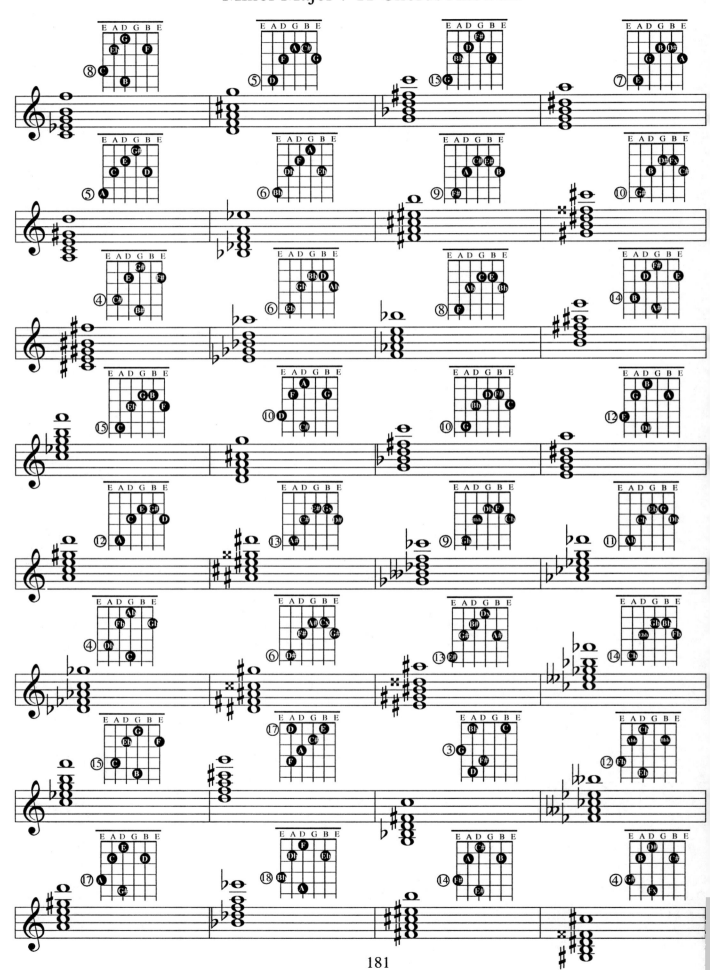

Minor Major 7 6 Chords Answers

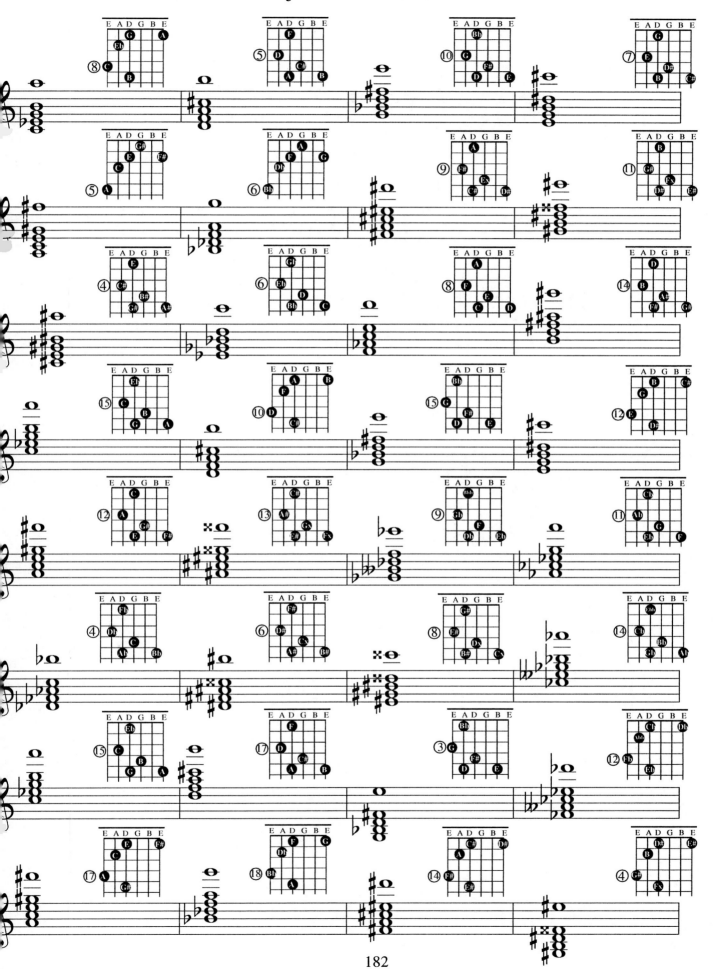

Minor Major 7 9 11 Chords Answers

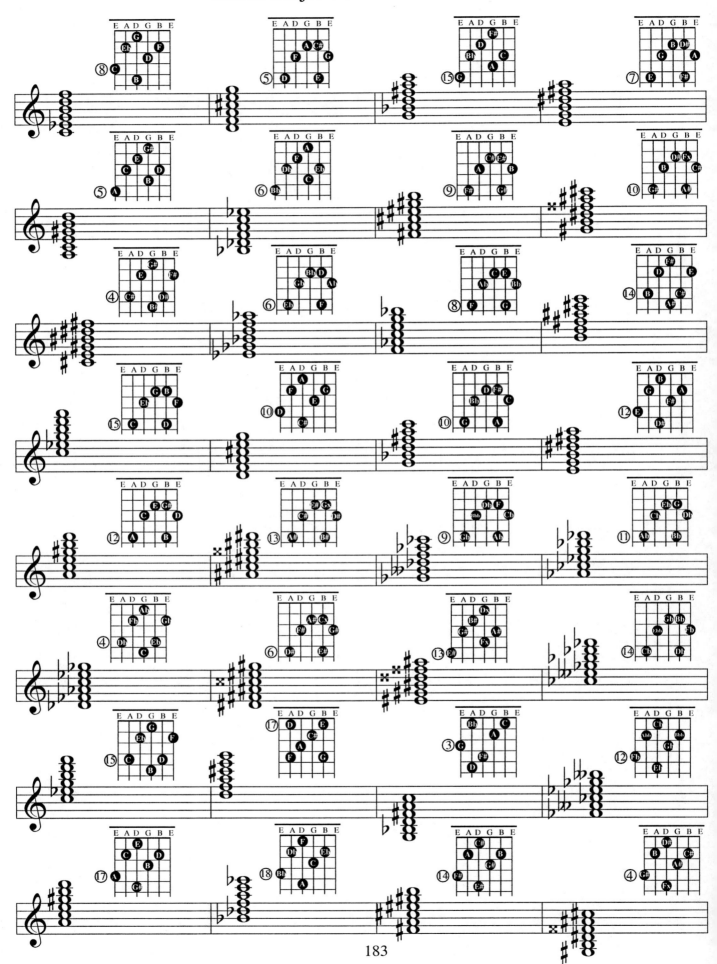

Minor Major 7 6 9 Chords Answers

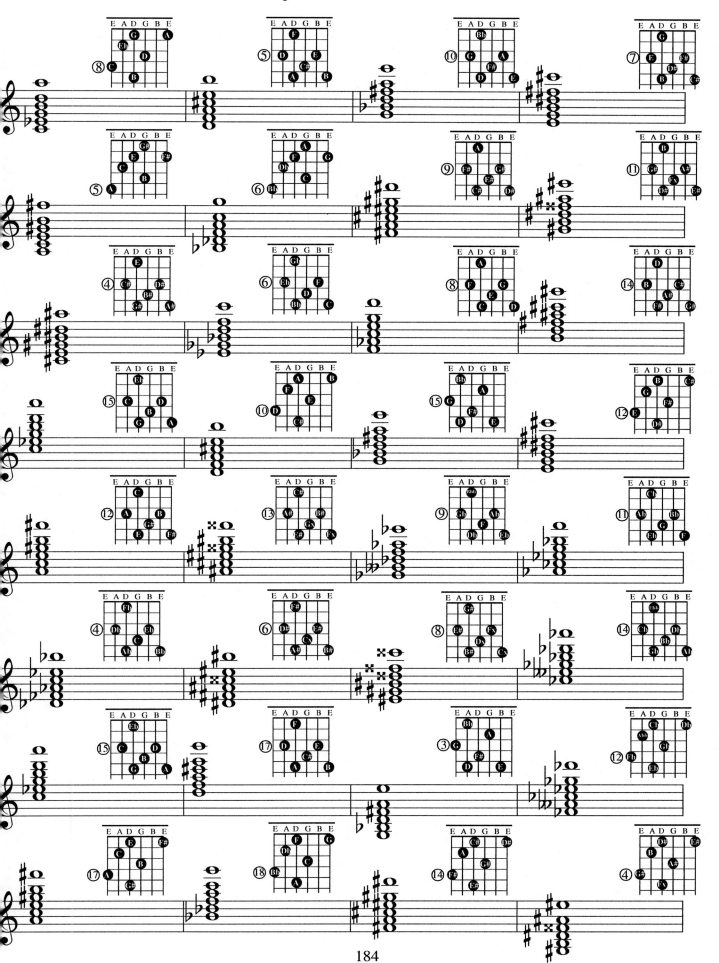

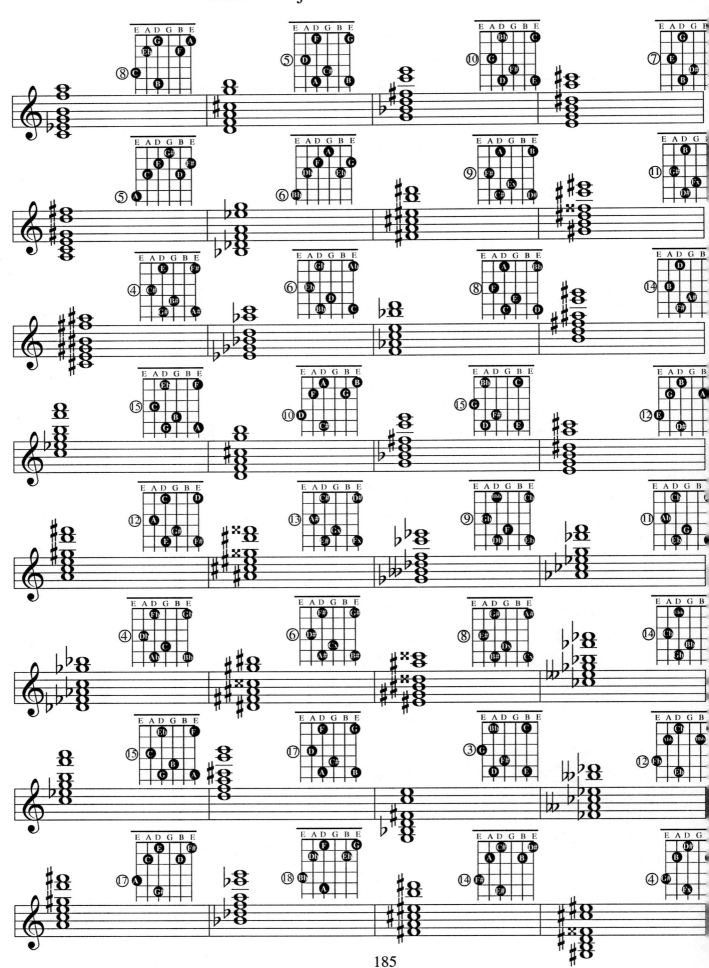

Minor Major 7b5 Chords Answers

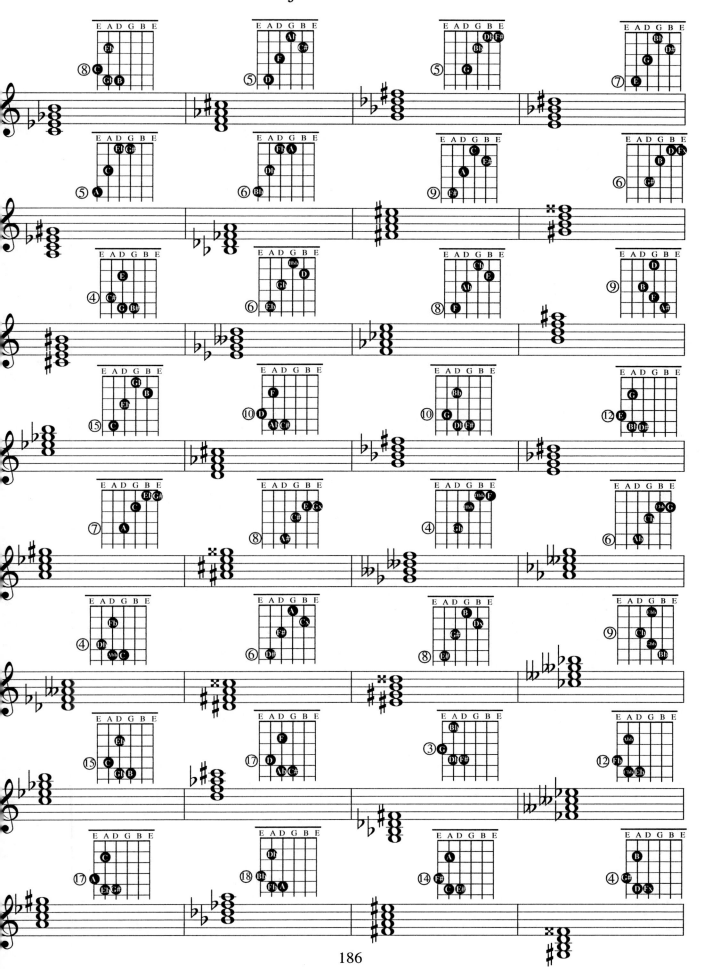

Minor Major 7b5 add 9 Chords Answers

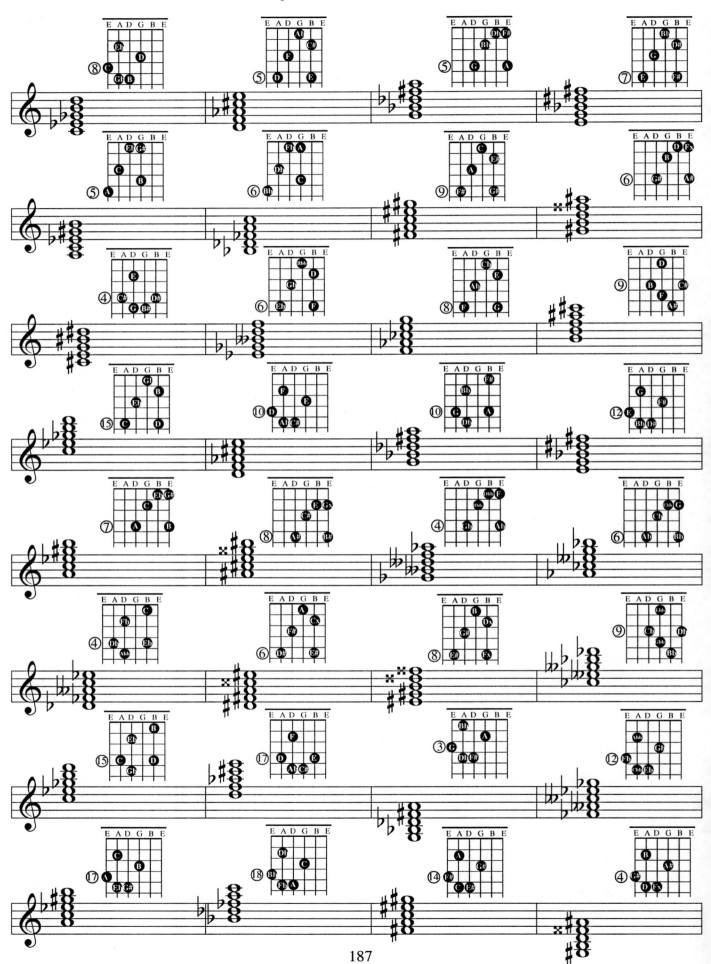

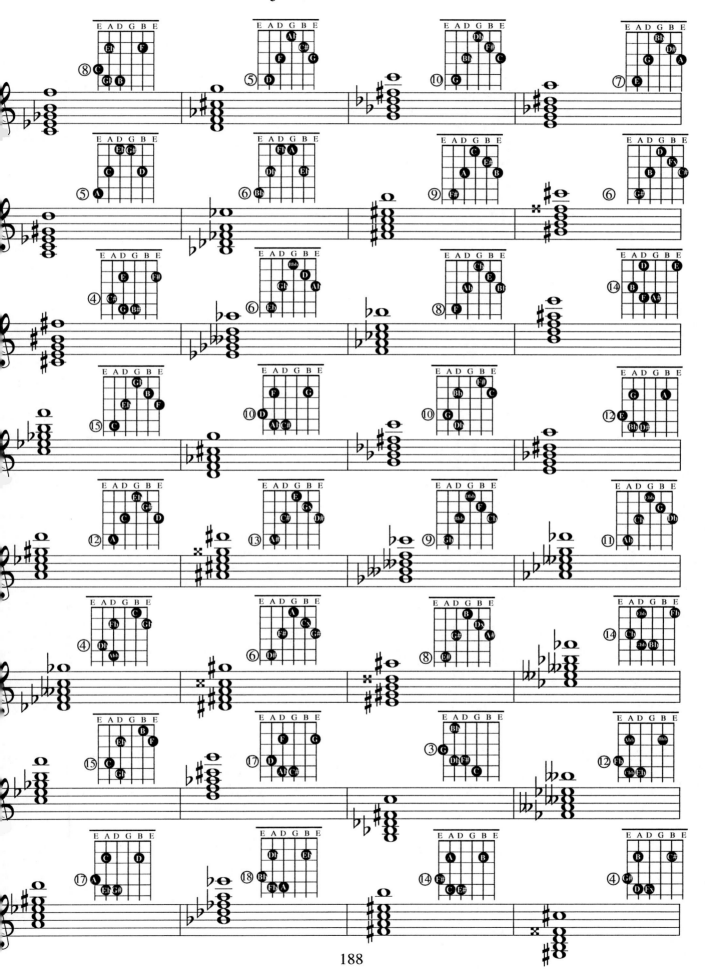

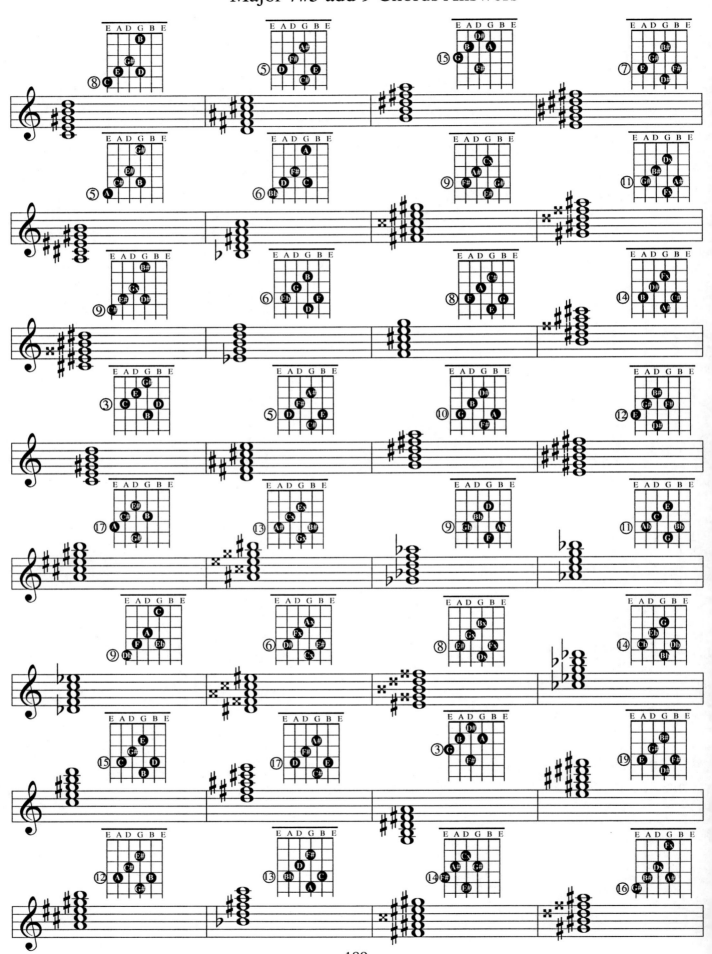

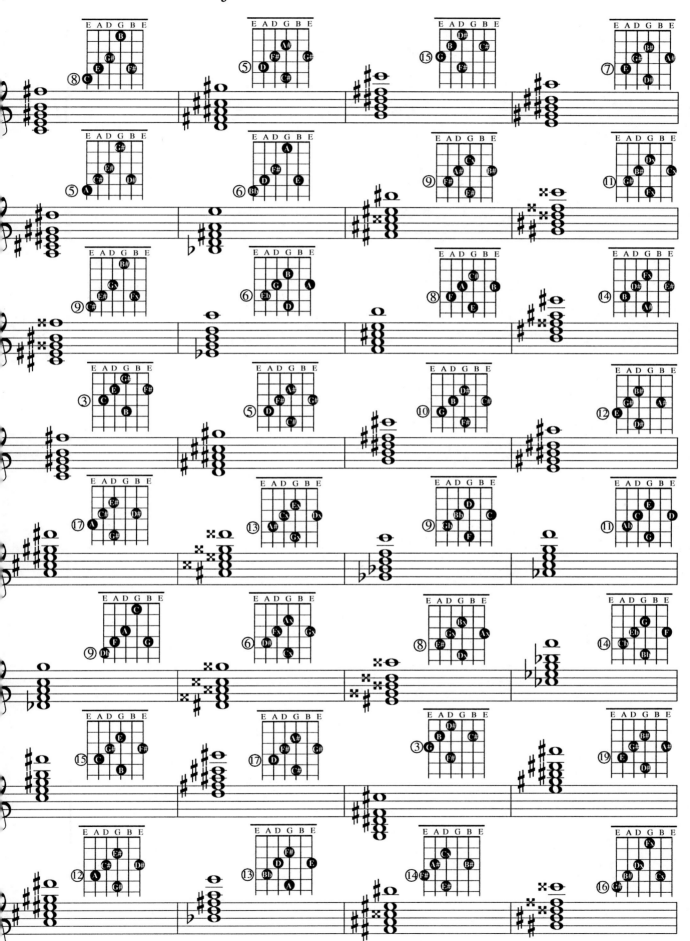

Blank Answer Worksheet for Further Study

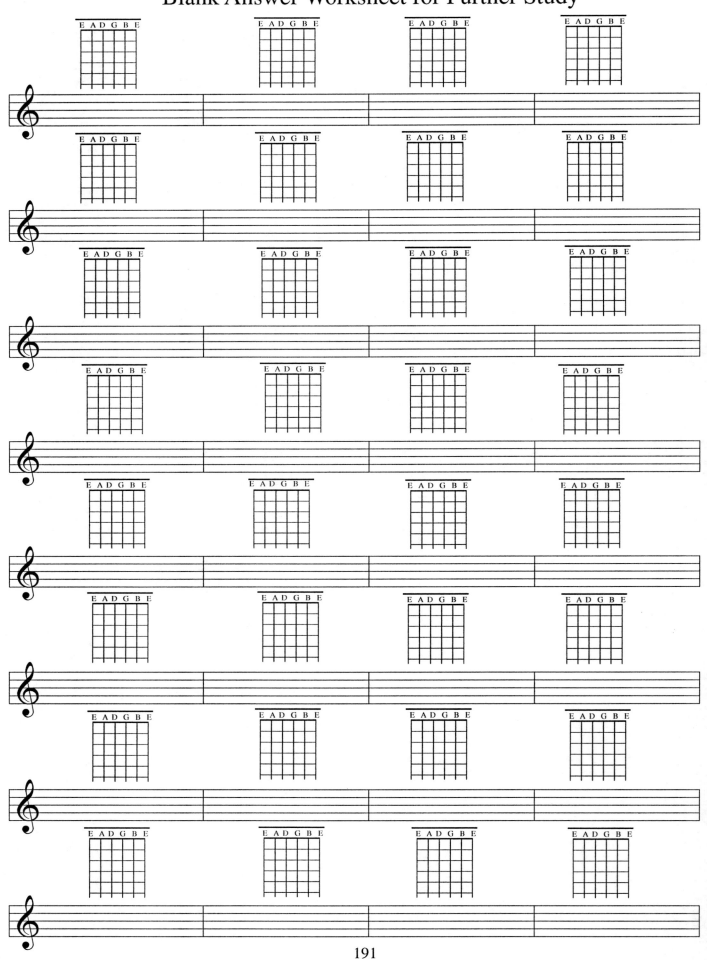

Note and Staff Location for Guitar Page One

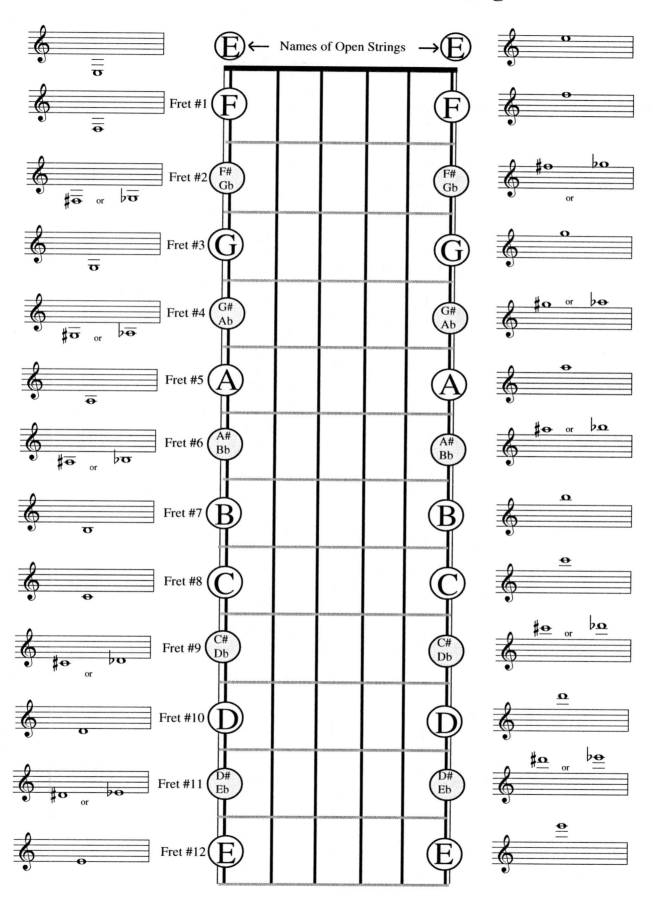

Note and Staff Location for Guitar Page Two

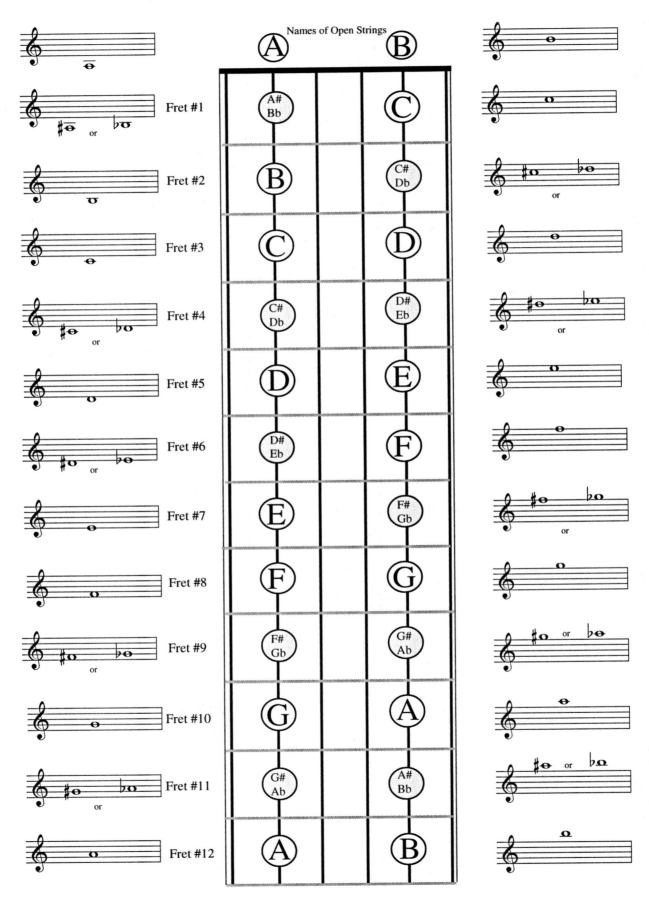

Note and Staff Location for Guitar Page Three

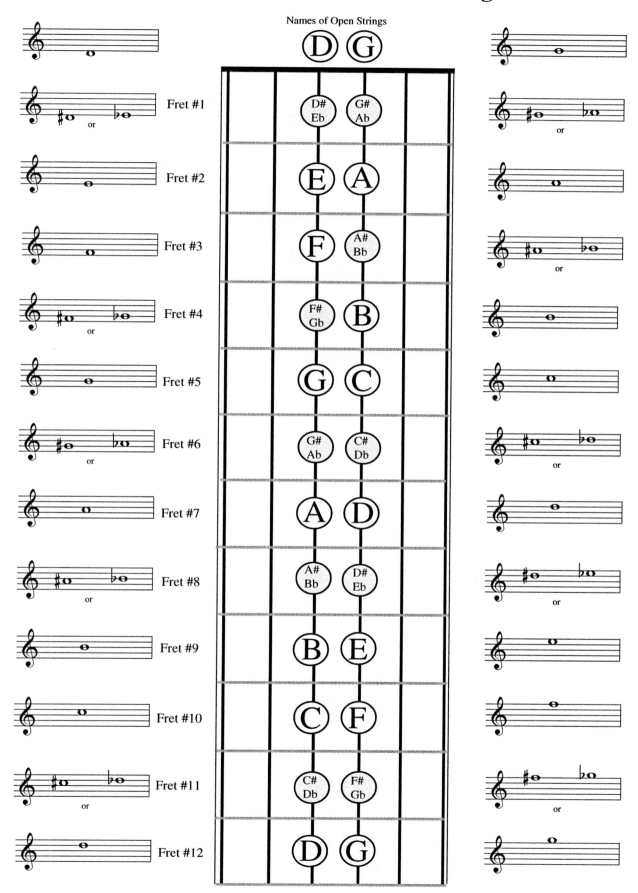

Note and Staff Location for Guitar Page Four

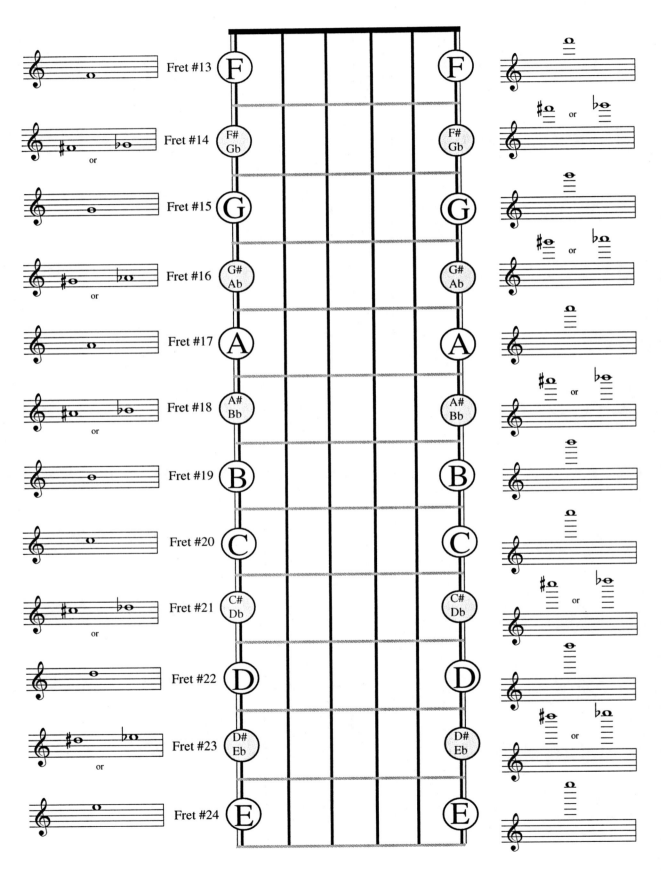

Note and Staff Location for Guitar Page Five

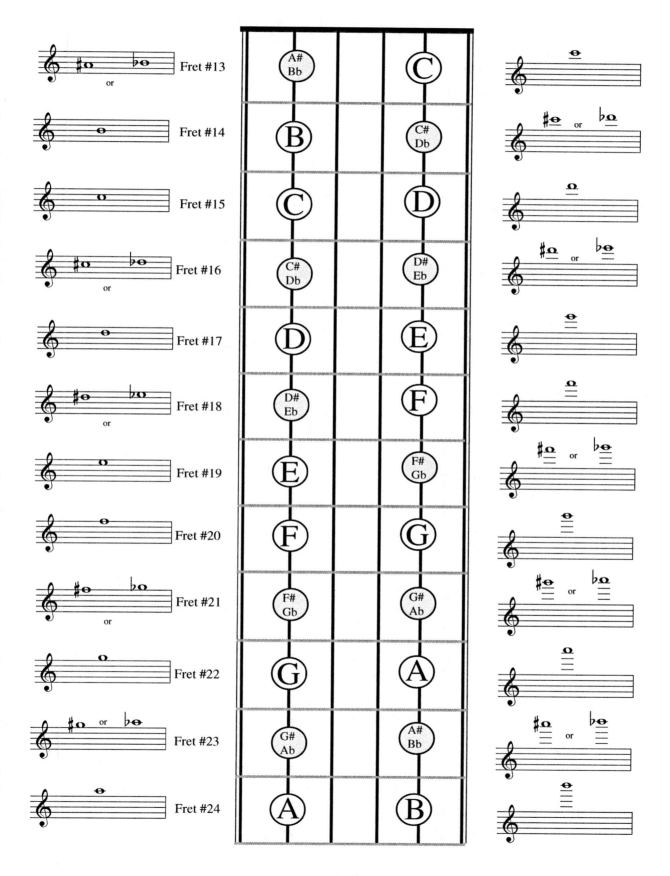

Note and Staff Location for Guitar Page Six

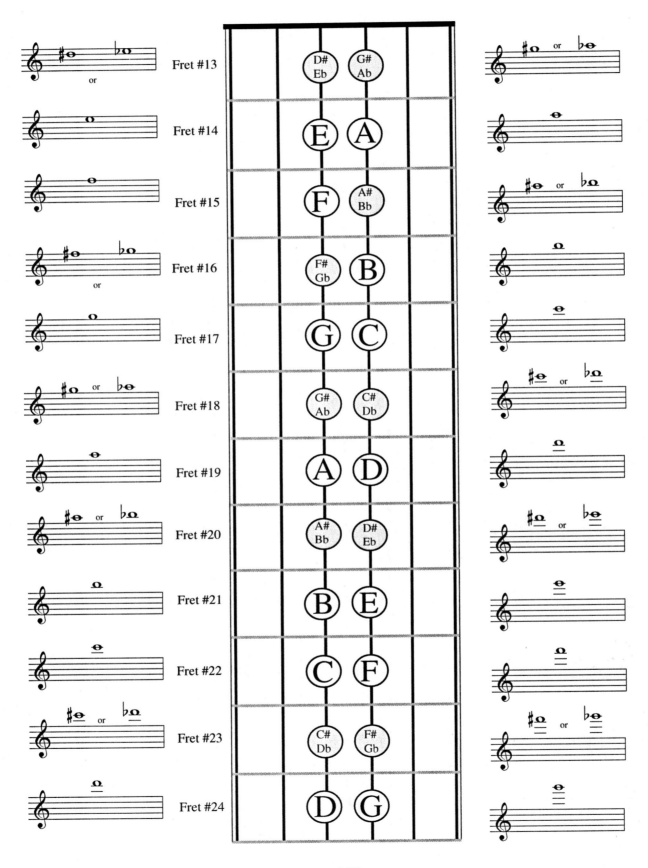

197

The Bruce Arnold series of instruction books for guitar are the result of 20 years of teaching. Mr. Arnold, who teaches at New York University and Princeton University has listened to the questions and problems of his students, and written forty books addressing the needs of the beginning to advanced student. Written in a direct, friendly and practical manner, each book is structured in such as way as to enable a student to understand, retain and apply musical information. In short, these books teach.

1st Steps for a Beginning Guitarist
Spiral Bound ISBN 1890944-90-4   Perfect Bound ISBN 1890944-93-9

"1st Steps for a Beginning Guitarist" is a comprehensive method for guitar students who have no prior musical training. Whether you are playing acoustic, electric or twelve-string guitar, this book will give you the information you need, and trouble shoot the various pitfalls that can hinder the self-taught musician. Includes pictures, videos and audio in the form of midifiles and mp3's.

Chord Workbook for Guitar Volume 1 (2nd edition)
Spiral Bound ISBN 0-9648632-1-9   Perfect Bound ISBN 1890944-50-5

A consistent seller, this book addresses the needs of the beginning through intermediate student. The beginning student will learn chords on the guitar, and a section is also included to help learn the basics of music theory. Progressions are provided to help the student apply these chords to common sequences. The more advanced student will find the reharmonization section to be an invaluable resource of harmonic choices. Information is given through musical notation as well as tablature.

Chord Workbook for Guitar Volume 2 (2nd edition)
Spiral Bound ISBN 0-9648632-3-5   Perfect Bound ISBN 1890944-51-3

This book is the Rosetta Stone of pop/jazz chords, and is geared to the intermediate to advanced student. These are the chords that any serious student bent on a musical career must know. Unlike other books which simply give examples of isolated chords, this unique book provides a comprehensive series of progressions and chord combinations which are immediately applicable to both composition and performance.

Music Theory Workbook for Guitar Series

The world's most popular instrument, the guitar, is not taught in our public schools. In addition, it is one of the hardest on which to learn the basics of music. As a result, it is frequently difficult for the serious guitarist to get a firm foundation in theory.

Theory Workbook for Guitar Volume 1
Spiral Bound ISBN 0-9648632-4-3   Perfect Bound ISBN 1890944-52-1

This book provides real hands-on application of intervals and chords. A theory section written in concise and easy to understand language prepares the student for all exercises. Worksheets are given that quiz a student about intervals and chord construction using staff notation and guitar tablature. Answers are supplied in the back of the book enabling a student to work without a teacher.

Theory Workbook for Guitar Volume 2
Spiral Bound ISBN 0-9648632-5-1   Perfect Bound ISBN 1890944-53-X

This book provides real hands-on application for 22 different scale types. A theory section written in concise and easy to understand language prepares the student for all exercises. Worksheets are given that quiz a student about scale construction using staff notation and guitar tablature. Answers are supplied in the back of the book enabling a student to work without a teacher. Audio files are also available on the muse-eek.com website to facilitate practice and improvisation with all the scales presented.

Rhythm Book Series

These books are a breakthrough in music instruction, using the internet as a teaching tool! Audio files of all the exercises are easily downloaded from the internet.

Rhythm Primer
Spiral Bound ISBN 0-890944-03-3   Perfect Bound ISBN 1890944-59-9

This 61 page book concentrates on all basic rhythms using four rhythmic levels. All examples use one pitch, allowing the student to focus completely on time and rhythm. All exercises can be downloaded from the internet to facilitate learning. See http://www.muse-eek.com for details

Rhythms Volume 1
Spiral Bound ISBN 0-9648632-7-8   Perfect Bound ISBN 1890944-55-6

This 120 page book concentrates on eighth note rhythms and is a thesaurus of rhythmic patterns. All examples use one pitch, allowing the student to focus completely on time and rhythm. All exercises can be downloaded from the internet to facilitate learning. See http://www.muse-eek.com for details.

Rhythms Volume 2
Spiral Bound ISBN 0-9648632-8-6   Perfect Bound ISBN 1890944-56-4

This volume concentrates on sixteenth note rhythms, and is a 108 page thesaurus of rhythmic patterns. All examples use one pitch, allowing the student to focus completely on time and rhythm. All exercises can be downloaded from the internet to facilitate learning. See http://www.muse-eek.com for details.

Rhythms Volume 3
Spiral Bound ISBN 0-890944-04-1   Perfect Bound ISBN 1890944-57-2

This volume concentrates on thirty second note rhythms, and is a 102 page thesaurus of rhythmic patterns. All examples use one pitch, allowing the student to focus completely on time and rhythm. All exercises can be downloaded from the internet to facilitate learning. See http://www.muse-eek.com for details.

Odd Meters Volume 1
Spiral Bound ISBN 0-9648632-9-4   Perfect Bound ISBN 1890944-58-0

This book applies both eighth and sixteenth note rhythms to odd meter combinations. All examples use one pitch, allowing the student to focus completely on time and rhythm. Exercises can be downloaded from the internet to facilitate learning. This 100 page book is an essential sight reading tool.
See http://www.muse-eek.com for details.

Contemporary Rhythms Volume 1
Spiral Bound ISBN 1-890944-27-0   Perfect Bound ISBN 1890944-84-X

This volume concentrates on eight note rhythms and is a thesaurus of rhythmic patterns. Each exercise uses one pitch which allows the student to focus completely on time and rhythm. Exercises use modern innovations common to twentieth century notation, thereby familiarizing the student with the most sophisticated systems likely to be encountered in the course of a musical career. All exercises can be downloaded from the internet to facilitate learning. See http://www.muse-eek.com for details.

Contemporary Rhythms Volume 2
Spiral Bound ISBN 1-890944-28-9   Perfect Bound ISBN 1890944-85-8

This volume concentrates on sixteenth note rhythms and is a thesaurus of rhythmic patterns. Each exercise uses one pitch which allows the student to focus completely on time and rhythm. Exercise use modern innovations common to twentieth century notation, thereby familiarizing the student with the most sophisticated systems likely to be encountered in the course of a musical career. All exercises can be downloaded from the internet to facilitate learning. See http://www.muse-eek.com for details.

Independence Volume 1
Spiral Bound ISBN 1-890944-00-9   Perfect Bound ISBN 1890944-83-1

This 51 page book is designed for pianists, stick and touchstyle guitarists, percussionists and anyone who wishes to develop the rhythmic independence of their hands. This volume concentrates on quarter, eighth and sixteenth note rhythms and is a thesaurus of rhythmic patterns. The exercises in this book gradually incorporate more and more complex rhythmic patterns making it an excellent tool for both the beginning and the advanced student.

Other Guitar Study Aids

Right Hand Technique for Guitar Volume 1
Spiral Bound ISBN 0-9648632-6-X   Perfect Bound ISBN 1890944-54-8

Here's a breakthrough in music instruction, using the internet as a teaching tool! This book gives a concise method for developing right hand technique on the guitar, one of the most overlooked and under-addressed aspects of learning the instrument. The simplest, most basic movements are used to build fatigue-free technique. Exercises can be downloaded from the internet to facilitate learning. See http://www.muse-eek.com for details.

Single String Studies Volume One
Spiral Bound ISBN 1-890944-01-7   Perfect Bound ISBN 1890944-62-9

This book is an excellent learning tool for both the beginner who has no experience reading music on the guitar, and the advanced student looking to improve their ledger line reading and general knowledge of each string of the guitar. Each exercise concentrates the students attention on one string at a time. This allows a familiarity to form between the written pitch and where it can be found on the guitar along with improving one's "feel" for jumping linearly across the fretboard. Exercises can be downloaded from the internet to facilitate learning. See http://www.muse-eek.com for details.

Single String Studies Volume Two
Spiral Bound ISBN 1-890944-05-X   Perfect Bound ISBN 1890944-64-5

This book is a continuation of Volume One, but using non-diatonic notes. Volume Two helps the intermediate and advanced student improve their ledger line reading and general knowledge of each string of the guitar. Each exercise concentrates the students attention on one string at a time. This allows a familiarity to form between the written pitch and where it can be found on the guitar along with improving one's "feel" for jumping linearly across the fretboard. Exercises can be downloaded from the internet to facilitate learning. See http://www.muse-eek.com for details.

Single String Studies Volume One (Bass Clef)
Spiral Bound ISBN 1-890944-02-5   Perfect Bound ISBN 1890944-63-7

This book is an excellent learning tool for both the beginner who has no experience reading music on the bass guitar, and the advanced student looking to improve their ledger line reading and general knowledge of each string of the bass. Each exercise concentrates a students attention of one string at a time. This allows a familiarity to form between the written pitch and where it can be found on the bass along with improving one's "feel" for jumping linearly across the fretboard. Exercises can be downloaded from the internet to facilitate learning. See http://www.muse-eek.com for details.

Single String Studies Volume Two (Bass Clef)
Spiral Bound ISBN 1-890944-06-8   Perfect Bound ISBN 1890944-65-3

This book is a continuation of Volume One, but using non-diatonic notes. Volume Two helps the intermediate and advanced student improve their ledger line reading and general knowledge of each string of the bass. Each exercise concentrates the students attention on one string at a time. This allows a familiarity to form between the written pitch and where it can be found on the bass along with improving one's "feel" for jumping linearly across the fretboard. Exercises can be downloaded from the internet to facilitate learning. See http://www.muse-eek.com for details.

Guitar Clinic
Spiral Bound ISBN 1-890944-45-9   Perfect Bound ISBN 1890944-86-6

Guitar Clinic" contains techniques and exercises Mr. Arnold uses in the clinics and workshops he teaches around the U.S.. Much of the material in this book is culled from Mr. Arnold's educational series, over thirty books in all. The student wishing to expand on his or her studies will find suggestions within the text as to which of Mr. Arnold's books will best serve their specific needs. Topics covered include: how to read music, sight reading, reading rhythms, music theory, chord and scale construction, modal sequencing, approach notes, reharmonization, bass and chord comping, and hexatonic scales.

Sight Singing and Ear Training Series

The world is full of ear training and sight reading books, so why do we need more?
This sight singing and ear training series uses a different method of teaching relative pitch sight singing and ear training. The success of this method has been remarkable. Along with a new method of ear training these books also use CDs and the internet as a teaching tool! Audio files of all the exercises are easily downloaded from the internet at www.muse-eek.com By combining interactive audio files with a new approach to ear training a student's progress is limited only by their willingness to practice!

A Fanatic's Guide to Ear Training and Sight Singing
Spiral Bound ISBN 1-890944-19-X   Perfect Bound ISBN 1890944-75-0

This book and CD present a method for developing good pitch recognition through sight singing. This method differs from the myriad of other sight singing books in that it develops the ability to identify and name all twelve pitches within a key center. Through this method a student gains the ability to identify sound based on it's relationship to a key and not the relationship of one note to another (i.e. interval training as commonly taught in many texts). All note groupings from one to six notes are presented giving the student a thesaurus of basic note combinations which develops sight singing and note recognition to a level unattainable before this Guide's existence.

Key Note Recognition
Spiral Bound ISBN 1-890944-30-0   Perfect Bound ISBN 1890944-77-7

This book and CD present a method for developing the ability to recognize the function of any note against a key. This method is a must for anyone who wishes to sound one note on an instrument or voice and instantly know what key a song is in. Through this method a student gains the ability to identify a sound based on its relationship to a key and not the relationship of one note to another (i.e. interval training as commonly taught in many texts). Key Center Recognition is a definite requirement before proceeding to two note ear training.

LINES Volume One: Sight Reading and Sight Singing Exercises
Spiral Bound ISBN 1-890944-09-2   Perfect Bound ISBN 1890944-76-9

This book can be used for many applications. It is an excellent source for easy half note melodies that a beginner can use to learn how to read music or for sight singing slightly chromatic lines. An intermediate or advanced student will find exercises for multi-voice reading. These exercises can also be used for multi-voice ear training. The book has the added benefit in that all exercises can be heard by downloading the audio files for each example. See http://www.muse-eek.com for details.

Ear Training ONE NOTE: Beginning Level
Spiral Bound ISBN 1-890944-12-2   Perfect Bound ISBN 1890944-66-1

This is a new method for developing instantaneous recognition of pitches within a key. This contextual-based ear training differs from interval based training by instilling a sense of key relationship; that is, a note is identified by it's characteristic sound within a key, and not by its distance from another note. This method has been used with great success and is now finally available on CD. There are three levels available depending on the student's ability. This beginning level is recommended for students who have little or no music training. A Complete Method book containing the Ear Training One Note Beginning, Intermediate and Advanced levels along with three accompanying CDs is also available for those students wishing to have a complete set of books and CDs under one cover.

Ear Training ONE NOTE: Intermediate Level
Spiral Bound ISBN 1-890944-13-0   Perfect Bound ISBN 1890944-67-X

This is a new method for developing instantaneous recognition of pitches within a key. This contextual-based ear training differs from interval based training by instilling a sense of key relationship; that is, a note is identified by it's characteristic sound within a key, and not by its distance from another note. This method has been used with great success and is now finally available on CD. There are three levels available depending on the student's ability. This intermediate level is recommended for students who have had some music training but still find their skills need more development.   A Complete Method book containing the Ear Training One Note Beginning, Intermediate and Advanced levels along with three accompanying CDs is also available for those students wishing to have a complete set of books and CDs under one cover.

Ear Training ONE NOTE: Advanced Level
Spiral Bound ISBN 1-890944-14-9   Perfect Bound ISBN 1890944-68-8

This is a new method for developing instantaneous recognition of pitches within a key. This contextual-based ear training differs from interval based training by instilling a sense of key relationship; that is, a note is identified by it's characteristic sound within a key, and not by its distance from another note. This method has been used with great success and is now finally available on CD. There are three levels available depending on the student's ability. This advanced level is recommended for advanced music students or those who have worked with the intermediate level and now wish to perfect their skills. A Complete Method book containing the Ear Training One Note Beginning, Intermediate and Advanced levels along with three accompanying CDs is also available for those students wishing to have a complete set of books and CDs under one cover.

Ear Training ONE NOTE: Complete Method
Spiral Bound ISBN 1-890944-47-5   Perfect Bound ISBN 1890944-48-3

This is a new method for developing instantaneous recognition of pitches within a key. This contextual-based ear training differs from interval based training by instilling a sense of key relationship; that is, a note is identified by it's characteristic sound within a key, and not by its distance from another note. This Complete Method book contains the Ear Training One Note Beginning, Intermediate and Advanced levels along with three accompanying CDsand is available for those students who wish to have a complete set of books and CDs under one cover.

Ear Training TWO NOTE: Beginning Level Volume One
Spiral Bound ISBN 1-890944-31-9   Perfect Bound ISBN 1890944-69-6

This Book and Audio CD continues the method of developing relative pitch ear training as set forth in the "Ear Training, One Note" series. There are six volumes in the beginning level series. Through practice, the student eventually gains the ability to recognize the key and the names of any two notes played simultaneously. Volume One concentrates on 5ths. Prerequisite: a strong grasp of the One Note method.

Ear Training TWO NOTE: Beginning Level Volume Two
Spiral Bound ISBN 1-890944-32-7   Perfect Bound ISBN 1890944-70-X

This Book and Audio CD continues the method of developing relative pitch ear training as set forth in the "Ear Training, One Note" series. There are six volumes in the beginning level series. Through practice, the student eventually gains the ability to recognize the key and the names of any two notes played simultaneously. Volume Two concentrates on 3rds. Prerequisite: a strong grasp of the One Note method.

Ear Training TWO NOTE: Beginning Level Volume Three
Spiral Bound ISBN 1-890944-33-5   Perfect Bound ISBN 1890944-71-8

This Book and Audio CD continues the method of developing relative pitch ear training as set forth in the "Ear Training, One Note" series. There are six volumes in the beginning level series. Through practice, the student eventually gains the ability to recognize the key and the names of any two notes played simultaneously. Volume Three concentrates on 6ths. Prerequisite: a strong grasp of the One Note method.

Ear Training TWO NOTE: Beginning Level Volume Four
Spiral Bound ISBN 1-890944-34-3   Perfect Bound ISBN 1890944-72-6

This Book and Audio CD continues the method of developing relative pitch ear training as set forth in the "Ear Training, One Note" series. There are six volumes in the beginning level series. Through practice, the student eventually gains the ability to recognize the key and the names of any two notes played simultaneously. Volume Four concentrates on 4ths. Prerequisite: a strong grasp of the One Note method.

Ear Training TWO NOTE: Beginning Level Volume Five
Spiral Bound ISBN 1-890944-35-1   Perfect Bound ISBN 1890944-73-4

This Book and Audio CD continues the method of developing relative pitch ear training as set forth in the "Ear Training, One Note" series. There are six volumes in the beginning level series. Through practice, the student eventually gains the ability to recognize the key and the names of any two notes played simultaneously. Volume Five concentrates on 2nds. Prerequisite: a strong grasp of the One Note method.

Ear Training TWO NOTE: Beginning Level Volume Six
Spiral Bound ISBN 1-890944-36-X   Perfect Bound ISBN 1890944-74-2

This Book and Audio CD continues the method of developing relative pitch ear training as set forth in the "Ear Training, One Note" series. There are six volumes in the beginning level series. Through practice, the student eventually gains the ability to recognize the key and the names of any two notes played simultaneously. Volume Six concentrates on 7ths. Prerequisite: a strong grasp of the One Note method.

Comping Styles Series

This series is built on the progressions found in Chord Workbook Volume One. Each book covers a specific style of music and presents exercises to help a guitarist, bassist or drummer master that style. Audio CDs are also available so a student can play along with each example and really get "into the groove."

Comping Styles for the Guitar Volume Two FUNK
Spiral Bound ISBN 1-890944-07-6   Perfect Bound ISBN 1890944-60-2

This volume teaches a student how to play guitar or piano in a funk style. 36 Progressions are presented: 12 keys of a Major and Minor Blues plus 12 keys of Rhythm Changes A different groove is presented for each exercise giving the student a wide range of funk rhythms to master.   An Audio CD is also included so a student can play along with each example and really get "into the groove." The audio CD contains "trio" versions of each exercise with Guitar, Bass and Drums.

Comping Styles for the Bass Volume Two FUNK
Spiral Bound ISBN 1-890944-08-4   Perfect Bound ISBN 1890944-61-0

This volume teaches a student how to play bass in a funk style. 36 Progressions are presented: 12 keys of a Major and Minor Blues plus 12 keys of Rhythm Changes A different groove is presented for each exercise giving the student a wide range of funk rhythms to master.   An Audio CD is also included so a student can play along with each example and really get "into the groove." The audio CD contains "trio" versions of each exercise with Guitar, Bass and Drums.

Bass Lines: Learning and Understanding the Jazz-Blues Bass Line
Spiral Bound ISBN 1-890944-94-7   Perfect Bound ISBN 1890944-95-5

This book covers the basics of bass line construction. A theoretical guide to building bass lines is presented along with 36 chord progressions utilizing the twelve keys of a Major and Minor Blues, plus twelve keys of Rhythm Changes. A reharmonization section is also provided which demonstrates how to reharmonize a chord progression on the spot.

Time Series

The Doing Time series presents a method for contacting, developing and relying on your internal time sense: This series is an excellent source for any musician who is serious about developing strong internal sense of time. This is particularly useful in any kind of music where the rhythms and time signatures may be very complex or free, and there is no conductor.

THE BIG METRONOME
Spiral Bound ISBN 1-890944-37-8   Perfect Bound ISBN 1890944-82-3

The Big Metronome is designed to help you develop a better internal sense of time. This is accomplished by requiring you to "feel time" rather than having you rely on the steady click of a metronome. The idea is to slowly wean yourself away from an external device and rely on your internal/natural sense of time. The exercises presented work in conjunction with the three CDs that accompany this book. CD 1 presents the first 13 settings from a traditional metronome 40-66; the second CD contains metronome markings 69-116, and the third CD contains metronome markings 120-208. The first CD gives you a 2 bar count off and a click every measure, the second CD gives you a 2 bar count off and a click every 2 measures, the 3rd CD gives you a 2 bar count off and a click every 4 measures. By presenting all common metronome markings a student can use these 3 CDs as a replacement for a traditional metronome.

Doing Time with the Blues Volume One:
Spiral Bound ISBN 1-890944-17-3   Perfect Bound ISBN 1890944-78-5

The book and CD presents a method for gaining an internal sense of time thereby eliminating dependence on a metronome. The book presents the basic concept for developing good time and also includes exercises that can be practiced with the CD. The CD provides eight 8 minute tracks at different tempos in which the time is delineated every 2 bars, and with an extra hit every 12 bars to outline the blues form. The student may then use the exercises presented in the book to gain control of their execution or improvise to gain control of their ideas using this bare minimum of time delineation.

Doing Time with the Blues Volume Two:
Spiral Bound ISBN 1-890944-18-1   Perfect Bound ISBN 1890944-79-3

This is the 2nd volume of a four volume series which presents a method for developing a musician's internal sense of time, thereby eliminating dependence on a metronome. This 2nd volume presents different exercises which further the development of this time sense. This 2nd volume begins to test even a professional level player's ability. The CD provides eight 8 minute tracks at different tempos in which the time is delineated every 4 bars with an extra hit every 12 bars to outline the blues form.   New exercises are also included that can be practiced with the CD. This series is an excellent source for any musician who is serious about developing an internal sense of time.

Doing Time with 32 bars Volume One:
Spiral Bound ISBN 1-890944-22-X   Perfect Bound ISBN 1890944-80-7

The book and CD presents a method for gaining an internal sense of time thereby eliminating dependence on a metronome. The book presents the basic concept for developing good time and also includes exercises that can be practiced with the CD. The CD provides eight 8 minute tracks at different tempos in which the time is delineated every 2 bars, with an extra hit every 32 to outline the 32 bar form. The student may then use the exercises presented in the book to gain control of their execution or improvise to gain control of their ideas using this bare minimum of time delineation.

Doing Time with 32 bars Volume Two:
Spiral Bound ISBN 1-890944-23-8   Perfect Bound ISBN 1890944-81-5

This is the 2nd volume of a four volume series which presents a method for developing a musician's internal sense of time, thereby eliminating dependence on a metronome..   This 2nd volume presents different exercises which further the development of this time sense. This 2nd volume begins to test even a professional level player's ability. The CD provides eight 8 minute tracks at different tempos in which the time is delineated every 4 bars with an extra hit every 32 bars to outline the 32 bar form.   New exercises are also included that can be practiced with the CD. This series is an excellent source for any musician who is serious about developing an internal sense of time.

Other Workbooks

Music Theory Workbook for All Instruments, Volume 1: Interval and Chord Construction
Spiral Bound ISBN 1890944-92-0   Perfect Bound ISBN 1890944-46-7

This book provides real hands-on application of intervals and chords. A theory section written in concise and easy to understand language prepares the student for all exercises. Worksheets are given that quiz a student about intervals and chord construction using staff notation. Answers are supplied in the back of the book enabling a student to work without a teacher.

E-Books

The Bruce Arnold series of instructional E-books is for the student who wishes to target specific areas of study that are of particular interest. Many of these books are excerpted from other larger texts. The excerpted source is listed for each book. These books are available on-line at www.muse-eek.com as well as at many e-tailers throughout the internet. These books can also be purchased in the traditional book binding format. (See the ISBN number for proper format)

Chord Velocity: Volume One, Learning to switch between chords quickly
E-book ISBN 1-890944-88-2   Traditional Book Binding ISBN 1-890944-97-1

The first hurdle a beginning guitarist encounters is difficulty in switching between chords quickly enough to make a chord progression sound like music. This book provides exercises that help a student gradually increase the speed with which they change chords. Special free audio files are also available on the muse-eek.com website to make practice more productive and fun. With a few weeks, remarkable improvement by can be achieved using this method. This book is excerpted from "1st Steps for a Beginning Guitarist Volume One."

Guitar Technique: Volume One, Learning the basics to fast, clean, accurate and fluid performance skills.
E-book ISBN 1-890944-91-2   Traditional Book Binding ISBN 1-890944-99-8

This book is for both the beginning guitarist or the more experienced guitarist who wishes to improve their technique. All aspects of the physical act of playing the guitar are covered, from how to hold a guitar to the specific way each hand is involved in the playing process. Pictures and videos are provided to help clarify each technique. These pictures and videos are either contained in the book or can be downloaded at www.muse-eek.com This book is excerpted from "1st Steps for a Beginning Guitarist Volume One."

Accompaniment: Volume One, Learning to Play Bass and Chords Simultaneously
E-book ISBN 1-890944-87-4   Traditional Book Binding ISBN 1-890944-96-3

The techniques found within this book are an excellent resource for creating and understanding how to play bass and chords simultaneously in a jazz or blues style. Special attention is paid to understanding how this technique is created, thereby enabling the student to recreate this style with other pieces of music. This book is excerpted from the book "Guitar Clinic."

Beginning Rhythm Studies: Volume One, Learning the basics of reading rhythm and playing in time.
E-book ISBN 1-890944-89-0   Traditional Book Binding 1-890944-98-X

This book covers the basics for anyone wishing to understand or improve their rhythmic abilities. Simple language is used to show the student how to read and play rhythm. Exercises are presented which can accelerate the learning process. Audio examples in the form of midifiles are available on the muse-eek.com website to facilitate learning the correct rhythm in time. This book is excerpted from the book "Rhythm Primer."

Printed in the United Kingdom
by Lightning Source UK Ltd.
104984UKS00001B/7